Vlad III

Dracula

The Life and Times of the Historical Dracula

Vlad III Dracula
(From a fifteenth century German manuscript)

Kurt W. Treptow

Vlad III Dracula

The Life and Times of the Historical Dracula

With Original Illustrations by Octavian Ion Penda

The Center for Romanian Studies
Iaşi ♦ Oxford ♦ Portland
2000

Published in Romania by

THE CENTER FOR ROMANIAN STUDIES
The Foundation for Romanian Culture and Studies
Oficiul Poştal I, Căsuţa Poştală 108
Str. Poligon nr. 11a
6600 Iaşi, Romania
www.romanianstudies.ro

Published in Great Britain by

THE CENTER FOR ROMANIAN STUDIES
c/o Drake International Services
Market House
Market Place
Deddington
Oxford OX15 0SE
Great Britain

Published in the United States of America by

THE CENTER FOR ROMANIAN STUDIES
c/o International Specialized Book Services
5804 N.E. Hassalo St.
Portland, Oregon 97213, USA
www.isbs.com

National Library of Romania Cataloging-in-Publication Data

TREPTOW, KURT W.
Vlad III Dracula: The Life and Times of the Historical Dracula / Kurt W. Treptow.
Iaşi, Oxford, Portland: The Center for Romanian Studies, 2000.
240 pp., 22 cm.
Illus., Bibliography, Index
ISBN 973-98392-2-3

1. Vlad Ţepeş, domn al Ţării Româneşti, 1456-1462 şi 1476

94(489.1)"14" Vlad Ţepeş
929 Vlad Ţepeş

Contents

Preface

The earth is a nursery in which men and women play at being heroes and heroines, saints and sinners; but they are dragged down from their fool's paradise by their bodies: hunger and cold and thirst, age and decay and disease, death above all, make them slaves of reality.

— George Bernard Shaw, *Man and Superman*[1]

The Middle Ages have produced numerous legends and heroes that remain very much a part of our contemporary culture; one need only refer to the tales of King Arthur and his Knights of the Round Table or of the outlaw Robin Hood, both familiar subjects of literary works and films, as examples. Amidst the struggle to halt the Ottoman onslaught in Southeastern Europe the historical figure of Vlad Dracula arose to become a legend in his own time, and has remained such throughout the centuries. He has, at different times and in different places, been portrayed as either a saint or a sinner, and in one sense or another continues to be seen in this way.

Vlad III Dracula, who at three different times (1448, 1456-1462, and 1476) occupied the throne of the small Romanian principality of

---

[1]George Bernard Shaw, "Man and Superman," Act III, in *Four Plays by Bernard Shaw* (New York, 1965), p. 377.

Wallachia to the north of the Danube, opposed Turkish efforts to dominate his land, launching an offensive against Ottoman strongholds along the Danube during the winter of 1461-1462 and trying to stand up to the massive invasion of Wallachia led by Mehmed the Conqueror in the following summer. Despite this, many sources portray Vlad as a man of demonic cruelty, the embodiment of all that is evil. For example, the German stories tell how

> he invented frightening, terrible, unheard of tortures. He ordered that women be impaled together with their suckling babies on the same stake. The babies fought for their lives until they finally died. Then he had the women's breasts cut off and put the babies inside head first; thus he had them impaled together.[2]

Instead of a hero who defended Christendom against the Turkish onslaught, these stories speak of a man who, on St. Bartholomew's day, "ordered that two churches be burned down and plundered of their riches and holy vessels."[3] Likewise, the Slavic stories about Dracula speak of "a devil, so evil, as was his name so was his life."[4]

The controversy surrounding his very name — *Dracula* — underlines the problem of the two contradictory images of the man. Vlad was called Dracula and signed his name as such in documents issued from his chancellory because he inherited the name from his father, who had been made a member of the Order of the Dragon by Holy Roman Emperor Sigismund of Luxemburg, a crusading order founded to halt the Turkish onslaught in Europe. While in modern

[2]See P.P. Panaitescu, "The German Stories about Vlad Ţepeş," in Kurt W. Treptow, ed., *Dracula: Essays on the Life and Times of Vlad Ţepeş* (New York, 1991), p. 190; and Matei Cazacu, *L'histoire du prince Dracula en Europe centrale et orientale (XVe siècle)* (Genève, 1988), p. 96. See appendix IV.

[3]See Panaitescu, "The German Stories about Vlad Ţepeş," in Treptow, *Dracula: Essays...*, p. 189; and Cazacu, *L'histoire du prince Dracula*, p. 96. See appendix IV.

[4]"Povestire despre Dracula voievod," pp. 197-214, in *Cronicele slavo-romîne din secolul XV-XVI publicate de Ion Bogdan*, P.P. Panaitescu, ed. (Bucureşti, 1959); and Anton Balotă, "An Analysis of the Dracula Tales," in Treptow, *Dracula: Essays...*, p. 168.

Vlad III Dracula

(From a sixteenth century German manuscript)

Romanian the name *dracul* means 'devil,' in the fifteenth century it also had the meaning of 'dragon.' Dracula meant 'son of the Dragon,' referring to his father Vlad II Dracul, while the etymological evolution of the word and the creation of the legend has transformed it to mean 'son of the devil' or a name that became synonymous with vampire in Western culture. While many Romanian scholars object to using the name Dracula because of its unfortunate evolution and prefer Vlad Ţepeş or the Impaler, I prefer to retain the name Dracula, the name which Vlad himself used and the name by which he, as well as the other sons of Vlad II, is referred to in fifteenth century chronicles. Despite its later evolution, Dracula was a prestigious name, part of the distinguished heritage of which Vlad was proud. The name 'Impaler,' by contrast, stresses his cruelty and plays into the myth of the demonic tyrant from which the vampire stories evolved.

The contradictory images of Vlad III Dracula present a paradox. How could the same man at once be seen as a hero fighting for the cause of Christianity, while at the same time be seen as a villainous agent of the Devil? The answers, of course, must be sought in the specific political, social, and economic contexts within which he pursued these policies. By looking at the problem in this manner it is possible to understand how these different images came into being, and to have a better understanding of the historical personality.

As we shall see, one of the key aspects of Vlad's career, and the one which provides us with the richest documentation, is his conflict with the Turks. Vlad lived in the age when the Ottomans were establishing themselves in Central Europe and threatening to expand into Central Europe and Italy. The question of resistance to Ottoman expansion has usually been studied from two distinct viewpoints: either as part of a general effort by the Christian states of Europe to stop the Ottoman advance into Europe or as an important moment in the national histories of the various peoples of Southeastern Europe. Neither approach is adequate. In the former case there is a tendency to underestimate the importance of the particular movement and no effort is made to understand its nature. Most often the causes and motivations of these movements are merely ascribed to the desire to defend Christendom against the Moslem assault. On the other hand, in the latter instance there is a tendency to overestimate the importance of these movements, as well as to ascribe to them ideals that they did not possess, as defenders of a national idea, precursors of the nineteenth century national movements in their respective lands.

This book presents the life and times of Vlad III Dracula, prince of Wallachia. His motivations and goals will be analyzed, and the reasons for its successes and failures will be investigated. At the same time, the context within which Vlad acted will also be analyzed as we shall investigate the situation of Wallachia in particular and Southeastern Europe in general during the fifteenth century, as well as present the structure of the Romanian principality at this important moment in history. All of these elements influenced and limited Vlad's course of action and the decisions he made. Nevertheless, this is also a study of a great, legendary personality. For history is, after all, the study of the evolution of human life. While nature and history impose limits on the actions of men, certain trends in historiography to renounce the role of great men in the historical process are misguided. While conditions impose limits on human actions, it is still ultimately the decisions and actions of political and social leaders which direct the course of human history. To assume that all is guided by greater forces, be they natural or supernatural, is ultimately to reject the very essence of history. Humans retain freedom of action and through their decisions shape their own destiny, for this reason it is essential that the so-called traditional narrative approach to history not be rejected. At the same time, this is not to claim for it superiority over other approaches to the study of history, it is merely an appeal for methodological interaction.

As we shall see, Vlad was both a heroic and a tragic figure. A man who tried to shape history, but also one who was shaped by it. Although he ultimately failed in his aims, Vlad's greatness lies in the fact that he sought to rise above the limits placed upon him by time and place. This, above all, is why he has carved out a place for himself in the history of Europe during the Middle Ages.

It must be remembered that the sources which historians use are also created by men. Especially for the medieval history of East-Central and Southeastern Europe, a large part of the sources available to the historian concentrate on the role of leaders and their actions. This is the framework within which the people living at the time understood their own contemporary history, and ultimately the way in which most people continue to perceive it in our own day. This is what makes Vlad III Dracula a legitimate subject for study in trying to understand the complex history of Southeastern Europe during the fifteenth century.

***

This book is the result of research begun during my years as a graduate student at the University of Illinois. It would not have been possible without the kind support of many people who have assisted me over the years. I would like to acknowledge the support of the International Research and Exchanges Board and the United States Department of Education Fulbright-Hays Program through their research exchange programs. In addition, I am grateful to Dr. Keith Hitchins of the University of Illinois for his encouragement and support throughout my career. I am indebted to Octavian Ion Penda for his original illustrations which are included in this volume. I would also like to thank my staff at the Center for Romanian Studies, Petronela Postolache, Viorica Rusu, and Dana Ungureanu. Last, but not least, I express my gratitude to wife Laura for her support and understanding.

Kurt W. Treptow

Vlad III Dracula

The Life and Times of the Historical Dracula

Hie facht sich an gar ein grausen

liche erschröckenliche Hystorien. von dem wilden wüt
rich Dracole weyde Wie er die leüt gespißt hot vnd
gepraten vñ mit den haüßtern yn einē kessel gesotten

(Scene from a German manuscript from 1500)

Chapter 1

Prologue

Dracula went into Braşov as far as the chapel of St. Jakob and ordered that the suburbs of the city should be burned down. And no sooner had he arrived there, when early in the morning he gave orders that the men and women, young and old alike, should be impaled next to the chapel, at the foot of the mountain. He then sat down at a table in their midst and ate his breakfast with great pleasure.

— From a fifteenth century German manuscript
on the life and deeds of Prince Dracula.[1]

One of the most controversial figures of fifteenth century Europe, the Romanian Prince Vlad III Dracula, also known as Ţepeş (the Impaler), remains obscured behind a veil of myths, the origins of which can be traced to his own lifetime. These

---

[1]See P.P. Panaitescu, "The German Stories about Vlad Ţepeş," pp. 185-196, in Treptow, *Dracula...*, p. 189. See appendix IV for a complete English translation of the German Stories about Vlad and appendix V for a translation of the fragment from the Hungarian Court Chronicler Antonius Bonfinius concerning the Wallachian prince.

legends have evolved throughout the centuries, right up to the present day. The picture of Dracula eating his breakfast with pleasure amongst the bodies of his impaled victims, handed down to us by fifteenth century German chronicles, evokes vivid images of the fictional vampire of the same name created by the Irish novelist Bram Stoker at the end of the nineteenth century. In fact, during the twentieth century the fictional vampire has often been confounded with the historical prince. The culmination of this could be seen in the 1992 film by Francis Ford Copola entitled *Bram Stoker's Dracula*, which, in its opening scenes, makes a direct connection between the vampire and the historical Dracula.

The origins of the myths about Vlad III Dracula can be traced back to his own lifetime. It is the growth of these legends throughout the following centuries that accounts for his remarkable international fame; the eminent Romanian historian Constantin C. Giurescu once stated, Romanian history has had "princes more important than Ţepeş, with longer reigns, and who realized greater accomplishments, such as Mircea the Old and Stephen the Great, but their fame did not become so great in Europe."[2]

While the dominant image of Dracula has been that of a bloody tyrant, later transformed into a bloodthirsty vampire, he has always been a highly controversial figure. Side by side with the image of the cruel tyrant described in the fifteenth century German Stories are tales of a strong and just leader who, like his Albanian contemporary George Castriota Scanderbeg, bravely opposed Turkish domination of his country. Antonius Bonfinius, the chronicler of King Matthias Corvinus of Hungary, described Dracula as being "a man of unheard of cruelty and justice... He behaved with such harshness in this barbarous country that everyone could have their things in safety, even in the middle of the forest."[3] The Slavic stories tell of a brave leader who, "when he set out against the Turks, addressed his entire army,

---

[2]Quoted in "Introduction" to Treptow, *Dracula...*, p. 8.

[3]See Appendix V.

saying: 'Whoever is afraid of death, he will not go with me, but will remain here.'"[4] Centuries later, this heroic image can also be found in the French writer Victor Hugo's *Légende des siècles*:

Vlad, a nobleman from Tarvis, called Beelzebub
Refused to pay tribute to the Sultan
And killed all the Turkish emissaries
Impaling them on thirty stakes along both sides
of the road.[5]

In Romania the prince has generally enjoyed a more positive image than elsewhere. While certain nineteenth century historians, such as Mihai Kogălniceanu and Ioan Bogdan,[6] had a negative impression of the prince, others saw in his strong leadership and cruel justice a solution for the problems of their own times. For example, the Romanian national poet Mihai Eminescu, in his well-known poem *Satire III*, decried the corruption and dishonesty that he saw all around him and called upon Vlad to bring down his wrath upon the guilty.[7] Likewise, Romanian oral tradition generally portrays Dracula as a stern but just prince.[8] Examples of this in art can be seen in several paintings by the nineteenth century Romanian artist Theodor

---

[4]Pandele Olteanu, *Limba povestirilor slave despre Vlad Ţepeş* (Bucureşti, 1960), p. 356.

[5]Quoted in Alexandru Duţu, "Portraits of Vlad Ţepeş: Literature, Pictures, and Images of the Ideal Man," in Treptow, *Dracula...*, p. 242. The French text reads:

Vlad, boyard de Tarvis, appelé Belzebuth
Refuse de payer au sultan son tribut
Prend l'ambassade turque et la fait périr toute
Sur trente pals, plantés aux deux bords de la route.

The French writer's reference to the satanic name Beelzebub is illustrative of the controversial nature of the Wallachian prince and reflect the confusion surrounding his name.

[6]See, for example, Ioan Bogdan, *Vlad Ţepeş şi naraţiunile germane şi ruseşti asupra lui* (Bucureşti, 1896), who considers Vlad to have been a deranged tyrant. His book was the first monograph on Dracula.

[7]"Satire III" in Kurt W. Treptow, ed., *Poems and Prose of Mihai Eminescu* (Iaşi: The Center for Romanian Studies, 2000).

Aman, one of which portrays a dignified Vlad refusing the offerings of the sultan's messengers.

In twentieth century Romanian historiography, especially under the communist regime, Vlad began to be portrayed in a nationalist manner, with strong socio-economic undertones. The fifteenth century prince became a sort of proto-Marxist thanks to the works of Barbu T. Câmpina and others who emphasized Dracula's alleged conflicts with the boyars and efforts to impose central control over the economy.[9] Official propaganda portrayed him as a champion of the lower classes, at times going so far as to dub him the father of centralized economic planning. As we shall see, documents were misused in an abusive manner to support wholly ideological conclusions. Our task is to reexamine the available evidence to test the validity of these interpretations.

The fame of Vlad III Dracula can be traced to the growth of the legends about him over the centuries. They have at their origin, in large measure, his resistance to Ottoman domination and his policies during his principal reign on the throne of Wallachia from 1456 to 1462, especially his relations with the Saxon cities of neighboring Transylvania and with the Kingdom of Hungary. Thus, to understand the fame of Dracula it is first necessary to study the historical figure of Vlad III Dracula and the times in which he lived. To do this it is also of vital importance to reexamine the prevalent conclusions about his reign, too often repeated, in light of the existent evidence. This is the scope of the present book.

---

[8]Radu R. Florescu and Raymond T. McNally, *Dracula: A Biography of Vlad the Impaler, 1431-1476* (New York: Hawthorn Books, 1973), p. 66; and Raymond T. McNally, "An Historical Appraisal of the Image of Vlad Țepeș in Contemporary Romanian Folklore," in Treptow, *Dracula...*, pp. 197-228.

[9]See, for example, Barbu T. Câmpina, "Complotul boierilor și răscoala din Țara Românească din iulie-noiembrie, 1462," pp. 599-624, in *Studii și referate privind istoria României*, pt. I (București, 1954); Barbu T. Câmpina, "Victoria oștii lui Țepeș asupra Sultanului Mehmed al II-lea (cu prilejul împlinirii a 500 de ani)," pp. 533-555, in *Studii. Revista de istorie*, XV:3 (1962); and Gustav Gündisch, "Cu privire la relațiile lui Vlad Țepeș cu Transilvania în anii 1456-1458," in *Studii. Revista de istorie*, XVI:3 (1963), pp. 681-696.

Chapter II

The Principality of Wallachia

This land was long ago inhabited by the Getae, who forced Darius, the son of Histape, to flee shamefully... Later they were defeated and subjugated by Roman forces. A colony of Romans was brought there, who ruled over the Dacians, under the leadership of one known as Flaccus, after whom the land was named Flacchia. Then, after a long period of time, the name was altered, as often happens, and it was called Wallachia, and instead of Flacchians [the inhabitants] were named Wallachians. These people have a Roman language that has changed a great deal so that it is very difficult for someone from Italy to understand it.

— Aeneas Silvius Piccolomini, *Cosmographia*[1]

he territory on the left bank of the Danube that for more than five hundred years formed the Principality of Wallachia has, since ancient times, been a crossroad between East and West, between Europe and Asia. This fact helps account for

---

[1]Aeneas Silvius Piccolomini, "Cosmographia," pp. 469-474, in Maria Holban, ed., *Călători străini despre țările române*, vol. I (București, 1968), p. 472.

its tumultuous history, a geopolitical reality that marked the reign of Vlad III Dracula, as the Danube represented the limit of Ottoman expansion in Europe during the fifteenth century.

The Principality of Wallachia came into existence at the beginning of the fourteenth century on a territory bordered by the Carpathian Mountains and the Danube, Siret, and Milcov rivers. When the unification of the smaller state formations that came to form Wallachia was completed during the reign of Mircea the Old (1386-1418) its territories included Muntenia, Oltenia, Dobrogea, a part of southern Bessarabia, as well as the duchies of Amlaş and Făgăraş in Transylvania. From the Carpathian Mountains in the northern part of the country, with their passes connecting Wallachia with Transylvania, the land gradually descended into an area of dense forests that opened into wide plains further south. The relief of the terrain made defense difficult, particularly from the south. The Danube could be crossed by bark or bridge, and during the winter it would often freeze over; thus it did not represent a formidable natural obstacle. From the north defense was easier as long as control of the mountain passes could be maintained. Yet, the terrain did not allow for the construction of fortresses that could be used to maintain and strengthen control over the region as a whole. As a result the country's most important military fortifications were all located in the border regions.

***

The Principality of Wallachia, which came into being during the late thirteenth and early fourteenth centuries, was the first Romanian state to take shape, but the history of this people on the territories in the Carpathian-Danubian region goes back much further.

In ancient times this region was populated by the Getae and the Dacians, two branches of the same tribe of Thracians. According to the geographer Strabo, the Getae lived in the area around the Danube River, while the Dacians dwelled in the Carpathian Mountain region in what is now Transylvania.[2] The first historical record of the existence of this people comes from Herodotus who describes them as "the bravest and most correct among the Thracians." He also provides two differing accounts of their religion and their worship of the god Zalmoxis.[3] The political formation of these people reached its peak during the first century when a powerful Dacian kingdom formed under the leadership of Burebista (70-44 B.C.), on a territory roughly corresponding to that of present-day Romania.

The Dacian King Decebal

The following century it again flourished under the rule of King Decebal (87-106 A.D.). The threat posed by the Dacian kingdom under the leadership of Decebal, who had defeated a Roman attack early in his reign, caused worry to the Roman Empire. During the reign of the Emperor Trajan Rome decided to take action against its neighbor to the northeast launching two attacks, the first in 101-102, the second in 105-106, which resulted in the complete destruction of the Dacian kingdom and its transformation into a Roman province. The conquest of Dacia marked the pinnacle of Roman power as it would be the last province added to the Empire and the first that it would abandon.

Roman rule in Dacia lasted for 165 years, from 106 to 271. During this time fortresses and cities were built and the province was colonized, usually by Roman veterans from diverse parts of the Empire, but bound by a common language — Latin. In fact, Latin had already had a strong influence in the Dacian lands as contacts between the Geto-Dacian peoples and the Romans dated back several centuries

[2]Strabo, *The Geography of Strabo*, vol. 3, trans. Horace Leonard Jones (Cambridge, MA, 1960), p. 215 (7.3.13).

[3]*Herodotus*, vol. 2, trans. A.D. Godley (Cambridge, MA, 1966), pp. 295, 297 (IV.94-95). For a comprehensive study of this religion see my "A Study in Geto-Dacian Religion: The Cult of Zalmoxis," pp. 5-22, in Kurt W. Treptow, *From Zalmoxis to Jan Palach*.

before the conquest of the province. In 271, Emperor Aurelian decided to withdraw Roman administration from the province. The decision was militarily sound, reducing the border area that needed to be manned and defended against the increasing number of Barbarian attacks from the northeast, establishing the Danube as a fortified line of defense for the Empire. Nevertheless, contacts with the former province did not cease. Rome sought to maintain the area as a buffer against the barbarian invasions, and the population that had settled there during the period of Roman administration for the most part remained. This mixing of Roman colonists and the native Geto-Dacian population laid the basis for the formation of the Romanian people.

***

Religion is an important aspect in the continuity of the Romanian people. The Romanians formed as a people not only with a common language, but also with a common religion. As Christianity spread throughout the Mediterranean region during the final centuries of the Roman Empire, it made its way to Dacia where it was adopted by the Latin speaking population. Its assimilation was made even easier in this region by the similarities that the new religion shared with the cult of Zalmoxis that had been the state religion of the Dacian kingdom prior to the Roman conquest. As the renowned scholar of the history of religions Mircea Eliade pointed out, the cult of Zalmoxis, perhaps more than any other pre-Christian cult, was easily adaptable to Christianity.[4] This helped facilitate the fusion of the two cultures that ultimately brought about the ethnogenesis of the Romanian people.

---

[4]Mircea Eliade, *Zalmoxis, the Vanishing God: Comparative Studies in the Religions and Folklore of Dacia and Eastern Europe*, trans. Willard R. Trask (Chicago, 1972), p. 69. On this topic see Kurt W. Treptow, "A Study in Geto-Dacian Religion: The Cult of Zalmoxis," pp. 5-22, in *From Zalmoxis to Jan Palach*.

Christianity began to enter the territories of former Dacia in the early fourth century as evidenced by the establishment of a bishopric in Tomis[5] (today Constanţa) on the Black Sea coast. The early spread of Christianity in this region, which coincided with the formation of the Romanian people, is further demonstrated by the fact that the core religious vocabulary in Romanian is of Latin origin: church = *biserică* (Lat. *basilica*), cross = *cruce* (Lat. *crux, -cis*), priest = *preot* (Lat. *presbiterum*), God = *Dumnezeu* (Lat. *dom(i)ne deus*), Easter = *Paşti* (Lat. *pascha, -ae*), Christmas = *Crăciun* (Lat. *creatio, -onis*), Bible = *Biblie* (Lat. *biblia*), angel = *înger* (Lat. *angelus*),[6] etc. If Christianity had not taken root early on among the Romanians this core vocabulary would certainly have been of Slavonic origin. As the Church developed a hierarchical structure in the centuries following the Slavic invasions of Southeastern Europe, it became Slavicized. Slavonic became the official language of the Church in the Romanian lands and many of the terms relating to the Church hierarchy, that had not existed up to that time, are derived from Slavonic (which had borrowed many of these terms from Greek) and not Latin: metropolitan = *mitropolit* (Slav. *mitropolită*), patriarch = *patriarh* (Slav. *patrijarhă*), abbot = *stareţ* (Slav. *starăcă*), monk = *călugăr* (Slav. *kalugeră*),[7] etc.

Evidence of the existence of a religious hierarchy during the Middle Ages on the territory that was to become Wallachia predate the formation of the principality. A letter from Pope Gregory XI to King Bela of Hungary in 1234 mentions a pseudo-bishop of the Greek rite in Wallachia.[8] After the formation of the principality around 1310 under the rule of Prince Basarab I (1310-1352) the

[5]This bishopric is mentioned down to the ninth century.

[6]See Academia Republicii Socialiste România, Institutul de lingvistică din Bucureşti, *Dicţionarul explicativ al limbii române DEX* (Bucureşti, 1975).

[7]*Ibid.*

[8]Constantin C. Giurescu, "Întemeierea mitropoliei Ungrovlahiei," pp. 673-697, in *Biserica ortodoxă romînă: Buletinul oficial al patriarhiei romîne*, LXXVII:7-10 (iulie-oct., 1959), pp. 676-677.

Church hierarchy began to develop further, playing an important role in the medieval state structure. Basarab I was buried in the church he built at Câmpulung. The Church was officially recognized by the patriarch in Constantinople in 1359 during the reign of his son and successor Nicolae Alexandru (1352-1364). The prince of Wallachia addressed the Patriarch of Constantinople, asking him to recognize the Metropolitanate of *Ungrovlahia*, because as the head of Orthodoxy only he could rightfully confer this title; at the same time he sought to strengthen ties with the Byzantine Empire,[9] as the threat to the existence of the young state posed by Catholic Hungary still lingered despite the defeat suffered by the latter at the battle of Posada in 1330.[10]

The residence of the new metropolitan was established in Curtea de Argeș, the capital of Wallachia at the time, in the Church of St. Nicolae Domnesc, built during the reign of Nicolae Alexandru.[11] Initially the metropolitan ruled over all of Wallachia, but in 1370 the border was modified together with the establishment of the Metro-

---

[9]Giurescu, "Întemeierea mitropoliei Ungrovlahiei," p. 685. On the history of the Romanian Orthodox Church generally, see Nicolae Iorga, *Istoria bisericii românești*, 3 vols. (București, 1932).

[10]The battle of Posada took place in November, 1330, when Carol Robert of Anjou, king of Hungary, who had led his army into Wallachia to bring the newly formed state under Hungarian rule, was defeated by Prince Basarab I in the Făgăraș Mountains along the border between Transylvania and Wallachia. The Wallachian victory secured the country's independence.

[11]B. Theodorescu and I. Barnea, "Cultura în cuprinsul mitropoliei Ungrovlahiei," pp. 827-888 in *Biserica ortodoxă romînă: Buletinul oficial al patriarhiei romîne*, LXXVII:7-10 (iulie-oct., 1959), p. 858. Although the capital of Wallachia was moved to Târgoviște early in the fifteenth century, the seat of the metropolitanate remained at Curtea de Argeș. It was only moved to Târgoviște in 1517, after the reforms suggested by St. Nifon to Prince Radu cel Mare (1495- 1508). It then moved to Bucharest in 1668, in modern times becoming the seat of the patriarch of the Romanian Orthodox Church. See Niculae Șerbănescu, "Titulatura mitropoliților, jurisdicția, hotarele și reședințele mitropoliei Ungrovlahiei," pp. 698-721, and "Mitropoliții Ungrovlahiei," pp. 722-826, in *Biserica ortodoxă romînă: Buletinul oficial al patriarhiei romîne*, LXXVII:7-10 (iulie-oct., 1959), pp. 716-717.

Nicolae Alexandru
Prince of Wallachia, 1352-1364

politanate of Severin (in what is today Drobeta-Turnu Severin), with the Olt River as the probable border between the two.[12] Until the fall of Constantinople to the Ottomans in 1453, the metropolitans of Wallachia, like those of Moldavia after the establishment of the Church in the neighboring principality, were appointed by Constantinople, most of them being Greeks.[13]

The princes of Wallachia patronized the Church, founding monasteries and churches, giving them land grants and exempting them from taxes, as well as making donations to the important center of Orthodoxy on Mount Athos. At times the metropolitan or certain abbots of important monasteries would participate as members of the *sfatul domnesc* (princely council), but during the fifteenth century this occurred only when matters directly affecting the Church were under consideration. In return the Church served as a moral and political support for the state internally, strengthening the authority of the prince, while also having a diplomatic function in the relations of the state with the rest of the Orthodox world. The importance of the Church in medieval society must

---

[12]Şerbănescu, "Titulatura mitropoliţilor, jurisdicţia, hotarele şi reşedinţele mitropoliei Ungrovlahiei," p. 713.

[13]*Idem*, pp. 730-740. The first metropolitan was Iachint de Vicina (1359-1372), a Greek from the north of Dobrogea. His known successors up to the time of Vlad III Dracula were: Hariton (1372-1381), a Greek who had been abbot of the Cutlumus Monastery at Mount Athos; Antim Critopulos (1381- c. 1402), a Greek who had served as metropolitan of Severin until then; Teodor (1402-before 1412), also a Greek; and Eftimie (1412-?), a Greek who also probably attended the Council of Constance (1414-1418). Following Eftimie we have no information about the metropolitans of Wallachia until the mid-fifteenth century.

not be underestimated. "The principal characteristic of the Romanian soul at the time was its religiousness," the Romanian historian Ilie Minea correctly pointed out, "a general phenomenon also common to other European peoples. Civilization had the color of the Church: literature was, with very few exceptions, religious. Art was also in the service of the Church."[14]

***

The feudal economic system in Wallachia was of uncertain origins. As a result it has been the source of much debate in Romanian historiography. Most likely, it began with the era of the great migrations when invaders would impose their rule on the native population and attempt to exploit their conquest. Several scholars, most notably P.P. Panaitescu, argue, on the basis of linguistic evidence, that the Slavic invasions led to the formation of a ruling class that gradually was Romanianized. This is also true of the Pechenegs in the tenth century and the Cumans in the eleventh and twelfth centuries, both migratory peoples of Turkish origin from Central Asia who entered Moldavia and Wallachia and settled on the fertile agricultural lands.[15] After establishing their rule over the native population these peoples were gradually assimilated by the native population, similar to the case of the assimilation of the Bulgars by the Slavic population in Bulgaria.

---

[14]Ilie Minea, "Vlad Dracul şi vremea sa," in *Cercetări istorice: revistă de istorie românească*, IV:1 (Iaşi, 1928), p. 195.

[15]P.P. Panaitescu, "Problema originii clasei boiereşti," in *Interpretări româneşti* (Bucureşti, 1994), pp. 50-51. Panaitescu agrees that the Cumans played an important role, although less than that of the Slavs, in the formation of the Romanian boyar class. As evidence he cites the Cuman origin of the name of the family dynasty, Basarab, that ruled Wallachia during the fourteenth and fifteenth centuries. See also Nicolae Iorga, *Imperiul cumanilor şi domnia lui Băsarabă*, Academia Română, [Mem.] secţia istorică, seria III, tom. VIII (Bucureşti, 1927-1928); P. Diaconu, *Les Petchénègues au Bas-Danube* (Bucureşti, 1970); and P. Diaconu, *Les Coumans au Bas-Danube aux XIe et XIIe siècles* (Bucureşti, 1978).

Other scholars stress the native origins of the boyar class, arguing that property rights were gradually usurped by village leaders, leading to the creation of a hereditary class.[16] While one can imagine that some native formation of a boyar class took place, most scholars agree on the Slavic origin of the boyars based upon linguistic evidence and the Slavic structure of feudal institutions in the Romanian lands.

The need for organizing a system of defense encouraged the extension of feudalism and the creation of the boyars as a social group. It must be noted that this process began in the plains which were more vulnerable to attack and richer in agricultural potential. It only gradually spread to other areas.

One of the factors that helped to speed up the process of feudalization was the fact that during the thirteenth and fourteenth centuries the Romanian lands found themselves located along thriving commercial routes linking East and West. As these routes brought with them a certain amount of wealth and hence required a defensive system, the extension of forms of feudalism naturally followed. This growing feudal social, political, and economic system led to the development of small state formations, such as voievodates and cnezates, that gradually united to create the principalities of Wallachia and Moldavia during the fourteenth century.[17] It must be remembered, however, that large communities of free peasants also existed within these states. Thus they cannot be considered wholly feudal, though the development of this system led to their creation. It is only with the extension of Ottoman domination into the Romanian lands and their increasing economic exploitation by the Porte during the sixteenth century that feudal relations between landlords and peasants in the Romanian lands significantly expanded.[18]

---

[16]See Radu Rosetti, *Pământul, sătenii şi stăpânii în Moldova* (Bucureşti, 1907).

[17]An excellent study of the period leading up to the creation of the Romanian principalities is Şerban Papacostea, *Românii în secolul al XIII-lea: Între cruciată şi imperiul mongol* (Bucureşti, 1993). See also, Şerban Papacostea, *Geneza statelor feudale româneşti* (Cluj-Napoca, 1989).

The process of consolidation of these smaller state formations was also enhanced by the extension of neighboring powers into the Romanian lands and the need to defend against them. This is especially true of the Kingdom of Hungary which, after conquering Transylvania, tried to extend its control over Wallachia and Moldavia, provoking the local population to organize itself politically and militarily to oppose the expansion of the Magyar kingdom.

As a result we encounter the emergence of principalities on the Romanian lands in the fourteenth century, first Wallachia to the south, bordering the Danube, around 1310, and later Moldavia to the east of the Carpathians, in 1359.

---

[18]Keith Hitchins aptly describes the impact of Ottoman domination on the Romanian lands during the sixteenth century: "a double process was at work: a reduction in the number of small peasant holdings, on the one hand, and, on the other, the extension of large estates. It must be emphasized, however, that this process had begun before the period of Ottoman vassalage; it was now simply accelerated." See Keith Hitchins, "Ottoman Domination of Moldavia and Wallachia in the Sixteenth Century," in *Asian Studies One: A Collection of Papers on Aspects of Asian History and Civilization,* Balkrishna G. Gokhale, ed. (Bombay, India, 1966), p. 141.

Chapter III

Wallachia before 1456:
The Threat Posed
by Ottoman Expansion

Basarabs, Muşats, in holy shadows you remain, a noble race,
Settlers of the land and givers of new laws, you who did trace
With spade and plow the new frontiers of a country large and free
Far extending from the mountains to the Danube and the sea.

— Mihai Eminescu, *Satire III*[1]

As we have seen, the Principality of Wallachia came into being at the beginning of the fourteenth century through the fusion of smaller state formations that had existed previously on this territory. The period of the completion of territorial expansion and the development and consolidation of the state institutions coincided with the reign of Prince Mircea the Old (1387-1418).[2] It is also at this

---

[1]From "Satire III" in Kurt W. Treptow, ed., *Poems and Prose of Mihai Eminescu* (Iaşi: The Center for Romanian Studies, 2000).

time that the Romanian principalities first came into contact with the
new power that would dominate this region of Europe for the next
500 years and would have a decisive impact upon the future development of the Romanian principalities and all of Southeastern Europe
— the Ottoman Turks.

The consolidation of Wallachia, both territorially and adminis-
tratively, had only just been completed when the Ottoman threat
appeared. The principality had come into existence around 1310. The
metropolitanate had been officially recognized by the patriarch only
in 1359, and the consolidation of its territories occurred during the
time when Ottoman expansion first touched the borders of the young
state toward the end of the fourteenth century.

One of the principal problems that the new state would face
when it encountered the Ottoman political and military threat at this
relatively fragile stage in its existence was the lack of any well-estab-
lished principle of succession to the throne. A hereditary-elective system of succession to the throne existed in which an assembly of
boyars proclaimed one of the male members of the ruling family as
prince. While it was usual for the oldest son of the prince to be chosen, followed by the next brother, theoretically all male offspring of
the ruling prince, both legitimate and illegitimate, could make a claim
to the throne.[3] The hereditary-elective system led to struggles among
royal offspring to garner support amongst factions of boyars in their
bids for the throne. It also created opportunities for outside interference in the internal dynastic struggles that were to plague the young
principality.

While some historians, such as R.W. Seton-Watson, have claimed
that no clear theory has been elaborated as to why royal power failed

---

[2]Mircea the Old, *cel Bătrân* in Romanian, was so-called with the sense "the Wise."
Village elders in Southeastern Europe were traditionally referred to as "old and wise men."

[3]See Alexandru A. Vasilescu, *Urmașii lui Mircea cel Bătrân până la Vlad Țepeș
(1418-1456): I, De la moartea lui Mircea cel Bătrân până la Vlad Dracul (1418-1437)*
(București, 1915), p. 16; and Ștefan Andreescu, *Vlad Țepeș (Dracula), între legendă și
adevăr istoric* (București, 1976), p. 19.

to be established on a secure and lasting basis, suggesting a variety of possibilities including a lack of worthy successors and Turkish intervention,[4] the problem is more fundamental. As we have seen, the state and religious structures in Wallachia, as well as the boyars, as a social group, were of Slavic origin; it is here that the explanation for the hereditary-elective system of choosing princes must be found. The problem that would plague Wallachia throughout the period under discussion is similar to that experienced by many Slavic states in Eastern Europe — the absence of primogeniture in Slavic customary law, meaning that all sons had a right to a share in an inheritance.[5]

The origins of this problem predated both the foundation of the state and the appearance of the Turks in Europe. It is true, however, that the hereditary-elective system of choosing princes, in fact, first became a serious problem with the appearance of the Ottoman threat. Several factors help to explain why. First of all, from the reign of Bogdan I to that of Mircea the Old, the number of royal offspring multiplied. In fact, the family can be divided into two branches from the time of Mircea's reign. Both Mircea and his brother Dan were sons of Prince Radu I (1377-1384). The oldest son, Dan, succeeded their father in 1384. When he died three years later, in 1387, his brother Mircea succeeded him on the throne. One chronicler, Chalkondyles, claims that Mircea killed his brother,[6] while other sources claim that Prince Dan was killed by Sisman, prince of the Serbs.[7] It seems unlikely that Mircea committed fratricide as Dan's son, the future Prince Dan II, is known to have served his uncle loyally and referred to him with reverence in several documents issued during his reigns.[8] Whatever the true circumstances of Dan's death may have been, the fact remains that following the death of Mircea the Old in January, 1418, the sons of both Mircea and his brother

---

[4]R.W. Seton-Watson, *A History of the Roumanians from Roman Times to the Completion of Unity* (Cambridge, 1934), pp. 31-32.

[5]See, for example, G. Vernadsky, *Kievan Russia* (New Haven, 1973), pp. 179-180.

[6]Laonic Chalcocondil, *Expuneri istorice*, trans. Vasile Grecu (Bucureşti, 1958).

Dan would contest the throne, each building support among boyar factions.

Interestingly, it was Mircea himself who realized the grave nature of this problem, especially after the appearance of the Turkish threat, and took measures to try and establish a sound principle of succession to the throne. He did this, much like Roman emperors attempted to do, by making his son Mihail associate ruler as early as 27 December 1391.[9] By 1416, Mihail had become de facto ruler of Wallachia and was securely placed to succeed his father who died on 31 January 1418. Despite his efforts, as we shall see, Mircea's attempt to establish a sound principle of succession failed for shortly after his death the struggle between his successors and those of his brother Dan broke out, and, as the great prince foresaw when he tried to find a solution to this dilemma, it would be used to full advantage by the Ottoman aggressor, as well as by his Saxon and Hungarian neighbors to the north.

The result of this increasing external interference in the internal affairs of Wallachia can be demonstrated statistically. From the founding of the principality in 1310 until the end of the reign of Mircea cel Bătrân in 1418, a period of 108 years, a total of seven princes sat on the throne of Wallachia, making an average reign of slightly more than 15 years:

Basarab I	c. 1310-1352
Nicolae Alexandru	1352-1364
Vladislav I (Vlaicu)	1364-1377

---

[7]Constantin Căpitanul Filipescu, *Istoriile domnilor Ţării Româneşti cuprinzînd istoria munteană de la început pănă la 1698*, N. Iorga, ed. (Bucureşti, 1902). This chronicle has been mistakenly attributed by the editor to Constantin Căpitanul Filipescu. It is in fact a shorter variant of *Letopiseţul cantacuzinesc* written by Radu Popescu, see Constantin Grecescu and Dan Simonescu, eds., *Istoria Ţării Romîneşti, 1290-1690. Letopiseţul cantacuzinesc* (Bucureşti, 1960), p. LXII. See also the Bulgarian Chronicle cited by Nicolae Iorga in *Studii şi documente*, vol. IV (Bucureşti, 1901), p. IV.

[8]See Ilie Minea, *Vlad Dracul şi vremea sa* (Iaşi, 1928), pp. 88-89.

[9]Alexandru Vasilescu, *Urmaşii lui Mircea cel Bătrân*, p. 16.

Radu I	1377-1384
Dan I	1384-1387
Mircea the Old	1387-1418
Vlad I	1394-1397

In contrast, the period from 1418 to the final reign of Vlad III Dracula in 1476, a period of 58 years, a total of 11 different princes sat on the throne, making an average reign of slightly over 5 years. The situation is even more grim when we consider that many of these eleven princes had several different reigns, including Vlad who reigned three times (1448, 1456-1462, and 1476). Thus we can identify 29 separate reigns during this 58 year period making for an average of reign of only 2 years:

Mihail I	1418-1420
Dan II	1420-1421
Radu II Prasnaglava	March-November, 1421
Dan II	1421-1423
Radu II Prasnaglava	Summer, 1423
Dan II	1423-1424
Radu II Prasnaglava	1424-1426
Dan II	1426-1427
Radu II Prasnaglava	January-March, 1427
Dan II	1427-1431
Alexandru I Aldea	1431-1436
Vlad II Dracul	1436-1442
Mircea	March-August, 1442
Basarab II	1442-1443
Vlad II Dracul	1443-1447
Vladislav II	1447-1448
Vlad III Dracula	October, 1448
Vladislav II	1448-1456
Vlad III Dracula	1456-1462
Radu cel Frumos	1462-1473
Basarab Laiotă	November-December, 1473
Radu cel Frumos	1473-1474
Basarab Laiotă	March, 1474

Radu cel Frumos	· March-September, 1474
Basarab Laiotă	1474-1476
Vlad III Dracula	November-December, 1476

While the impact of the Ottoman threat can be seen in the political instability that characterized Wallachia throughout the fifteenth century, it cannot be said that the threat posed by Ottoman expansion created this condition; it was inherent in the hereditary-elective system of choosing princes. The Ottoman danger merely amplified it as the Porte consciously exploited this fundamental weakness.

Several historians have tried to explain the instability that characterized Wallachian politics during this period as resulting from an ongoing struggle for the throne between the successors of Dan I and those of Mircea the Old, following the death of the latter in 1418. It has been argued that the conflict was initially a personal rivalry between members of the two families, but that later on it became a struggle along territorial lines, the Dănești faction (originally descendants of Dan I) being boyars from Oltenia, while the Drăculești faction (originally descendants of Mircea the Old) were boyars from Muntenia.[10] The so-called Drăculești-Dănești rivalry, while providing a nice framework for trying to understand the problem, is difficult to prove when confronting the evidence. For example, while the struggle between Mihail, Mircea the Old's eldest son and successor, and Dan II, son of Dan I, may be interpreted in this way, as is also true of the ongoing struggle during the 1420s between Dan II and another of Mircea's sons, Radu Praznaglava, it fails to explain the conflict between Alexandru Aldea and Vlad Dracul during the 1430s as both were sons of Mircea. Likewise, it cannot explain the conflict between Vlad III and Radu cel Frumos in 1462, which we will examine in detail later, as both were sons of Vlad Dracul, grandsons of Mircea. It seems an artificial construction to interpret the ongoing struggles for the throne that characterized fifteenth century Wallachia in terms of the Drăculești-Dănești rivalry.[11]

---

[10]See A.D. Xenopol, "Lupta dintre Dănești și Drăculești," in *Analele Academiei Române mem. sect. ist.*, seria II, tom. XXX (București, 1907), p. 2 (184) and 84 (266).

Family loyalty appears not to have been an impediment for asserting claims to the throne against brothers. The conflicts are best understood as being attempts by those who had a legitimate claim to the throne to gain support among a faction of the boyars and/or support from a foreign power to take control of the country. These were personal conflicts. Family ties nevertheless played a powerful role in creating factions among the boyars, and certainly princes, once installed on the throne, sought to secure benefits for their relatives and supporters.

***

As we mentioned earlier, the first contact between Wallachia and the Ottomans came during the reign of Mircea the Old. Following the great Ottoman victory over the Serbs at Kosova in 1389, Mircea agreed to pay tribute to the Ottomans, although he did not become a vassal and maintained his country's independence.[12] Nevertheless, conflicts with the Ottomans ensued. He won a great victory over the Turks, defeating Sultan Bayezid I in the marshes at Rovine in 1394. The following year he allied himself with Emperor Sigismund of Luxembourg, king of Hungary, and joined the emperor in the ill-fated Crusade that ended in a disastrous defeat for the Christian forces, made up of French, Burgundian, and German knights, at Nicopolis in 1396. The collapse of the Ottoman Empire following the invasion by Tamerlane in 1402 and the outbreak of the Ottoman Civil War gave Mircea a respite. He tried to intervene in the civil war between the sons of Bayezid to gain advantages for Wallachia by supporting Musa. The eventual victory of Mehmed I meant a rebirth of Ottoman power. The new sultan seized several Danubian fortresses from Walla-

---

[11]This is also the position taken by Alexandru Vasilescu, *Urmașii lui Mircea cel Bătrân*, p. 19.

[12]See the text of the treaty from 1391 in Dimitrie A. Sturdza and C. Colescu-Vartic, *Acte și documente relative la istoria renascerei României*, vol. I (1391-1841) (Bucuresci, 1900), doc. I, pp. 1-2.

chia, and took control of Dobrogea, making it a Turkish province.[13] In addition, Mircea had to agree to pay an annual tribute of 3,000 ducats. Nevertheless, he maintained Wallachia's independence as the agreement did not recognize the Ottoman Empire as a suzerain power and in exchange for tribute the Ottomans were obligated to defend Wallachia against unauthorized raids north of the Danube. Through his skillful political maneuvering and military prowess Mircea earned the respect of his formidable enemy to the south, being characterized by the Turkish chronicler Leunclavius as "the bravest and cleverest among the Christian princes."[14] He died on 31 January 1418 and was buried in the church at the Monastery of Cozia, which he had built, on 4 February 1418.[15] His reign would become the point of reference for all of his successors during the fifteenth century, who, in many of their official acts, refer back to the reign of Mircea. It was he who strengthened Wallachia, developed its institutions, and maintained its independence in face of the Ottoman threat.

Mircea the Old
Prince of Wallachia, 1387-1418
By Octavian Ion Penda

Mircea's handpicked successor, his eldest son Mihail I, was acting as prince of Wallachia even before his father's death. He is mentioned as associate ruler in documents as early as 1391, but consistently after 1415 when he used the title "I Mihail, voievod and

---

[13]It would remain so until its incorporation into Romania as a result of the Russo-Turkish War, also known as the Romanian War for Independence, in 1877.

[14]"*Princeps... inter Christianos fortissimus et acerrimus,*" in Leunclavius, *Historia Musulmana Turcorum de monumentis ipsorum exscripta* (1591), f. 418.

[15]The most complete study of the reign of Mircea cel Bătrân is P.P. Panaitescu, *Mircea cel Bătrân* (Bucureşti, 1944). See also N. Şerbănescu and N. Stoicescu, *Mircea cel Mare (1386-1418)* (Bucureşti, 1987); Ion Pătroiu, ed., *Marele Mircea Voievod* (Bucureşti, 1987); *Io Mircea mare voievod şi domn* (Bucureşti, 1988); R.W. Seton-Watson, *History of the Roumanians,* pp. 32-34; and Ioan Bogdan, *Luptele romînilor cu turcii pănă la Mihai Viteazul* (Bucureşti, 1898), pp. 16-17.

prince."[16] Nevertheless, Mircea's efforts to ensure a smooth transition to the throne to protect the independence of Wallachia failed completely. While the first year of Mihail's reign went smoothly as he maintained close relations with the Hungarians, and Sultan Mehmed I was busy consolidating his newly refounded empire, the new prince failed to preserve the delicate balance between the two neighboring powers that his father had sought to establish.

Although the reasons are unclear, Mihail, from the time of his co-regency in 1417, stopped paying tribute to the Turks. In addition, he participated alongside the Hungarian Army in a battle against the Ottomans along the Danube in September 1419. This led the sultan to launch an attack against Wallachia in which Mihail was defeated in the fall of 1419 and forced to pay the tribute he had neglected to send during the three previous years, as well as to promise to pay promptly in the future. In addition, he was forced to cede the fortress of Giurgiu and the left bank of the Danube to the Black Sea to the Ottomans, and to give his sons Mihail and Radu as hostages. These concessions weakened Mihail's position among the boyars, some of whom defected to a rival claimant to the throne, Dan II, son of Mircea the Old's brother Dan I.[17] Perhaps the opposition from the boyars led Mihail not to respect the terms of the new treaty. This created an opportunity exploited by Dan II who sought to enlist the sultan's help in his effort to gain the throne. A war broke out between Mihail and Dan in the spring of 1420. At first it appeared that Mihail would have sufficient strength to repel the invasion of his rival, but Turkish intervention in May turned the tide in favor of Dan II. Mihail was forced to retreat and to seek help from his Hungarian allies. When the two forces met again in the summer of 1420 Dan's forces, aided by the

---

[16]"Io Mihail, voievod şi domn," see documents in *Documenta Romaniae Historica B. Ţara Românească*, vol. I (Bucureşti, 1966). See also Alexandru Vasilescu, *Urmaşii lui Mircea cel Bătrân*, pp. 6-9. The term *voievod* is a title given to a military leader.

[17]Among the boyars who defected to Dan we can identify Albul and Utmeş from existent documents.

Turks, defeated Mihail and his Hungarian contingent. Mihail was killed in the fighting and Dan II assumed the Wallachian throne.[18]

This first conflict between the successors of Mircea the Old is illustrative of the subsequent struggles for the throne in Wallachia during the fifteenth century. The country would become a battle-ground between the Hungarian Kingdom and the Ottoman Empire in their struggle for supremacy in the Danubian region. Each side would support claimants to the throne in this Romanian principality in order to gain influence and the upper hand in the struggle with the other power. At the same time, claimants to the throne would regularly appeal to one of these two powers for assistance in gaining the throne. The result was that the position of any prince was at best pre-carious and the struggle to preserve the principality's independence, as it had been established by Mircea the Old, would become ever more difficult. It is in this light that we must also view the reign of Vlad III Dracula.

During the 1420s the ongoing struggle for the throne between Dan II and Radu II Praznaglava characterized Wallachian politics. While Dan had initially gained the throne with the aid of the Turks, his rival Radu sought assistance from the king of Hungary, Emperor Sigismund of Luxembourg. As each prince found it necessary to make overtures to one or the other of the opposing neighboring powers, his rival could easily appeal to the other side in his effort to retake the throne. Thus, Dan regained the throne for the second time in 1421-1422 with the aid of Hungary. This led Radu Praznaglava to appeal to yet another source for support in his effort to oust his cousin Dan from the throne, Prince Alexander the Good (1400-1432) of neighboring Moldavia.

Like his contemporary Mircea the Old in Wallachia, Alexander the Good realized the administrative and territorial consolidation of the second Romanian principality, Moldavia. Following Mircea's

---

[18]Alexandru Vasilescu, *Urmaşii lui Mircea cel Bătrân*, pp. 14-20; A.D. Xenopol, "Lupta dintre Dăneşti şi Drăculeşti," p. 5 (187); and Ştefan Nicolaescu, *Domnia lui Alexandru Vodă Aldea, fiul lui Mircea Vodă cel Bătrân, 1431-1435* (Bucureşti, 1922), pp. 231-233.

death, he used the occasion of the struggles in Wallachia to secure the southern border of his principality and to improve its economic situation by seizing the strategic Danubian fortress of Chilia in 1421 which was also an important customs point through which a great deal of Moldavian trade passed.

The ongoing conflict between the two rivals for the throne finally came to an end in 1427 when Radu II Praznaglava was ousted from the throne, after a brief reign, by Dan II, with the aid of Hungary, and killed, together with his sons.[19] This was clearly a precautionary measure taken by Dan II to eliminate potential rivals to the throne. Nevertheless, other claimants remained. When Dan II attempted to regain possession of the fortress of Chilia, Moldavian Prince Alexander the Good decided to assist another of Mircea the Old's sons, Alexandru Aldea, in his attempt to claim his father's throne.[20]

In 1430, with the outcome of the Ottoman-Venetian conflict over Salonika clear, Dan II once again reoriented his foreign policy toward the Porte. This caused a reaction from Hungary which began to support Dan's rivals for the throne. Alexandru Aldea was not the only pretender. Another son of Mircea, Vlad, also sought to lay claim to the throne. Realizing that an opportune moment had arrived, Vlad, who had established himself in Transylvania in 1429 to garner support for his bid, quickly made his way to the court of Emperor Sigismund of Luxembourg in Nuremburg in January 1431 to gain the emperor's support for an attack on Wallachia.

As a boy Vlad had been sent by his father as a hostage to the court of Emperor Sigismund in 1395-1396 when he allied with Hungary on the eve of the ill-fated Nicopolis Crusade. He later spent time in Constantinople at the court of the Byzantine emperor, before coming to Transylvania in 1429 to pursue his claim to the Wallachian throne. When Vlad arrived in Nuremburg in 1431 he received a

---

[19]Alexandru Vasilescu, *Urmaşii lui Mircea cel Bătrân*, pp. 20-36.

[20]*Ibid.*, pp. 37-40.

warm welcome from the emperor who formally invested him as prince of Wallachia. At the same time, in a great ceremony, the *Draconorden* (The Order of the Dragon), a crusading order founded by Sigismund in 1418 to fight the Turkish Infidels and perpetuate the condemnation of Jan Hus, was bestowed upon the would-be prince.[21]

It is as a result of this distinction that Vlad became known as *Dracul* which in Romanian at that time meant "the Dragon." The name *Dracula* (*Drăculea* in its old Romanian form), by which his son Vlad Ţepeş was known both in his own time and up to the present day, is derived from this title, the *-a/-ea* suffix meaning "son of." Thus Dracula means "son of Dracul," referring to his father Vlad II.[22] Because the term *dracul* also has another meaning, that of "the devil," some scholars attributed it to an alleged brutality demonstrated by Vlad II that would be surpassed by his son Vlad III, about whom rumors of excessive cruelty would circulate throughout Europe. The name Dracula was interpreted in this sense already in the fifteenth century when stories of Vlad Ţepeş's cruelty had spread in the German and Russian speaking lands. For example, the Slavic stories concerning Vlad III Dracula begin: "There was in Wallachia a Christian prince of the Greek faith by the name of Dracula in the Romanian language, while in ours the Devil, so evil was he. As was his name so was his life." [23] This is clearly a literary invention as fifteenth century

---

[21]Alexandru Vasilescu, *Urmaşii lui Mircea cel Bătrân*, pp. 42-43; Radu Florescu and Raymond T. McNally, *Dracula: A Biography of Vlad the Impaler*, pp. 29-31; and C.C. Giurescu, "The Historical Dracula," in Kurt W. Treptow, *Dracula: Essays...*, p. 14.

[22]On this see Grigore Nandriş, "A Philological Analysis of Dracula and Romanian Place-Names and Masculine Personal Names in -a/ea," pp. 229-237, in Kurt W. Treptow, ed., *Dracula: Essays....*

[23]See Pandele Olteanu, *Limba povestirilor slave despre Vlad Ţepeş* (Bucureşti, 1960), p. 355 for the original Slavic version and a Romanian translation; likewise, P.P. Panaitescu, ed., *Cronicele slavo-romîne din sec. XV-XVI publicate de Ion Bogdan* (Bucureşti, 1959), pp. 200 and 207; and Matei Cazacu, *L'histoire du Prince Dracula en Europe centrale et orientale (XVᵉ siècle)* (Genève, 1988), pp. 172-173 for the original Slavic version and a French translation. There are no sources which portray Vlad Dracul as having been excessively cruel, and he is known to have had good relations with the boyars.

documents refer to all three of Vlad Dracul's sons — Mircea, Vlad, and Radu — as Dracula, with the sense of "son of Dracul."

Vlad's hopes of becoming prince of Wallachia soon faded as he set out from Nuremburg. At the urging of the Lithuanian Prince Swidrigaillo, Sigismund had a change of heart and decided instead to support Alexandru Aldea, Alexander the Good's candidate for the throne.[24] With Moldavian support, Aldea launched an invasion of Wallachia in the summer of 1431 and ousted Dan II. The latter fled to the Ottomans who lent him troops to attempt to retake the throne. In the ensuing conflict, Alexandru Aldea again emerged victorious, once more assisted by Moldavian forces, and secured his place on the throne. Dan II was killed in the fighting.[25] The result left Vlad Dracul in Transylvania where he remained a pretender to the throne, waiting for favorable circumstances to permit him again to pursue his goal.

Alexandru Aldea (1431-1436) is a controversial prince who assumed the throne amidst difficult circumstances. The death of Alexander the Good in January 1432 brought a period of political instability to Moldavia not unlike that which characterized Wallachian politics after the death of Mircea the Old. This left the new prince without his most ardent ally. In addition, Turkish power in Southeastern Europe was on the rise with the defeat of Venice in the war over Salonika in 1430 and the conquest of southern Albania in 1432. Within Wallachia, Aldea pursued a policy of reconciliation, maintaining many of the members of the *sfatul domnesc* (princely council) of Dan II in their posts.[26]

---

[24]Ilie Minea, *Vlad Dracul şi vremea sa*, p. 96. Alexander the Good had reoriented his foreign policy away from Poland during the final year of his reign, allying himself with Lithuania and Hungary, rivals of the Polish Kingdom.

[25]Alexandru Vasilescu, *Urmaşii lui Mircea cel Bătrân*, pp. 42-44, 47.

[26]See doc. 72 in *Documenta Romaniae Historica, B. Ţara Românească*, vol. I, pp. 133-134. For example, among the boyars listed in the *sfatul domnesc* in the *hrisov* issued by Alexandru Aldea at Târgovişte on 17 November 1431 *jupan* Albul, *jupan* Radu al lui Sahac, Nan Pascal, *jupan* Iarciul, *jupan* Toxaba, all had been supporters of Dan II.

Alexandru Aldea
Prince of Wallachia, 1431-1436
By Octavian Ion Penda

Failing to receive support from his allies, he was forced to negotiate with Sultan Murad II. He went to Adrianople, the Ottoman capital at that time, and, in addition to accepting to pay an annual tribute to the sultan, he also had to agree to render military assistance when requested to do so, as well as to send hostages to the Porte. Thus, his reign is often seen as the beginning of Wallachia's vassalage to the Ottomans.[27] Although it is true that he joined an Ottoman invasion that plundered southern Transylvania in 1432, he generally tried to preserve a balance of power between his two rival neighboring empires, respecting the agreements that he had concluded with the sultan while, at the same time, sending messengers to Sigismund trying to renew relations with Hungary.[28] He failed in the latter, giving Vlad Dracul the occasion again to promote his candidacy for the Wallachian throne. Already when Aldea was at Adrianople, Vlad Dracul, joined by some of Aldea's boyars, who had abandoned their prince, tried to gain support from Braşov to invade Wallachia. Unfortunately for him, in Aldea's absence his chief boyar Albu proved capable of protecting the country[29] and Emperor Sigismund showed

---

[27]Keith Hitchins, "Ottoman Domination of Moldavia and Wallachia in the Sixteenth Century," p. 124.

[28]On the reign of Alexandru Aldea see Alexandru Vasilescu, *Urmaşii lui Mircea cel Bătrân*, pp. 44-54. Ştefan Nicolaescu, *Domnia lui Alexandru Vodă Aldea*, presents a very positive image of the prince usually accused of being an Ottoman pawn. The author concludes, "Alexandru Aldea appears to me... as a young voievod, a brave prince, wholly devoted to the Christian cause... In my opinion Alexandru Vodă Aldea is a small hero of his time" (p. 238).

[29]The political importance of Albu is revealed by two letters he sent to Braşov published by Nicolae Iorga in *Scrisori de boieri, scrisori de domni* (Vălenii-de-Munte, 1925), pp. 11-12.

little interest in this corner of his vast empire. Nevertheless, as a result of Aldea's cooperation with the Ottoman attack on Transylvania, after 1432 Braşov began receiving refugees from Wallachia and lending support to Vlad Dracul.

Despite everything, Alexandru Aldea, aided by his powerful boyar Albu, proved capable of maintaining the delicate balance necessary to ensure a relative autonomy and secure his position on the throne. In fact, Alexandru Aldea would be the only prince from the death of Mircea the Old in 1418 to that of Vlad III Dracula in 1476 to die a natural death while on the throne.

Vlad Dracul led an invasion of Wallachia in the summer of 1436, but with Ottoman assistance Aldea repulsed the attack. Shortly after this, however, the prince, who had been suffering from an unknown illness since 1435, died naturally, leaving no heir.[30] This left the door open for his brother, Vlad Dracul, to reenter the country and install himself on the throne in the fall of 1436.

Sultan Murad II
By Octavian Ion Penda

The reign of Vlad II Dracul, in some ways, resembles that of his predecessor. Like Aldea, circumstances forced Vlad to try to maintain a careful balance between the two neighboring empires who struggled for supremacy in the lower Danube region. The new prince hastily renounced the terms of the treaty concluded by Aldea with the sultan, but after an Ottoman attack on Wallachia in November 1436 and the death of his protector, Sigismund of Luxembourg, the following year, he was compelled to seek an accommodation with Sultan Murad II who was then preparing to take advantage of the difficulties faced by the Hungarian

---

[30]Alexandru Vasilescu, *Urmaşii lui Mircea cel Bătrân*, pp. 52-55; and Ilie Minea, *Vlad Dracul şi vremea sa*, p. 141. The last known document from the reign of Alexandru Aldea was issued in Târgovişte on 25 June 1436, see doc. 77 in *Documenta Historica Romaniae, B. Ţara Românească*, vol. I, pp. 138-140.

Kingdom in the aftermath of Sigismund's death and the violent peasant uprising that took place in Transylvania in 1437-1438. Dracul paid homage to the sultan at Adrianople and had to accept terms similar to those agreed to by Aldea under similar circumstances in 1432.[31] Thus, when the sultan decided to launch an attack on Transylvania in 1438 Vlad joined the Ottoman Army with a contingent of Wallachian troops.

The campaign of 1438, the most significant Ottoman attack on Transylvania up to that time, took place in August.[32] Sultan Murad set out from Adrianople with his army and marched north to Vidin where he crossed the Danube into Wallachia. The initial objective of the campaign may have been an attack on Hungary itself, but the sultan decided instead to invade Transylvania.[33] In Wallachia he joined forces with Vlad and the two armies crossed the mountains into Transylvania. Near Hațeg they encountered resistance led by a Romanian nobleman named Cândea; after forcing him to retreat, they went on and captured Câlnic and Sebeş without resistance. While besieging Sibiu with part of his forces, Murad sent detachments in other directions, plundering Alba Iulia, and reaching the outskirts of Sighişoara. After 8 days the siege of Sibiu was lifted and the Ottoman and Wallachian forces reunited and withdrew from Transylvania through Țara Bârsei, plundering the suburbs of Braşov along the way. The entire campaign had the character of a raid; Ottoman forces met little or no resistance in the open field and they took back with them to Wallachia a vast amount of plunder and numerous prisoners which they

---

[31]Hitchins, "Ottoman Domination in Moldavia and Wallachia," p. 125; Virgil Ciocîltan, "Între sultan şi împărat: Vlad Dracul în 1438," pp. 1767-1790, in *Revista de istorie*, XXIX:11 (Noiembrie, 1976), p. 1778; see also the report of Ioan de Raguza in Nicolae Iorga, ed., *Notes et extraits pour servir à l'histoire des croisades au XV siècle. Quatrième série (1453-1476)* (Bucarest, 1915), p. 26.

[32]On this campaign see Ilie Minea, *Vlad Dracul şi vremea sa*, pp. 159-161; and Ciocîltan, "Între sultan şi împărat." According to Ciocîltan, who has undertaken the only comprehensive analysis of this campaign, it began on 7 August and lasted approximately 23 days.

[33]Ciocîltan, "Între sultan şi împărat," pp. 1775-1776.

divided upon their return. The Ottoman forces then marched back to Adrianople, crossing the Danube at Nicopolis.[34]

Like his predecessor, Alexandru Aldea, who had joined an Ottoman raid on Transylvania in 1432, Vlad Dracul began making peace overtures to Hungary almost immediately upon his return. The Romanian prince offered to set free Antonie of Sebeş and 50 other nobles, who, together with their families, had been taken prisoner during the campaign. The new king, Albrecht of Hapsburg, however, refused to allow them to repatriate as they had surrendered their cities without resistance in face of the invaders.[35] Vlad's efforts to maintain a balance between the two powers provoked suspicion on both sides. His overtures to Hungary following the campaign of 1438 made the sultan wary of Vlad's intentions, while the Hungarians had even more reason not to trust him after he had joined the sultan in the attack on Transylvania. After this, a new pretender to the Wallachian throne, Basarab II, the son of Dan II, began to serve in Emperor Albrecht's army.[36]

Vlad II Dracul
Prince of Wallachia, 1436-1442; 1443-1447
By Octavian Ion Penda

Like Aldea before him, Vlad Dracul pursued a policy of reconciliation within Wallachia. He retained many of the boyars who had served on the *sfatul domnesc* during the reign of his predecessor.[37] Indeed, his reign is characterized by a remarkable stability in his rela-

---

[34]On the itinerary of the campaign see Ciocîltan, "Între sultan şi împărat," pp. 1772-1773.

[35]See doc. 2330 in Gustav Gündisch, *Urkundenbuch zur Geschichte der Deutschen in Siebenbürgen*, vol. V (1438-1457) (Bukarest, 1975), p. 22.

[36]Minea, *Vlad Dracul şi vremea sa*, pp. 162-164.

[37]Among these we are able to identify Stanciul, Mircea, Nan Pascal, and Tatul Sârbul, see docs. 77 and 80 in *Documenta Romaniae Historica, B. Ţara Românească*, vol. I, pp. 138-140 and 142-144.

tions with the major boyars.[38] A significant member of Aldea's *sfatul domnesc* not to be found during Dracul's reign is Albul, who had been his predecessor's closest counsellor and had become an implacable enemy of Vlad.

It is in documents from the early part of Vlad Dracul's reign that we find the first mention of his sons. In a deed issued on 20 January 1437, the Wallachian prince speaks of his "first born sons, Mircea and Vlad."[39] There are three more documents that refer to Mircea and Vlad, all issued in August 1437.[40] The next document we possess that mentions Dracul's sons is dated 2 August 1439 in which, in addition to Mircea and Vlad, the prince mentions his youngest son, Radu,[41] born sometime between 23 August 1437 and the date this deed was issued. From contemporary accounts we know that Mircea was about 15 years old in 1443.[42] Likewise, for Vlad Dracula to have been a serious candidate for the throne in 1448 he must have been at least 18 at that time. As a result, most scholars conclude, based on this and the famous portrait of Dracula from Ambras Castle in Austria, that Vlad Țepeș was born sometime between 1429 and 1431, probably in Transylvania.[43]

---

[38]Docs. 80-99 in *Documenta Romaniae Historica, B. Țara Românească*, vol. I, pp. 142-175, are the existent internal documents from the reign of Vlad Dracul. Documents 80, 81, 82, 83, 84, 85, 86, 87, 89, 91, 93, 94, 95, 98, and 99 list the members of the *sfatul domnesc*.

[39]Doc. 80 in *Documenta Romaniae Historica, B. Țara Românească*, vol. I, pp. 142-143.

[40]Docs. 83, 85, and 87 in *Documenta Romaniae Historica, B. Țara Românească*, vol. I, pp. 146-153.

[41]Doc. 89 in *Documenta Romaniae Historica, B. Țara Românească*, vol. I, pp. 154-156.

[42]Nicolae Iorga, "Cronica lui Wavrin și Românii," in *Buletinul comisiei istorice a României*, IV (București, 1927), pp. 60-63.

[43]See, for example, Radu R. Florescu and Raymond T. McNally, *Dracula: A Biography of Vlad the Impaler, 1431-1476*, pp. 31-32.

With the union of the Hungarian and Polish crowns as a result of the election of the Polish King Ladislas as king of Hungary following the death of Albrecht of Hapsburg in 1440, crusading efforts were renewed. As a result, Vlad Dracul began to stray from his alliance with the sultan and lend support to the anti-Ottoman efforts of the Transylvanian governor John Hunyadi. After Hunyadi defeated Ottoman forces in Transylvania in March 1442 Dracul was called to Adrianople to demonstrate his loyalty to his suzerain, leaving his eldest son, Mircea, as governor in Wallachia. As a result of what he considered to be Dracul's treachery, the sultan imprisoned the prince at Gallipoli and ordered an attack on Wallachia.[44] This new Ottoman assault was again repulsed by Hunyadi who used the occasion to install his protege, Basarab II, on the throne. Realizing the danger posed to the empire if Hunyadi controlled Wallachia, the sultan decided to release Vlad Dracul at the end of 1442, but required him to leave his two youngest sons as hostages. Thus, Dracul's sons Vlad and Radu remained as Ottoman prisoners to ensure their father's continued loyalty to the Porte. The young princes were imprisoned at Egrigoz in an isolated part of Anatolia.[45]

Early in 1443, Vlad Dracul invaded Wallachia and took back his throne.[46] Basarab II was probably killed in the fighting as he is not to be heard from again. The strong base Dracul had established amongst the nobility made his return an easy one as he enjoyed popular support. Likewise, many probably feared and resented the threat posed by the growing interference of Catholic Hungary in the internal affairs of the country.

His experience of the previous year and the sultan's promise to return his sons led Dracul to remain neutral in the fall of 1443 when

---

[44]Minea, *Vlad Dracul și vremea sa*, p. 179.

[45]Minea, *Vlad Dracul și vremea sa*, p. 180; and Florescu and McNally, *Dracula: Essays on the Life and Times of Vlad Țepeș*, p. 35.

[46]We know Basarab II was on the Wallachian throne on 9 January 1443 when he issued a deed at Argeș confirming to the Monastery of Cozia its villages and Gypsy slaves, see doc. 96 in *Documenta Romaniae Historica, B. Țara Românească*, pp. 167-168.

Hunyadi organized the anti-Ottoman expedition in Serbia. Despite the great Christian victory at the battle of Nis on 3 November 1443, which restored Serbia under the rule of George Brankovic and marked the beginning of the Albanian rebellion led by Scanderbeg, Dracul remained cautious about joining the crusade being organized by King Ladislas and John Hunyadi in 1444.

As the Romanian historian Ilie Minea pointed out, "Vlad Dracul did not intend to exchange Turkish suzerainty for a Hungarian one. At the end of a trail blazed with great sacrifices he wanted to see the resurrection of Wallachian independence."[47] Dracul himself is said to have advised King Ladislas not to undertake this campaign, adding that the sultan went hunting with more attendants than the king had troops.[48] Nevertheless, he sent a contingent of 4,000 troops, under the command of his son Mircea, to participate in the ill-fated Varna campaign. The crusade ended in total disaster at Varna on 10 November 1444 when the Christian army was defeated and King Ladislas and the Papal legate Cardinal Cesarini were killed in the fighting.[49] Dracul intercepted the Christian forces as they retreated northward and arrested Hunyadi whom he blamed for the military fiasco; the Wallachian prince did not hide his fury with the Transylvanian governor and was on the verge of killing him when others intervened and paid a large ransom to free Hunyadi.[50]

---

[47]Minea, *Vlad Dracul și vremea sa*, p. 221.

[48]*Ibid.*, p. 211; Ilie Minea, *Informațiile românești ale cronicii lui Ian Dlugosz* (Vălenii-de-Munte, 1926); and Ioan Bogdan, *Luptele romînilor cu turcii pănă la Mihai Viteazul*, pp. 18-19.

[49]On the Varna Campaign see L.S. Stavrianos, *The Balkans since 1453*, pp. 52-54; R.W. Seton-Watson, *A History of the Roumanians from Roman Times to the Completion of Unity*, p. 38; and Oskar Halecki, *The Crusade of Varna: A Discussion of Controversial Problems* (New York, 1943). An important source of information on the events of 1443-1444 is the poem of the Hungarian court minstrel Michael Beheim who received his information from Hans Magest, a Saxon soldier who fought in the Christian Army at Varna and fell prisoner to the Turks. See Constantin I. Karadja, *Poema lui Michel Beheim despre cruciadele împotriva turcilor din anii 1443 și 1444* (Vălenii-de-Munte, 1936).

The Ransoming of John Hunyadi from Vlad II Dracul, 1444

By Octavian Ion Penda

The situation of Dracul's sons, Vlad and Radu, is unknown during this period. It is known that during the peace negotiations which led to the short-lived Peace of Seghedin in June 1444 the sultan promised to free Dracul's sons.[51] We cannot be certain, however, if they were freed during this time. In any event, the problem of the captivity of the two young princes remains unclear from the available evidence.

After the disaster at Varna, Vlad decided to participate actively in planning the Danubian expedition organized by the Burgundian crusader Walerin de Wavrin. Initially conceived of as an attempt to rescue King Ladislas who many believed had survived the battle of Varna, Dracul clearly saw in this campaign the chance to secure his southern border against increasing Ottoman power. In August 1445 the Christian forces started out from Brăila, with Wallachian cavalry units, led by Mircea, accompanying the Burgundian fleet, under Wavrin's command, up river. They were to join up with an army led by John Hunyadi at Nicopolis in early September.[52]

After an unsuccessful attack on Silistria, the Wallachian and Burgundian forces liberated Turtucaia and the strategic fortress of Giurgiu. Dismayed by the lack of support from Hungary, Dracul wrote to Braşov, asking them to:

> help us with arcs and arrows and guns and powder to arrange ·
> them in the fortress, [in all likelihood referring to Giurgiu]
> because it is the strongest [fortress] of ours and yours, and all
> the Christians. And again, what the servant of my majesty,
> Dragomir, has said to you, believe him as they are the words of
> my majesty.[53]

---

[50]I. Christian von Engel, *Geschichte der Moldau und Wallachey* (Halle, 1804), pp. 167-173.

[51]Minea, *Vlad Dracul şi vremea sa*, p. 236. Ştefan Andreescu maintains that Vlad and Radu returned to Wallachia at this time, see Andreescu, *Vlad Ţepeş (Dracula)*, p. 33.

[52]For details on this campaign see Nicolae Iorga, "Cronica lui Wavrin şi românii," pp. 103-145; and Minea, *Vlad Dracul şi vremea sa*, pp. 254-266.

Shortly after the capture of Giurgiu, the Ottoman commander at Rusciuc, across the Danube, surrendered that fortress to the Christian forces. It was here that Vlad Dracul granted asylum to 12,000 Bulgarians who no longer wanted to live under Turkish rule. He is said to have declared that:

> had nothing else been accomplished [during this campaign] than to save these 11,000 or 12,000 Christian souls who escaped from bondage... this in and of itself was a great achievement.[54]

Despite these successes, the campaign came to an end shortly after the Christian forces reached Nicopolis. The Turks avoided a direct engagement and, with their supplies running low and winter rapidly approaching, the Christians were compelled to abandon the campaign around 1 October; the Burgundian fleet had to withdraw from the Danube, which froze over during the winter, and made its way back to Constantinople.

The conflict between John Hunyadi and Vlad Dracul had its origins in 1442 when Hunyadi placed Basarab II on the Wallachian throne during the time when Dracul was imprisoned at Gallipoli; the situation was probably aggravated in 1443 when the Wallachian prince refused to join Hunyadi's Christian coalition. The Transylvanian governor certainly never forgave Dracul for detaining him after the Varna disaster. The uneasy cooperation between the two during the Danubian campaign in 1445, in which Hunyadi played only a minor role, could not erase the animosity between the Wallachian prince and the Transylvanian governor who had also become the royal governor of Hungary following the ascension to the throne of Ladislas the Posthumous, the infant son of Albrecht of Hapsburg, after the death of King Ladislas in the battle of Varna. Relations with

---

[53]Doc. LV in Ioan Bogdan, *Documente privitoare la relaţiile Ţării Româneşti cu Braşovul şi Ţara Ungurească în secolul XV şi XVI*, vol. I (1413-1508) (Bucureşti, 1905), p. 80.

[54]Wavrin quoted in Maria Holban, ed., *Călători străini despre ţările române*, vol. I, pp. 111-113. See also Minea, *Vlad Dracul şi vremea sa*, p. 262.

Hungary continued to deteriorate as the two men supported opposite sides in the ongoing struggle for the throne of Moldavia. It was probably during late 1445 that Dracul wrote to Braşov, complaining:

> please understand me; I have left my little children to be butchered for Christian peace so that I and my country can be subjects of our King and join with you. Thus I expected that my poor men would be treated better by you, and that both our peoples could eat freely, both here and there. Now I still see that my poor men [merchants] are not allowed to eat freely because the governors of your fortresses plunder them and skin them alive without cause. Tell me, why are my poor men being killed? Why can I not assure justice for my poor men? Please, therefore, as my friends, tell the governors of these [fortresses] that, if they are my friends, to listen to the advice of God and not force me to break away from our lord, the King, and the Holy Crown, as this would not be of my own desire. Tell them to treat my poor men well and to give back to each one what they took from them...[55]

The cool relations between Wallachia and Hungary forced Vlad Dracul to again make peace with the sultan in 1446. In addition to renewing the old terms of the treaty with the sultan, he had to return the 12,000 Bulgarians who took refuge in Wallachia during the Danubian campaign of the previous year.[56] We are also informed, in the above letter, that his sons, Vlad and Radu, remained as Ottoman hostages during the 1445 campaign.[57] Although Dracul feared for the lives of his sons at this time, clearly the sultan preferred to keep the

---

[55]Doc. LIV in Ioan Bogdan, *Documente privitoare la relaţiile Ţării Româneşti cu Braşovul şi Ţara Ungurească în secolul XV şi XVI*, vol. I (1413-1508), pp. 78-79; and doc. 62 in Gr. Tocilescu, *534 documente istorice slavo-române din Ţara Românească şi Moldova privitoare la legăturile cu Ardealul, 1346-1603* (Bucureşti, 1931).

[56]Minea, *Vlad Dracul şi vremea sa*, pp. 269-270.

[57]The last mention of his sons Mircea, Vlad, and Radu in internal documents from the reign of Vlad Dracul is in a deed issued in Târgovişte on 7 August 1445. See doc. 99 in *Documenta Romaniae Historica, B. Ţara Românească*, vol. I, pp. 173-175.

Wallachian prince's sons in good health to use as bargaining chips in his relations with Vlad II.

As relations between Hunyadi and Dracul worsened, the Transylvanian governor wrote to the councilors of Braşov on 20 July 1447 telling them to lend aid to a new pretender, Vladislav, another son of Dan II.[58] Later that year he organized an attack on Wallachia aimed at ousting Vlad. Hunyadi set out from Braşov after 23 November and made a violent assault on the Romanian principality; Vlad was killed near Bălteni[59] and his eldest son Mircea was buried alive by the magnates of Târgovişte. After installing his protege, Vladislav II, on the throne, the Transylvanian governor returned to Braşov in mid-December.[60]

Again we cannot be sure of the status of Vlad and Radu during this time. Most likely, they remained as hostages at the Ottoman court, but a passage from Kritoboulos suggests that they may have returned to Wallachia after their father made peace with the sultan in 1446. The Greek chronicler tells us that:

> This man [Vlad] and his brother [Radu] had fled when John the Getan,[61] ruler of the Paenonians and Dacians, had come with a considerable force and had murdered their father and given the governorship to another man. The father of the present Sultan had then welcomed these two fugitives who had fled to him...[62]

In any event, the situation of the two royal offspring changed after the death of their father. The oldest, Vlad, now became a pre-

---

[58]Letter in Hurmuzaki-Iorga, *Documente*, vol. XV₁, p. 34.

[59]Mention of this is made in a deed issued on 3 April 1534, see *Documenta Romaniae Historica*, B. *Ţara Românească*, vol. II, p. 289.

[60]On this campaign see the study of Francisc Pall, "Intervenţia lui Iancu de Hunedoara în Ţara Românească şi Moldova în anii 1447-1448," pp. 1049-1072, in *Studii. Revista de istorie*, XVI:5 (1963); and Camil Mureşan, *Iancu de Hunedoara şi vremea sa* (Bucureşti, 1968), pp. 141-143.

[61]So-called because Hunyadi was a Romanian.

The Executions of Vlad II Dracul at Bălteni
and his son Mircea by the magnates of Târgoviste

By Octavian Ion Penda

tender to throne; it would not be long before, with Ottoman support, he would make his bid to take his father's throne.

**

Dracula's opportunity came in the fall of 1448, less than a year after his father's death, when Hunyadi organized what was to be the last great anti-Ottoman crusade before the fall of Constantinople in 1453. Accompanied by Vladislav II,[63] Hunyadi crossed the Danube into Serbia in September with a Christian army that reached Kosovo in mid-October where they encountered the Ottoman forces commanded by Sultan Murad II. Chalkondyles tells us that at Kosovo:

> On the left wing there was Dan [Vladislav II] who was his [John Hunyadi's] great friend whom he had brought to the throne of the Land of the Dacians [Wallachia] because of his animosity for Dracula [Vlad Dracul]... [Vladislav] brought 8,000 Dacians with him to make war.[64]

The battle ended in another disaster for the Christian forces, and in their hasty retreat Hunyadi was taken prisoner by the Serbian Prince George Brankovic.

Hoping to create difficulties for the Christian offensive, the Ottomans supported Vlad, who, in early October, invaded Wallachia in the absence of Vladislav II and took the throne. Amidst the uncertainty surrounding the outcome of the battle of Kosovo and the fate

---

[62]See the translation by Raymond T. McNally in his study, "The Fifteenth Century Manuscript by Kritoboulos of Imbros as an Historical Source for the History of Dracula," pp. 1-13, in *East European Quarterly,* vol. XXI:1 (Spring, 1987), p. 7; and Kritovoulos, *History of Mehmed the Conqueror,* trans. Charles T. Riggs (Princeton, 1954), p. 178 [IV.58].

[63]See the letter of Hunyadi to the Saxons of Transylvania dated 7 August 1448 in Barabas Szamu, *Székely Oklevéltar,* vol. VIII (Budapest, 1934), pp. 75-76, announcing that Vladislav was on his way to Transylvania to join his troops.

[64]Chalcocondil, *Expuneri istorice,* p. 210.

of the Christian leaders, the new prince, Vlad III Dracula, wrote to the councilors of Braşov:

> We bring you news that Mr. Nicolae from Ocna Sibiului writes to us and asks us to be so kind as to come to him until John [Hunyadi], the Royal Governor of Hungary, returns from the war. We are unable to do this because an emissary from Nicopolis came to us this past Tuesday [29 October] and said with great certainty that Murad, the Turkish Sultan, made war for three days against John [Hunyadi] the Governor, and that on the last day he [Hunyadi] formed a circle with his caravan, then the Sultan himself went down among the janissaries and they attacked this caravan, broke through their lines, and defeated and killed them. If we come to him now, the Turks could come and kill both you and us. Therefore, we ask you to have patience until we see what has happened to John. We do not even know if he is alive. If he returns from the war we will meet with him and we will make peace with him. But if you will be our enemies now, and if something happens, you will have sinned and you will have to answer for it before God.[65]

An anonymous Ottoman chronicle also mentions Vlad's invasion of Wallachia, but mistakenly places these events in 1449.[66] A letter from Constantinople, dated 7 December 1448, also mentions Dracula's invasion of Wallachia, supported by Ottoman troops; though it confuses many events, it clearly indicates that by this date he had been removed from the throne.[67] According to Chalkondyles, upon his return from Kosovo, Vladislav II, aided by Petru II, prince of Moldavia, forced Vlad III to abandon the throne.[68] This would imply that by

---

[65]Nicolae Iorga, *Scrisori de boieri, scrisori de domni*, 3rd ed. (Vălenii-de-Munte, 1931), pp. 160-161. This document is mistakenly attributed by Iorga to Vladislav II.

[66]*Cronici turceşti privind ţările române, extrase, vol. I, sec. XV-mijlocul XVII*, Mihail Guboglu and Mustafa Mehmet, eds. (Bucureşti, 1966), p. 185.

[67]Cited by Ilie Minea, *Vlad Dracul şi vremea sa*, p. 275.

[68]Chalcocondil, *Expuneri istorice*, p. 158.

Stem des selben ars ist er gesetzt wo erden: de n zu ein,
em herrn in der walehei zu hand lies er todten den Laszla weyde der

Vlad III Dracula assumes the throne of Wallachia in 1448

By Octavian Ion Penda

late November Dracula's first reign as prince of Wallachia had come
to an end.

We have little information about Vlad III from the end of his
first reign in November 1448 to the beginning of his second reign in
1456. It is clear that he returned to the Ottoman capital, but after a
short time, for reasons unknown, he went to Moldavia where his
uncle, Bogdan II,[69] had come to the throne in the fall of 1449. The
new Moldavian prince allied himself with John Hunyadi against
Poland;[70] thus, through his uncle, Dracula would be reconciled with
his father's murderer.

Meanwhile, relations between Hunyadi and Vladislav II had
cooled after the latter had made his way back from Kosovo directly to
Wallachia, failing to try and free the royal governor who ultimately
escaped from George Brankovic's prison at Semendria in December
1448. Although the reasons for these new tensions between the royal
governor and the prince of Wallachia are unclear, internal documents
from Vladislav's reign reveal that, for an unknown period of time
between 2 January 1450 and July 1451, Hunyadi seized the Transylvanian lands of Amlaş and Făgăraş, traditional duchies of the Wallachian prince, from Vladislav.[71] Although these territories were

---

[69]Vlad Dracul had been married to a daughter of Alexander the Good, a sister of
Bogdan II. Bogdan II was also the father of Stephen the Great. Thus, Vlad Dracula and
Stephen the Great were cousins.

[70]Andreescu, *Vlad Ţepeş (Dracula)*, p. 47. Andreescu states that Dracula set out for
Moldavia because he saw the Turks had little interest in ousting Vladislav. Although the reasons for his departure from Adrianople are unknown, it seems unlikely that this would have
been his principal motivation as he could not hope for support from Moldavia which was in
the midst of a dynastic struggle and, during the reign of Bogdan II, an ally of Hunyadi.

[71]This can be seen in the formula used by the prince to refer to himself in these deeds.
Thus in documents dated 2 January 1450 and again in July, 1451, we find the prince using
the formula: "I, Vladislav, by the grace and will of God, ruler and Prince over all of Wallachia, and of the areas across the mountains on our borders, the duchies of Amlaş and
Făgăraş." In a deed issued on 28 March 1451, however, he refers to himself merely as
"Prince over all of Wallachia," no longer mentioning Amlaş and Făgăraş, clearly something
too important to have been merely an omission.

Vladislav II
Prince of Wallachia, 1447-1456
By Octavian Ion Penda

restored to him, Vladislav clearly realized that he faced the same difficult task, as his predecessors Alexandru Aldea and Vlad Dracul had, of maintaining the delicate balance of power between Hungary and the Ottoman Empire.

Dracula's situation again changed when his uncle, Bogdan II, was murdered by Petru Aron at Rǎuşeni in October, 1451. Together with his cousin Stephen, he sought refuge in Transylvania where he hoped to take advantage of the tensions between Hungary and Wallachia and convince Hunyadi to support his bid for the throne. Unfortunately for Vlad, shortly after he arrived in Transylvania, the royal governor concluded a three-year peace treaty with the Porte that recognized the independence of Wallachia. This treaty created a kind of collective suzerainty of Hungary and the Ottoman Empire over the Romanian principality.[72] The status quo was accepted by both sides and they agreed that, if Vladislav died, neither side would intervene and the new prince would be chosen by an assembly of the boyars. Thus, the treaty represented a setback for Vlad in his efforts to regain the throne.

Shortly after the conclusion of this treaty Hunyadi wrote to the councilors of Braşov telling them not to give aid or shelter to Vlad, but to arrest him and send him away.[73] On 30 March 1452 Hunyadi

---

[72]Ştefan Pascu, et al., eds., *Documenta Romaniae Historica, D. Relaţii între ţările române*, vol. I (1222-1456) (Bucureşti, 1977), p. 420. See also Veniamin Ciobanu, "The Equilibrium Policy of the Romanian Principalities in East Central Europe, 1444-1485," pp. 29-52, in Treptow, *Dracula: Essays...*, pp. 37-38.

[73]Letter dated 6 February 1452 in *Documenta Romaniae Historica, D. Relaţii între ţările române*, vol. I, p. 424.

informed Braşov that Dracula had returned to Moldavia[74] where another of his cousins, Alexăndrel, had come to the throne.

Vlad's activities during this time are not known, but he would again leave Moldavia and return to Transylvania to pursue his bid for the Wallachian throne as relations between Vladislav and Hunyadi soon deteriorated. A monetary reform attempted by the Wallachian prince in 1452 strained relations with Hungary so that in October 1452 Hunyadi wrote to the councilors of Braşov ordering them not to accept the new coins struck by Vladislav II.[75] Although peace between the two was soon restored, relations again cooled and a new dispute broke out at the end of 1454. While Hunyadi was busy fighting the Turks in Serbia, it was known that Wallachia was swarming with Turkish merchants and the councilors of Sibiu believed an Ottoman military threat was imminent.[76] Hunyadi reacted by again seizing the duchies of Amlaş and Făgăraş from Vladislav.[77] This prompted the Wallachian prince to complain to the councilors of Braşov that:

> [Although] I, my boyars, and my country have spilled our blood for the Holy Crown, for Hungary, and for Christianity, no matter how much we have sworn, our father, John voievod, does not care, and he was not pleased with my work, because it is not enough for him to be Governor of Hungary, but he also had to take from me my estates and my territories of Făgăraş and Amlaş, and he acted badly toward me; and you can see that he broke the oaths and promises he made to me.[78]

---

[74]See *Documenta Romaniae Historica, D. Relaţii între ţările române*, vol. I, p. 425.

[75]Hurmuzaki, *Documente*, vol. II₂, pp. 15-16. On this issue see Matei Cazacu, "L'impact ottoman sur les pays roumains et ses incidences monétaires (1452-1504)," in *Revue roumaine d'histoire*, XII:1 (1973), pp. 175-176.

[76]See *Documenta Romaniae Historica, D. Relaţii între ţările române*, vol. I, p. 442.

[77]See doc. 112 (dated 20 September 1454 or 1455) and doc. 113 (15 April 1456) in *Documenta Romaniae Historica, B. Ţara Românească*, vol. I, pp. 195-197, where Vladislav once again refers to himself only as "prince over all of Wallachia."

[78]Doc. 66 in Tocilescu, *535 documente slavo-române*, pp. 63-64.

A new peace was concluded between Hunyadi and Vladislav in the fall of 1455,[79] but by December of that year hostilities had again broken out as Hunyadi had received word of a Turkish and Wallachian raid in Transylvania.[80] As the conflict between Hungary and Wallachia worsened, Vlad Dracula began to receive support from the royal governor in his efforts to regain his father's throne. As a result, on 6 April 1456 King Ladislas of Hungary ordered the Saxons to protect the Transylvanian borders and the possessions of John Hunyadi, who was then preparing to defend

John Hunyadi
Royal Governor of Hungary
From a contemporary engraving

Belgrade from an Ottoman assault, against continuing attacks by Vladislav II.[81] Preoccupied with the defense of Belgrade, Hunyadi gave Vlad military support, entrusting him to defend the borders of Transylvania[82] and allowing him the possibility of launching an invasion of Wallachia to take the throne for a second time.

The circumstances under which Dracula reclaimed the throne of Wallachia are unknown. From the available evidence we can infer that sometime between the beginning of July and the end of August, Vlad

---

[79]See the letter of Hunyadi to Braşov, dated 15 November 1455, doc. 328 in *Documenta Romaniae Historica, D. Relaţii între ţările române*, vol. I, pp. 447-448.

[80]See the letter of John Hunyadi to Braşov, dated 23 December 1455, doc. 329 in *Documenta Romaniae Historica, D. Relaţii între ţările române*, vol. I, pp. 449-450.

[81]See the letter of King Ladislas, dated 6 April 1456, doc. 329 in *Documenta Romaniae Historica, D. Relaţii între ţările române*, vol. I, pp. 449-450.

[82]See the letter of Hunyadi to Braşov, dated 3 July 1456, doc. 336 in *Documenta Romaniae Historica, D. Relaţii între ţările române*, vol. I, p. 455.

III invaded Wallachia and seized the throne. Vladislav II was killed in the fighting.[83] Meanwhile, John Hunyadi, the man who, ironically, was responsible both for the assassination of his father as well as for allowing Vlad the chance to regain the throne of Wallachia, died of the plague while defending Belgrade from an Ottoman assault. The first known document from Dracula's principal reign is dated 6 September 1456.[84] Now that the son of Vlad Dracul had achieved his goal of regaining his father's throne, a more difficult task awaited him: to find a way to maintain the autonomy of his principality against the threats posed by its two powerful neighbors. This was a problem that had plagued all of his predecessors since the reign of his grandfather Mircea the Old.

[83]Tradition holds that Vladislav was killed at Târgşor on 20 August. See Nicolae Stoicescu, *Vlad Ţepeş* (Bucharest, 1978), p. 25; Ştefan Andreescu, *Vlad Ţepeş (Dracula)*, pp. 57-58, speculates that Dracula took the throne between 15 April (the date of the last document from Vladislav's reign) and 3 July (the date of Hunyadi's letter to Braşov, interpreting this document to mean that Dracula was, at that date, already prince of Wallachia). Hunyadi's letter, however, refers to Vlad only as *voievod*, a title given to a military leader, and does not indicate that he had yet claimed the throne of Wallachia.

[84]See doc. 338 in *Documenta Romaniae Historica, D. Relaţii între ţările române*, vol. I, pp. 456-458; and doc. CCLVII in Bogdan, *Documente privitoare la relaţiile Ţării Româneşti cu Braşovul şi Ţara Ungurească*, pp. 316-317.

Chapter IV

The Political Structure of Wallachia in the mid-Fifteenth Century

...we cannot make peace with the Turks because they wish to pass through our country to attack and plunder you... This is why we have retained the Turkish messenger until you receive this news. You can judge for yourselves that when a man or a prince is strong and powerful he can make peace as he wants to; but when he is weak, a stronger one will come and do what he wants to him... you should think about what we and ours deserve in fairness and in honor, as there are some people who think badly of us and who are working against us. You should be enemies of such men, as we are toward your enemies.

— Vlad Dracula to Braşov, 10 September 1456[1]

Several social groups made up Wallachian society during the time of Vlad III Dracula. The most important politically were the landed aristocracy of the country, called *boyars*. It was a hereditary class, although the prince could create new boyars by

---

[1]Letter of Vlad Ţepeş to Braşov dated 10 September 1456 in Nicolae Iorga, *Scrisori de boieri, scrisori de domni*, 2nd ed. (Vălenii-de-Munte, 1925), pp. 164-165. An English translation of this letter can be found in Appendix I.B.

bestowing this title upon them and granting them lands and privileges. This was by no means a uniform group, some boyars had vast land holdings, others only small estates. In addition, the power of each individual boyar also depended upon his family ties, something of great significance, although often difficult for us to demonstrate due to the scarcity of documents for this period, in the relations between the prince and the boyars, as well as among the boyars themselves.

The next group was the clergy. As we have previously mentioned, the Church played a very important cultural, moral, and spiritual role in society, in addition to being influential politically. Many princes founded churches and monasteries, and almost all gave tax exemptions and land grants to them. Thus, the Church, through its monasteries, was also an important economic force in the country. Of the four existent *hrisoave* (deeds) from the second reign of Vlad III Dracula, two are land grants to two of the most important monasteries in the country: on 16 April 1457, at Târgoviște, Dracula confirmed the village of Troianești, on both banks of the Olt River, to the Monastery of Cozia, which had purchased the village from a boyar named Drăgoi for 50 florins, and exempted it from taxes on these holdings;[2] on 5 March 1458, during a visit to the Monastery of Tismana, in the northwestern part of the country, the prince confirmed all of the villages the monastery had held during the reign of his father, exempting them from taxes.[3] Sometimes the *metropolitan*, the title given to the chief spiritual leader of the country, would also participate as a member of the *sfatul domnesc* when matters directly affecting the Church were discussed.[4] It must also be mentioned that the clergy, like the boyars, was not a uniform group, thus we find lesser and higher members of the clergy included in this group.

---

[2]Doc. 115 in *Documenta Romaniae Historica, B. Țara Românească*, vol. I, pp. 198-200.

[3]Doc. 117 in *Documenta Romaniae Historica, B. Țara Românească*, vol. I, pp. 201-202.

The vast majority of the population was formed of peasants. Subjugated peasants who worked the lands held by the boyars were known as *rumâni* or *vecini*. The number of peasants in this class would increase during the second half of the fifteenth century in part due to increasing Ottoman economic exploitation of the country — a process that would reach its peak during the sixteenth century. A significant portion of the peasantry was made up of free peasants, owners of a landed estate, *moşie*, inherited from a real or imaginary ancestor. The *moşneni*, also called *moşteni*, had individual property rights, although pastures were held in common by the village community. Farm land was divided into plots that were distributed periodically, usually by drawing lots, according to a system known as *devălmăşie*.[5]

The final group that needs to be mentioned are inhabitants of the cities. While Wallachia did not experience significant urban development at this time, thereby inhibiting the exchange of goods between the cities and the villages, the latter remaining essentially self-sufficient, a number of important urban centers existed in the country. Most of these had significant commercial and defensive roles, such as Chilia, Brăila, and Giurgiu on the Danube. Another important city was Curtea de Argeş, the capital of the country during the fourteenth century and the seat of the metropolitanate during this time. The capital of Wallachia, and its most important urban center during this time, was Târgovişte. In addition, it is during the reign of Vlad III Dracula that we find the first mention in documents of the locality which would become the country's most important urban center — Bucharest.[6]

---

[4]See, for example, the deed issued by Radu cel Frumos for the Monastery of Snagov in Bucharest on 28 October 1464 that lists Metropolitan Iosif as a participant in the *sfatul domnesc* (doc. 127 in *Documenta Romaniae Historica, B. Ţara Românească*, vol. I, pp. 215-219), and the deed issued by Basarab cel Tânăr at Gherghiţa on 23 March 1482 that lists Metropolitan Macarie among the participants in the *sfatul domnesc* on that occasion (see doc. 179 in *ibid.*, pp. 288-292).

[5]Detailed explanations of these terms can be found in Ovid Sachelarie and Nicolae Stoicescu, *Instituţii feudale din ţările române. Dicţionar* (Bucureşti, 1988).

The Wallachian capital of Târgoviște from a sixteenth century engraving

Although it existed as a settlement already during the fourteenth century, it was during the reign of Vlad III Dracula that the city on the Dâmbovița River was fortified and became a princely residence. While Târgoviște would remain the capital of the country until the seventeenth century, already by 1476, the year of Dracula's third and final reign, Bucharest would be referred to by King Matthias Corvinus of Hungary as "the most powerful fortified town in Wallachia, strengthened both by works of art and by nature."[7] Its importance is also attested to by the fact that from the time of its first mention in 1459, the majority of deeds issued by the princes of Wallachia during the rest of the fifteenth century emanate from Bucharest and not Târgoviște as had been true prior to that date.[8] The reasons for this have more to do with economics than politics. With the decline of Saxon commerce due to Ottoman expansion in the Middle East and Southeastern Europe, economic ties with the Ottoman Empire began

---

[6]Doc. 118 in *Documenta Romaniae Historica, B. Țara Românească*, vol. I, pp. 203-204.

[7]Quoted in Constantin C. Giurescu, *History of Bucharest*, trans. Sorana Gorjan (Bucharest, 1976), p. 24.

[8]See the documents in *Documenta Romaniae Historica, B. Țara Românească*, vol. I.

to grow in importance. In addition, Bucharest was located on an important trading point between the forests and the plains and was also close to rich monasteries, such as Snagov.[9]

Little is known of the political and administrative organization of the cities of Wallachia during this period. Most likely, as with the Transylvanian cities, they were autonomous communes, governed by a council of 12 leading citizens,[10] under the rule of the prince, with restricted citizenship rights. As the cities were usually fortified, the prince generally would appoint a military governor, called a *pârcălab*, responsible for their defense.[11] Unlike medieval cities in the West, however, Wallachian cities produced very little, depending mainly upon commerce for their economic livelihood.[12]

From this brief survey of the social groups of Wallachia during the time of Vlad III Dracula it becomes apparent that within each of these larger groups there existed a variety of conflicting interests. It is inconceivable to speak of "class interests" as such in fifteenth century Wallachian society, much less of a class conflict between boyars and peasants. The ties of serfdom were not yet exceedingly oppressive and

[9]See the study of P.P. Panaitescu, "Cum au ajuns Bucureştii capitala ţării," pp. 161-169, in *Interpretări româneşti*. Constantin C. Giurescu, in his *History of Bucharest*, prefers to stress political motives, saying that Vlad made Bucharest a prominent princely residence as part of his struggle against the Turks, while his brother, Radu cel Frumos, continued to foster the growth of the city because he depended upon Turkish support (pp. 23-24). He admits, however, that it may have been "justified not only by strategic considerations but also, perhaps, by its higher economic opportunities" (p. 23).

[10]For example, a letter sent by the leading boyars of Basarab Laiotă to Braşov shortly after Dracula's death in its address refers to "our good neighbors and friends from the county of Braşov, and to the twelve councilors...," see doc. CCXXI in Bogdan, *Documente privitoare la relaţiile Ţării Româneşti cu Braşovul şi Ţara Ungurească*, pp. 267-269.

[11]One such *pârcălab* was Cârstian, one of Dracula's boyars, who, as military governor of Târgovişte, wrote to Braşov telling of Vlad's victory over the Turks in 1476. See Bogdan, *Documente privitoare la relaţiile Ţării Româneşti cu Braşovul şi Ţara Ungurească*, pp. 357-358.

[12]P.P. Panaitescu, "Comunele medievale în principatele române," pp. 119-159, in *Interpretări româneşti*, pp. 152-153 and 158.

bonds of loyalty often transcended social categories. As is true in the Balkans today, family ties were of far greater importance in creating bonds among members of a society than any theoretical "class interest."

***

As we have mentioned, by the end of the reign of Mircea the Old the state institutions of Wallachia had been fully developed, although they would be gradually altered throughout the fifteenth century in response to the changing needs of the Romanian principality.[13] For all intents and purposes the prince exercised absolute power in the country, aided by an advisory council known as the *sfatul domnesc.* Among the members of this princely council we find several of the most powerful and influential boyars, supporters of the prince, and a number of officials, known as *dregători,* also drawn from the ranks of the boyars. Throughout the fifteenth century, including during the reigns of Vlad III Dracula, the most important members of the *sfatul domnesc* were the great boyars who served on the council solely in their quality as great landowners, usually followed by lesser boyars who were also court officials.[14] This gradually changed so that by the late fifteenth and early sixteenth century, the *sfatul domnesc* was comprised almost exclusively of boyars who were also court officials.[15]

When the administrative organization of the state came into being during the fourteenth century essentially Byzantine institutions were adopted, borrowed from the older South Slav states, that met the specific needs of the new country.[16] Among the titles given to

---

[13]For a detailed study of social, cultural, economic, and political life in Wallachia during this time see Dinu C. Giurescu, *Țara Românească în secolele XIV-XV* (București, 1973).

[14]This can be determined because, in a *hrisov* [deed], the members of the *sfatul domnesc,* who are recorded as witnesses to the document, are listed in their order of importance.

[15]Nicolae Stoicescu, *Sfatul domnesc și marii dregători din Țara Românească și Moldova, sec. XIV-XVII* (București, 1968), p. 54.

members of the *sfatul domnesc* during the time of Vlad III Dracula we find the following:

♦ JUPAN — An old Slavic word meaning *lord* or *master*. A title given to great boyars, usually members of the *sfatul domnesc*.[17]

♦ VORNIC — First mentioned in a document from 1389, the *vornic* was the most important *dregător* in the princely council. He served as a magistrate, having juridical functions which he could exercise throughout the country. At times there would be two *vornici* on the council, the second being of a lesser rank.[18]

♦ LOGOFĂT — First appeared between 1390-1400, the *logofăt* was the head of the prince's chancellery, responsible for drawing up correspondence and documents.[19]

♦ SPĂTAR — First mentioned in a document from 1415, the *spătar* was a military officer, usually commander of the cavalry. At times two *spătari* would serve on the princely council.[20]

♦ STOLNIC — First mentioned in a document from 1392, the *stolnic* was responsible for providing the court with food. He would also taste the food before the prince would eat.[21]

♦ PAHARNIC — First mentioned in a document from 1392, the *paharnic* becomes a regular member of the *sfatul domnesc* after 1424. He was charged with providing drink at the court; he would also be responsible for the prince's wine cellars.[22]

---

[16]Stoicescu, *Sfatul domnesc și marii dregători din Țara Românească și Moldova*, p. 45.

[17]*Idem*, pp. 27-28.

[18]*Ibid.*, pp. 185-204.

[19]*Ibid.*, pp. 170-185.

[20]*Ibid.*, pp. 243-247.

[21]*Ibid.*, pp. 280-284.

♦ COMIS — First mentioned in a document from 1415. The *comis* was charged with the care of the prince's horses, and for transporting the tribute and other gifts to the sultan.[23]

♦ VISTIER — First mentioned in a document from 1392, the *vistier* was the court treasurer, responsible for recording all monies received and spent by the chancellery. He would also be charged with providing furs and clothes both for the prince's personal wardrobe and for gifts. He would keep a register of all villages in the country and the taxes owed, in addition to recording all gifts received by the prince.[24]

♦ STRATORNIC — First mentioned as a member of the *sfatul domnesc* in a document from the reign of Dracula's father Vlad Dracul, dated 18 July 1437, under the name *postelnic.* He was responsible for the prince's living quarters.[25]

In addition, we can identify three other court officials during the time of Vlad III Dracula who were not, however, members of the *sfatul domnesc:*

♦ ARMAŞ — Two undated letters sent by Vlad III to Braşov, that probably date from his second reign (1456-1462), mention "Stoica *armaşul.*"[26] The *armaş* first appeared in documents as a member of the *sfatul domnesc* in a *hrisov* issued on 3 June 1478. He was responsible for carrying out punishments ordered by the prince and had some military functions. He also oversaw the prince's Gypsy slaves.[27]

♦ PÂRCĂLAB — First mentioned in Wallachia in 1368, the *pârcălab* was the military governor of a castle or fortified city.[28]

---

[22] *Ibid.,* pp. 273-280.

[23] *Ibid.,* pp. 293-298. When he issued a deed the prince would traditionally receive a horse from the beneficiary of the act. In addition, horses would often be given as gifts.

[24] *Ibid.,* pp. 217-227.

[25] *Ibid.,* pp. 263-271.

♦ GRĂMĂTIC — A court servant, not necessarily a boyar, who worked under the *logofăt* and had the duty to write out all official documents and correspondence issued by the court. The name of the *grămătic* would usually appear in a separate phrase, following the list of the members of the *sfatul domnesc,* where he would include the place where the *hrisov* was issued and the date on which it was promulgated.

Such was the structure of Wallachian society and the organization of the Wallachian state during the reigns of Vlad III Dracula, the subject of our study.

---

[26]See doc. LXIX in Bogdan, *Documente privitoare la relaţiile Ţării Româneşti cu Braşovul şi Ţara Ungurească,* p. 92. Bogdan dates this document between 1456 and 1459. His conclusion seems likely because the document refers to goods left by Stoica *armaşul* at Chever Paul in Braşov that have not been returned to him, asking that justice be done for his servant. Since all documents referring to economic conflicts with Braşov date from this period it seems likely that this document is no exception. Nevertheless, the same document is presented by Tocilescu as probably being from 1476, see doc. 105 in Tocilescu, *534 documente istorice slavo-române,* pp. 99-100. Likewise, the second document, although it only mentions that Stoica *armaşul* was sent to Braşov to deliver a message on behalf of the prince, is dated by Bogdan between 1456-1459, while Tocilescu places it in 1476. See doc. LXVIII in Bogdan, *Ibid.,* p. 91; and doc. 104 in Tocilescu, *op.cit.,* p. 99.

[27]Stoicescu, *Sfatul domnesc şi marii dregători din Ţara Românească şi Moldova,* pp. 227-233.

[28]*Ibid.,* pp. 204-217.

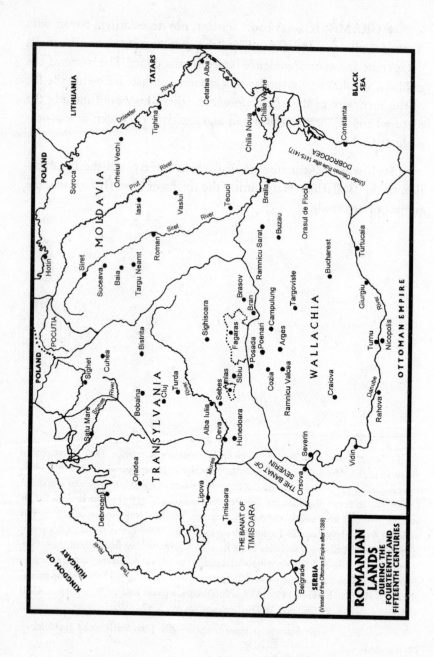

ROMANIAN LANDS
DURING THE
FOURTEENTH AND
FIFTEENTH CENTURIES

SERBIA
(Vassal of the Ottoman Empire after 1389)

POLAND

LITHUANIA

TATARS

BLACK SEA

KINGDOM OF HUNGARY

POLAND

POCUTIA

Hotin

Debrecen

Oradea

Satu Mare

Sighet

Cuhea

Bobalna

Bistrita

Sighisoara

Brasov

Bran

Fagaras

Posada

Amlas

Sibiu

Sebes

Alba Iulia

Turda

Cluj

Deva

Hunedoara

Lipova

Timisoara

THE BANAT OF TIMISOARA

Belgrade

TRANSYLVANIA

Soroca

Orheiul Vechi

Tighina

Cetatea Alba

Chilia Veche

Chilia Noua

Constanta

DOBRODGEA
(Under Ottoman Rule after 1415-1417)

MOLDAVIA

Iasi

Vaslui

Tecuci

Suceava

Baia

Targu Neamt

Roman

Braila

Orasul de Floci

Ramnicu Sarat

Buzau

Bucharest

Targoviste

Campulung

Poenari

Arges

Cozia

Ramnicu Valcea

Craiova

WALLACHIA

Giurgiu

Turnu

Nicopolis

Rahova

Vidin

Severin

Orsova

THE BANAT OF SEVERIN

Turtucaia

OTTOMAN EMPIRE

Dniester

River

Prut

River

Siret

River

Siret

Mures

River

Somes

River

Danube

River

Tisa

River

Olt

River

Chapter V

Vlad's Relations with the Boyars

C ommunist historiography created the image of Dracula as a class hero who struggled to curb the abuses of the evil boyars. This thesis has been repeated so often that it is usually taken for granted, without realizing the political motives that inspired it. Precisely for this reason the relationship between Vlad III and his boyars must be reconsidered — especially in light of recent political changes in Romania and Eastern Europe that free the question of any ideological constraints.

Vlad III Dracula has often been presented not only as a crusader against the expansion of the Ottoman Turks in Southeastern Europe, but also against the increasing power of the rich boyars in his country. The thesis developed by Barbu T. Câmpina that Ţepeş defeated the armies of Sultan Mehmed II in the summer of 1462, and only lost his throne later that year as a result of a revolt by the great boyars who joined Radu cel Frumos against the prince who had impinged upon their feudal privileges throughout the preceding six years,[1] has been accepted and further elaborated in many other recent works.[2] It is, nevertheless, a question which merits further discussion.

Literary sources from the fifteenth century provide some information concerning the relations between the Romanian prince and his boyars. For example, the Byzantine chronicler Laonic Chalkondyles wrote:

> To strengthen his power, he killed, in a short time, twenty-thousand men, women, and children; he surrounded himself with a number of distinguished and devoted soldiers and servants to whom he gave the money, wealth, and social positions of those he had killed, so that, in a short time, he brought about a radical change, and this man completely altered the organization of Dacia [Wallachia].[3]

The German stories about Vlad give even more specific information:

> he asked his boyars to come to his house for a feast. When the feast was over, Dracula went to the oldest of them and asked how many princes he thought the country had had? And then he asked the others, one by one, the same question. They all said what they knew; one answered fifty, another thirty, but none of them answered that there had been seven of them, so he had them all impaled. There were five hundred of them altogether.[4]

Native chronicles also tell of Dracula's efforts to assert his authority vis-à-vis the boyars:

> He did something to the citizens of Târgovişte because he found that the boyars of Târgovişte had buried his brother

[1]See Barbu T. Câmpina, "Complotul boierilor şi răscoala din Ţara Românească din iulie-noiembrie, 1462," pp. 599-624, in *Studii şi referate privind istoria României*, pt. I-a. This idea was originally suggested by Gh. Ghibănescu at the end of the nineteenth century, see "Vlad Ţepeş (studiu critic)" in *Arhiva, organul societăţii ştiinţifice şi literare din Iaşi*, vol. VIII, nos. 7-8, pp. 373- 417, and vol. VIII, nos. 9-10, pp. 497-520 (1897). Câmpina's version is heavily dosed in Marxist-Leninist ideology.

[2]See, for example, Nicolae Stoicescu, *Vlad Ţepeş, Prince of Wallachia*; and Radu Florescu and Raymond T. McNally, *Dracula, A Biography of Vlad the Impaler, 1431-1476*.

[3]Laonic Chalcocondil, *Expuneri istorice*, p. 283 [Bk. IX]. An English translation of the section of Chalkondyles's chronicle concerning Vlad III Dracula can be found in Appendix III.

[Mircea] alive. As he wanted to know the truth he looked for his brother in the ground and found him buried face down.

So when it was Easter and all the citizens were at the feast and while the young were dancing, he unexpectedly captured all of them. All those who were old he had impaled around the city, while those who were young, together with their wives and children, all dressed up for Easter, he had taken to Poienari where they worked to build the fortress there until their clothes fell off and they all remained naked. For this reason he was called the Impaler [Ţepeş].[5]

This evidence all points to the fact that Dracula sought to strengthen the central authority of the state in order to preserve his position and enhance his power, a policy that explains Chalkondyles's account according to which:

he sent for some of his boyars, one by one, whom he thought might be treasonous and plot to overthrow him, and he had

[4]See P.P. Panaitescu, "The German Stories about Vlad Ţepeş," pp. 185-196, in Treptow, *Dracula: Essays...*, p. 191. Ştefan Andreescu argues that in the story Vlad answers 7 because this is the number of princes he would have considered as being legitimate in the line of succession from the founding of Wallachia: Basarab I, Nicolae Alexandru, Vladislav I, Radu I, Mircea the Old, Vlad Dracul, and himself. This seems like a stretch for Vlad would not have had any reason to consider, for example, Mihail I, who had been Mircea's designated successor, as being illegitimate (see Ştefan Andreescu, *Vlad Ţepeş (Dracula)*, p. 81).

[5]*Istoria Ţării Româneşti, 1290-1690. Letopiseţul cantacuzinesc*, p. 205. For other variants see *ibid*, p. 4 and Căpitanul Constantin Filipescu [Radu Popescu], *Istoriile domnilor Ţării Româneşti cuprinzînd istoria munteană de la început până la 1688*, pp. 15-16. This certainly does not refer to all the citizens of Târgovişte but to a group whom Vlad suspected of having betrayed his father during the Hungarian invasion led by John Hunyadi in 1447. Ştefan Andreescu convincingly argues that this occurred on Sunday, 17 April 1457 (see Andreescu, *Vlad Ţepeş (Dracula)*, p. 83). We know from documentary sources that Vlad was in Târgovişte on 16 April 1457 and, as this was the first Easter of his reign, it is likely that he would have taken revenge on his father's opponents fairly soon after coming to the throne. This episode is also recounted by the Saxon chronicler Johann Filstich (1684-1743), *Tentamen Historiae Vallachicae/Încercare de istorie românească*, Adolf Armbruster, ed., trans. Radu Constantinescu (Bucureşti, 1979), p. 103.

Vlad punishing the citizens of Târgoviste for the murder
of his brother Mircea

By Octavian Ion Penda

them mutilated and impaled, together with their wives, children, and servants...[6]

Vlad himself alluded to such a program in a letter to the officials of Braşov on 10 September 1456, shortly after coming to the Wallachian throne for the second time:

> You can judge for yourselves that when a man or a prince is strong and powerful he can make peace as he wants to; but when he is weak, a stronger one will come and do what he wants to him.[7]

While these sources give us some indications about the relationship between Vlad and his boyars, they, by themselves, are inadequate to draw any conclusions. Literary works, in general, are filled with exaggerations. Chalkondyles, for example, presents his account of Dracula's domestic policy merely as an introduction to the main part of his story — the war with the Turks in 1462. The Byzantine chronicler had never been to Wallachia and cannot be considered as a reliable source concerning domestic matters. He also had an interest in portraying Vlad as a formidable enemy who merited the personal attention of the Ottoman sultan. Likewise, the German Stories were themselves written to justify Matthias Corvinus's imprisonment of Dracula in 1462. They are also extremely biased in light of Vlad's conflicts with the German cities of Transylvania. Thus, only by using the available documents in conjunction with these literary sources can we gain an understanding of the true nature of Vlad III Dracula's relations with the boyars.

Unfortunately, only four internal documents from Vlad's reign still exist that list the members of the *sfatul domnesc*. Nevertheless, an examination of these documents does provide us with some evidence about his relations with the boyars. First of all, these documents sup-

---

[6]Chalcocondil, *Expuneri istorice*, p. 283.

[7]Nicolae Iorga, *Scrisori de boieri, scrisori de domni*, 2nd ed. (Vălenii-de-Munte, 1925), pp. 164-165. An English translation of this letter can be found in Treptow, *Dracula, Essays...*, Appendix IV.B, pp. 313-314.

port the literary evidence which claims that Dracula's domestic policies were directed toward consolidating his authority. Only two members of the *sfatul domnesc* on 16 April 1457 remained on the *sfatul domnesc* on 10 February 1461: Voico Dobriţa, who appears to have been the most influential boyar at Vlad III's court, and Iova *vistier*.[8] The significance of this is illustrated by the fact that the composition of the *sfatul domnesc* of other fifteenth century Wallachian princes does not indicate any comparable trends over a similar period of time. Thus, it can be said that Vlad's attempts to exert his authority over the *sfatul domnesc* were unique in fifteenth century Wallachian politics, thereby supporting the literary evidence.

A careful examination of the internal documents also tells us that the changes in the *sfatul domnesc* were the result of a carefully planned policy, gradually introduced throughout the reign of the Wallachian prince. Of the twelve boyars on Dracula's *sfatul domnesc* on 16 April 1457, at least three — Manea Udrişte, Stan al lui Negre, and Cazan al lui Sahac[9] — also served in the *sfatul domnesc* of his predecessor, Vladislav II. This is not at all surprising as the same situation is encountered whenever there was a change of princes in the fifteenth century, with one notable exception, even when the transition occurred as part of a military conflict, such as was the case when Vlad III Dracula seized the throne and ordered the execution of his predecessor.

The following table helps to illustrate this evolution. The *sfatul domnesc* from 5 March 1458, comprised of nine names, includes 4 new ones (in bold). That of 20 September 1459, comprised of 11

[8] Docs. 115 and 120 in *Documenta Romaniae Historica, B. Ţara Românească, vol. I (1247-1500)*, P.P. Panaitescu and Damaschin Mioc, eds. (Bucureşti, 1966), pp. 198-200, 205-206.

[9] The best work on the structure and function of the *sfatul domnesc* is Nicolae Stoicescu, *Sfatul domnesc şi marii dregători din Ţara Românească şi Moldova, sec. XIV-XVII* (Bucureşti, 1968). The standard reference book for the high officials serving on the *sfatul domnesc* in Wallachia and Moldavia is Nicolae Stoicescu, *Dicţionar al marilor dregători din Ţara Românească şi Moldova* (Bucureşti, 1971).

names, includes 3 changes (in bold). The final list from 10 February
1461 includes 4 new names (in bold) among the members of the
sfatul domnesc:[10]

Members of the Sfatul Domnesc
during the Reign of Vlad III Dracula, 1456-1462

16 April 1457	5 March 1458	20 Sept. 1459	10 Feb. 1461
Manea Udrişte	*jupan* Dragomir Ţacal	*jupan* Dragomir Ţacal	*jupan* Voico Dobriţa
Codrea *vornic*	*jupan* Voico Dobriţa	*jupan* Voico Dobriţa	*jupan* **Galeş** *vornic*
Dragomir Ţacal	*jupan* Stan al lui Negre *vornic*	*jupan* Stan *vornic*	*jupan* Stepan Turcul
Voico Dobriţa	Iova *vistier*	*jupan* **Stepan Turcul**	*jupan* Cazan *logofăt*
Stan al lui Negre	Buda *stolnic*	*jupan* Oprea	**Buriu** *spătar*
jupan Duca	**Gherghina** *comis*	*jupan* ?	Iova *vistier*
Cazan al lui Sahac	**Stoica** *paharnic*	**Bratul de la Milcov**	Opriţa (Oprea) *paharnic*
Oprea *logofăt*	**Pătru** *stratornic*	Moldovean *spătar*	**Linart** *stolnic*
Moldovean *spătar*	**Cazan** *logofăt*	Iova *vistier*	Gherghina *comis*
Buda *stolnic*	xxx	? *spătar*	**Radul** *stratornic*
Milea *paharnic*	xxx	**Tocsaba** *stolnic*	xxx
Iova *comis*	xxx	Stoica *paharnic*	xxx
xxx	xxx	Gherghina *comis*	xxx

[10]Docs. 115, 117, 118, and 120 in *Documenta Romaniae Historica, B. Ţara Românească*, vol. 1, pp. 198-206.

It is interesting to note the presence of Radul *stratornic*, a member of Vladislav II's court,[11] in the final list. It must also be mentioned that the absence of a particular boyar from a list may only mean that for any number of reasons he could not be present when a specific document was issued. For example, this most likely explains the absence of Oprea from the list of 1458, although he reappears on the two subsequent lists and continues to be a loyal supporter of Dracula even after his overthrow in 1462.[12]

Evidence of Vlad's efforts to eliminate his opponents from the *sfatul domnesc* is also found in a letter dated 23 April 1459 referring to a boyar *Koldra* who had 3,000 gold florins worth of property in Braşov. This may refer to Codrea, who is no longer found among the members of the *sfatul domnesc* after 16 April 1457 and was either killed by Dracula[13] or died in exile. Likewise, a letter from King Matthias Corvinus of Hungary to Braşov, dated 4 July 1458, orders the councilors of the city to turn over all the wealth of Mihail *logofăt*, a member of the *sfatul domnesc* during the reign of Vladislav II, who had been killed by Vlad.[14]

Thus, these documents make it clear that Dracula conducted a policy aimed at strengthening his authority, but at the same time they indicate that his efforts in this direction were not as sudden or drastic

---

[11]Docs. 112 and 113 in *Documenta Romaniae Historica, B. Ţara Românească*, vol. 1, pp. 195-197.

[12]See the letter of Basarab Laiotă to Braşov dated 9 May 1476, doc. CCLXXVIII in Bogdan, *Documente privitoare la relaţiile Ţării Româneşti cu Braşovul şi Ţara Ungurească*, p. 333, complaining that they lend support to his enemies Oprea *logofăt* and Voico al Tatului. Oprea *logofăt* is also mentioned in a letter of Radu cel Frumos to Braşov, pardoning certain boyars who fled after the war of 1462, but not Oprea (see doc. LXXXI in *Ibid.*, pp. 104-106; and doc. 77 in Tocilescu, *534 documente istorice slavo-române*, pp. 73-74).

[13]This is the conclusion of Ştefan Andreescu, *Vlad Ţepeş (Dracula)*, p. 83, but the circumstances of Codrea's removal from the *sfatul domnesc* and death are unknown, therefore any such conclusion is speculation. For the original document see Hurmuzaki, vol. XV/1, p. 52.

[14]Doc. 3128 in Gustav Gündisch, *Urkundenbuch zur Geschichte der Deutschen in Siebenbürgen,* vol. VI (1458-1473) (Bukarest, 1981), pp. 18-19.

as described in the literary sources. They also contradict the theory put forth by some historians that 1459 marks the turning point when Vlad succeeded in consolidating his authority over the boyars,[15] indicating instead that it was a policy gradually implemented throughout his reign.

A deed issued by Prince Mircea Ciobanul on 1 April 1551 sheds further light on Vlad III Dracula's relations with the boyars. It refers to a revolt led by a boyar, Albu cel Mare, against Vlad a century before:

> In the time of Vlad Voievod Țepeș there was a boyar called Albu cel Mare, who took the above mentioned villages [Glodul and Hințea] by force and devastated the holy monastery [Govora]... In the days of Vlad Voievod Țepeș, this boyar, Albu cel Mare, tried to take the throne from him, but Vlad Voievod went with his army against him and killed him together with his whole family. When Vlad Voievod saw the holy monastery devastated, he granted these villages, Glodul and Hințea, to it.[16]

While this document may indicate an organized resistance on the part of some of the great boyars against Dracula's policy of strengthening the authority of the prince, it may just as well merely indicate a continuation of the conflict between the two families that had its origins in the days of Prince Alexandru Aldea, who, together with his leading boyar Albu, opposed Vlad Dracul's attempts to take the throne.[17] It is also possible that the document in fact refers to Vlad Dracul instead of his son.[18] Given these circumstances it cannot be relied upon as a source of evidence about Vlad III Dracula's relations with the boyars.

---

[15]See, for example, Ştefan Andreescu, *Vlad Țepeș (Dracula)*, pp. 84-85; and Radu Florescu and Raymond T. McNally, *Dracula: A Biography of Vlad the Impaler, 1431-1476*, p. 61.

[16]"Doc. 3, Mircea Ciobanul, prince of Wallachia, confirms to the monastery of Govora the villages of Glodul and Hințea," in *Documente privind istoria României, veacul XVI, B. Țara Românească, vol. III (1551-1570)*, (Bucureşti, 1952), pp. 3-5.

Therefore, the available evidence tells us that Vlad did in fact gradually implement a policy aimed at increasing the authority of the prince. The evidence, however, to indicate an open conflict between the prince and the boyars is quite limited. Indeed, most of his opponents were in exile in Transylvania as reflected in the prince's letters to Braşov and Sibiu. For example, in an undated letter to Braşov, Dracula complains:

> And again I say to your graces as my good friends: there is to be found in your midst Mihail logofăt and Pardo, my enemies. I have forgiven all the others, but these I have not forgiven, and as I have not forgiven them, so you should banish them if you are friends of my majesty.[19]

There also exists a letter to Braşov dated 4 June 1460 in which Vlad asks the councilors of Braşov to turn over his enemies to Voico Dobriţa, one of his leading boyars, or if they would not come with

---

[17]Ştefan Andreescu argues that Albu cel Mare was in fact the son of Albu Taxabă, the most influential boyar at the court of Prince Alexandru Aldea, who attacked the Monastery of Govora in revenge for Vlad Dracul's depriving his family of Glodul and Hinţea (see Ştefan Andreescu, *Vlad Ţepeş (Dracula)*, p. 82). Yet it seems quite possible that Albu cel Mare refers to the same Albu who was the leading boyar at Aldea's court and a fierce opponent of Vlad Dracul, and that the events described in the document from the mid-sixteenth century occurred during the reign of Vlad Dracul, they being confused over one hundred years later with the reign of Vlad Ţepeş.

[18]As Vlad Dracul is credited with founding the Monastery of Govora, he may also have donated the above-mentioned villages to it.

[19]Doc. LXVII in Ioan Bogdan, *Documente privitoare la relaţiile Ţării Româneşti cu Braşovul şi Ţara Ungurească în secolul XV şi XVI, vol. I, 1413-1508* (Bucureşti, 1905), pp. 90-91. Bogdan dates this document between 1456 and 1458. As is known, from the letter of Matthias Corvinus cited earlier, Mihail *logofăt* was killed by Dracula prior to July 1458. We are able to date this letter more precisely thanks to another document in which Mihail Szilagyi orders Braşov and Sibiu to receive Mihail *logofăt* and other refugees from Wallachia and Moldavia, together with their families, and to shelter them and protect them from harm (see Annex II in Gündisch, "Cu privire la relaţiile lui Vlad Ţepeş cu Transilvania," pp. 692-695). Szilagyi's letter is dated 28 March 1458, therefore this letter from Vlad most likely dates from the period April-June, 1458; Pardo is unknown, not being mentioned in other sources. This document is also found in Gr. Tocilescu, *534 documente istorice slavo-române*, doc. 70, pp. 67-68.

him, to expel them from the city in his presence. The text indicates that this request was in accord with an agreement negotiated by the prince's emissary, Cârstian.[20]

The situation faced by Vlad III was not unusual. Almost every prince of Wallachia during the fifteenth century faced a similar situation.[21] Even when relations between the two were good, the Saxon cities preferred to maintain some political leverage over their larger neighbor to the south; therefore, they regularly harbored pretenders to the throne or their supporters, regardless of who was the actual prince. There is no indication in the documents that the problem faced by Vlad was substantially greater than that faced by other rulers of Wallachia during this period. Yet, for a variety of political reasons and his unusual zeal for dispensing with his enemies, he responded to this threat with far greater violence than most others.

A review of the internal documents from Dracula's reign also shows that they preserve all of the formulae common to such land grants in the fifteenth century, including the traditional exemption clauses from feudal dues. For example, in a *hrisov* issued by the prince on 20 September 1459, through which he granted to Andrei and his sons lands in Poiana of Stev and in Ponor, we find the following clauses:

> And if one of them will die, the land will remain with the others, without any taxes... All of this is to be their land and to be inherited by their children, grandchildren, and great-grandchildren, without any taxes such as for sheep, pigs, water, and wine, or any special services, such as cutting hay, trees, etc., that is to say all great and small services. And no one should dare cause any trouble for them, no clerk or tax collector, and

[20]Doc. CCLXII in Bogdan, *Documente privitoare la relaţiile Ţării Româneşti cu Braşovul şi Ţara Ungurească*, pp. 320-321.

[21]For example, see the letter of Basarab Laiotă to Braşov dated 9 May 1476, doc. CCLXXVIII in Bogdan, *Documente privitoare la relaţiile Ţării Româneşti cu Braşovul şi Ţara Ungurească*, p. 333, complaining that they lend support to his enemies Oprea *logofăt* and Voico al Tatului.

¶ Ein wunderliche vnd erschröckenliche
hystori von einem großen wüttrich genant
Dracole wayda Der do so gar vnkristen-
liche marter hat an gelegt die menschē. als
mit spissen. auch oy leüt zu tod geslyffen ꝛc

Getruckt zu bamberg im Lxxxxi. iare.

Vlad III Dracula
From a German manuscript published in 1491

none of the boyars or servants of my realm, because whoever dares to harm them will be severely punished.[22]

Thus, it can be said with certainty that although Vlad III attempted to increase his own authority, he had no intention of doing so by encroaching upon the traditional feudal prerogatives of the boyars. Instead, he sought to strengthen his own faction among the nobility, promoting the interests of his relatives and friends — a normal policy for his time although he pursued it with more vigor than others. Thus, it is not possible to see Dracula as some sort of class hero or even to assert that he tried to infringe upon the social status of the boyars. It is clear that he had no such intention.

As we shall see, there is no evidence to indicate that Dracula's boyars helped Radu cel Frumos to attain the throne. It is only in the summer of 1464 that one of Vlad's boyars, Voico Dobriţa, is reconciled with the new prince and rejoins the *sfatul domnesc*.[23] The unusual loyalty of Dracula's boyars is also confirmed by letters of Radu cel Frumos to Braşov and Sibiu, complaining that they were harboring boyars, loyal to his brother, who had taken refuge there.[24] Likewise, some of the boyars loyal to Vlad during his second reign can also be identified among his supporters in 1476 as he prepared to take the throne for a third time. Thus, we find Basarab Laiotă, in a letter dated 9 May 1476, complaining to Braşov that they were supporting his enemies, especially Oprea *logofăt*, a member of Dracula's *sfatul domnesc*, 1456-1462.[25] There is also a letter from Cârstian, *pârcălab* of Târgovişte, announcing the victory of Vlad III Dracula over Basarab Laiotă in 1476 to the citizens of Braşov.[26] This is the

---

[22]Doc. 118 in *Documenta Romaniae Historica, B. Ţara Românească*, vol. I, pp. 203-204.

[23]Doc. 124 in *Documenta Romaniae Historica, B. Ţara Românească*, vol. I, pp. 209-213, dated 10 July 1464.

[24]See doc. LXXXI in Bogdan, *Documente privitoare la relaţiile Ţării Româneşti cu Braşovul şi Ţara Ungurească*, pp. 104-106; and doc. 4 in S. Dragomir, *Documente nouă privitoare la relaţiile Ţării Româneşti cu Sibiul* (Bucureşti, 1935), p. 13.

same Cârstian referred to in the letter of Vlad to Braşov, dated 4 June 1460, mentioned earlier.

Therefore, the little information that the documents provide about Dracula's relations with the boyars clearly contradicts the accepted image. Although Vlad tried to strengthen his authority, this cannot be construed as an attack on the privileges of the boyars; after all, the prince and the boyars had essentially the same interest — the consolidation and strengthening of the power of the state which protected their status and privileges. Thus, it is better to view Dracula's policy as being one aimed at strengthening and securing the positions of his family and friends — typical behavior for his times — instead of being one directed against the boyars as a social class. Vlad's boyars on the whole appear to have been remarkably loyal to him, even during the great Ottoman invasion in the summer of 1462.

---

[25] Doc. CCLXXVIII in Bogdan, *Documente privitoare la relaţiile Ţării Româneşti cu Braşovul şi Ţara Ungurească*, p. 333. The document also mentions Voico al lui Tatu who is not identified in the existent documents from Vlad's second reign, but whose father, Tatu Sârbul, was among the loyal supporters of Dracula's father, Vlad Dracul. See Nicolae Stoicescu, *Dicţionar al marilor dregători din Ţara Românească şi Moldova (sec. XIV-XVII)* (Bucureşti, 1971), pp. 25, 28. There is also a similar letter dated 28 February 1476 in which Basarab Laiotă calls on Braşov to expel his enemies, see doc. CI in Bogdan, *Documente privitoare la relaţiile Ţării Româneşti cu Braşovul şi Ţara Ungurească*, pp. 126-127.

[26] Doc. CCCXII in Bogdan, *Documente privitoare la relaţiile Ţării Româneşti cu Braşovul şi Ţara Ungurească*, pp. 357-358. The same Cârstian is also referred to in a letter of Vlad to Sibiu dated 4 August 1475, see doc. CCLXV in Bogdan, *op.cit.*, pp. 322-323.

Chapter VI

Dracula and the Church

While there are few documents that shed light on Vlad III Dracula's relations with the Church, certain aspects need to be pointed out for, as we noted earlier, the Church, as an institution, was an important support for the state, providing it both legitimacy and strength. As in other countries, it also was an important part of the feudal socio-economic system. Unlike his relations with the boyars, Vlad's ties with the Church have been neither a source of significant investigation nor of dispute.

He is credited with building a church in Târgşor, and possibly founding the Monastery of Comana.[1] Likewise, he granted tax exemptions to the monasteries of Cozia and Tismana,[2] and may have expanded the important monastery at Snagov.[3] It is also known that, like other fifteenth century princes in the Romanian lands, he made donations to monasteries on Mount Athos, the spiritual center of Orthodoxy.[4] Thus, on the whole, his relations with the Church appear to have been without incident and quite similar to those of other fifteenth century Wallachian princes.

Nevertheless, an important change in the structure of the Church hierarchy took place in the mid-fifteenth century and the evi-

dence we have for this comes from the reigns of Vlad III Dracula and
his brother Radu cel Frumos. It is clear that after the fall of Constantinople to the Ottomans in 1453, the metropolitan of the Wallachian
Church is no longer appointed by the patriarch, but is selected from
among the native clergy. Exactly how this was done is unclear from
existent documents.

It seems that from this time, at least until the reorganization of
the Church at the beginning of the sixteenth century,[5] the *stareţ*
(abbot) of the Monastery of Cozia, which had been founded by Mircea the Old, was selected as the head of the Wallachian Orthodox

[1]In 1922 the Romanian historian Constantin C. Giurescu found a votive inscription
in Slavonic in the village of Strejnicu in the county of Prahova attesting to the foundation of
the church at Târgşor in 1461 by Vlad Ţepeş, see Constantin C. Giurescu, "O biserică a lui
Vlad Ţepeş la Târgşor," in *Buletin com. mon. ist.*, XVII (1924), pp. 74-75. See also B. Theodorescu and I. Barnea, "Cultura în cuprinsul mitropoliei Ungrovlahiei," pp. 827-888, in
Biserica ortodoxă romînă: Buletinul oficial al patriarhiei romîne, LXXVII:7-10 (iulie-octombrie, 1959), p. 863.

Radu Florescu and Raymond T. McNally have tried to explain the building of the
Church of St. Nicholas at Târgşor in 1461 as being done in atonement for the murders of his
predecessor Vladislav II in 1456 and Dan the Pretender in 1460 (see Radu Florescu and
Raymond T. McNally, *Dracula: A Biography of Vlad the Impaler*, p. 65), but it seems
unlikely that Vlad would have been overcome by such sentiments. In fact, he may have built
it there in celebration of his victories over his opponents, Vladislav II and Dan III, both of
whom are known to have perished at Târgşor.

[2]"Doc. 115, 16 April 1457 (6965), Târgovişte, Vlad Ţepeş voievod întăreşte m-rii
Cozia satul Troianeşti, pe ambele maluri ale Oltului, scutindu-l de slujbe şi dăjdii,"
pp. 198-200, and "Doc. 117, 5 March 1458 (6966), M-rea Tismana, Vlad Ţepeş voievod
întăreşte m-rii Tismana toate satele ei, pe care le-a avut în timpul tatălui său, Vlad Dracul,
scutindu-le de slujbe şi munci domneşti," in *Documenta Romaniae Historica, B. Ţara
Românească*, vol. I, pp. 201-202.

[3]The chronicle of Cantacuzino states that Dracula founded the Monastery at Snagov
(see *Istoria Ţării Româneşti, 1290-1690. Letopiseţul cantacuzinesc*, pp. 4, 205), but its
existence is already attested to during the reign of Mircea the Old (see *Documenta Romaniae Historica, B. Ţara Românească*, vol. I, pp. 34-35). Thus, it may be that Vlad rebuilt or
strengthened this important stronghold. It is also interesting to note that Snagov is traditionally accepted as Dracula's burial place, although no grave has ever been found. On efforts to
locate Vlad's tomb at Snagov see Dinu V. Rosetti, *Săpăturile arheologice de la Snagov*
(Bucureşti, 1925), vol. I, pp. 44-45.

Church. This conclusion is based on
the following evidence: a *hrisov* issued
by Vlad III Dracula on 16 April 1457
(6965) at Târgovişte confirms to the
Monastery of Cozia the village of
Troianeşti, on both sides of the Olt
River, which the monastery and its
abbot, Iosif, bought from Drăgoi, son
of Drăgoi, for 50 florins. The deed
exempts the monastery from taxes and
services normally due to the prince on
this land.[6] The same Iosif will become
metropolitan, and is mentioned as such
as a participant in the *sfatul domnesc*
when Radu cel Frumos issued a deed
confirming lands to the Monastery of
Snagov on 28 October 1464. Iosif is

The Monastery of Cozia
Founded by Mircea the Old

the first metropolitan mentioned in documentary sources since
Eftimie in 1412. He is also found as abbot at the Monastery of Cozia
in a document issued by Vladislav II on 7 August 1451.[7] Thus, we

---

[4]See "Doc. 116, 12 June 1457, Vlad Ţepeş voievod acordă privlegii m-rii Rusicon de
la Athos," p. 201 and "Doc. 119 (1 September 1460-31 August 1461), Vlad Ţepeş voievod
dăruieşte m-rii Filoteu de la Athos un oboc anual de 4000 aspri," in *Documenta Romaniae
Historica, B. Ţara Românească*, vol. I, p. 205.

[5]This practice undoubtedly ended after the Church reforms proposed by St. Nifon to
Prince Radu cel Mare (1495-1508), which included moving the metropolitanate from
Curtea de Argeş to Târgovişte and to create two bishoprics, one at Râmnic and the other at
Buzău, were implemented (1517). See Niculae Şerbănescu, "Mitropoliţii Ungrovlahiei,"
pp. 722-826, in *Biserica ortodoxă romînă: Buletinul oficial al patriarhiei romîne*, LXX-
VII:7-10 (iulie-octombrie, 1959), p. 744.

[6]"Doc. 115, 16 April (6965) 1457, Vlad Ţepeş voievod întăreşte m-rii Cozia satul
Troianeşti, pe ambele maluri ale Oltului, scutindu-l de slujbe şi dăjdii," in *Documenta Romaniae Historica, B. Ţara Românească*, vol. I, pp. 198-200.

[7]"Doc. 106, 7 August 1451 (6959), Târgovişte, Vladislav al II-lea voievod scuteşte
căruţele m-rii Cozia de orice fel de vamă, la târguri, la vaduri sau pe drumurile munţilor," in
Documenta Romaniae Historica, B. Ţara Românească, vol. I, pp. 186-187.

may conclude that he was probably the first native metropolitan and may have been named to the position either by Vlad III Dracula or by Radu cel Frumos since he became Metropolitan sometime between 16 April 1457 and 28 October 1464. He reigned perhaps until 1477 when Macarie is metropolitan. Macarie, likewise, had been abbot at Cozia, as shown in a document dated 15 July 1475. His successor, Ilarion, is mentioned as abbot at Cozia on 9 January 1478. Ilarion became metropolitan sometime before 17 April 1488 when Visarion is listed as abbot at Cozia.[8]

If we assume that the fall of Constantinople brought about the change in practice of naming the metropolitan, as appears likely,[9] we can then infer that Iosif was the first native clergyman named to the highest post in the Wallachian Orthodox Church as we have documentary evidence that shows him as abbot at Cozia before this time. Thus, the practice of naming the head of the most important monastery in the country as metropolitan began with the reign of Vlad III Dracula or Radu cel Frumos, sometime between 1457 and 1464.

It seems likely that this change in the traditional practice of the Church occurred during the reign of Dracula who undertook a determined policy to strengthen the prince's control over the institutions of the state and to increase its autonomy; he would have also viewed the Church in this light. Radu cel Frumos, who had just come to the throne thanks to Ottoman power, would more likely have accepted a metropolitan named by the patriarch at Constantinople if the practice

---

[8]Niculae Şerbănescu, "Mitropoliţii Ungrovlahiei," pp. 722-826, in *Biserica ortodoxă romînă: Buletinul oficial al patriarhiei romîne*, LXXVII:7-10 (iulie-octombrie, 1959), pp. 741-745.

[9]Another possible moment for this radical change in Church practice would be as a reaction against the Council of Florence, which proclaimed the union of the Orthodox and Catholic Churches in 1439. The Union provoked outrage in many Orthodox countries, and the inhabitants of Constantinople are said to have shouted "Better Islam than the Pope," when the union dictum was read (see L.S. Stavrianos, *The Balkans since 1453*, p. 56). It seems unlikely, however, that either Vlad Dracul or his successor Vladislav II would have taken such an extreme measure given the delicate nature of their relations with Catholic Hungary and their political ties to Constantinople.

Vlad installing Iosif, the abbot of Cozia,
as metropolitan of Wallachia

By Octavian Ion Penda

of naming the abbot of Cozia had not begun during Vlad's reign.
Thus, Dracula can, perhaps, be credited with strengthening the autonomy of the Church which he would regard as equivalent to strengthening state autonomy, a policy clearly reflected throughout his reign,
as we have seen from our discussion of his relations with the boyars.

Chapter VII

Vlad III Dracula's Foreign Relations, 1456-1461

As we have also seen in our survey of the history of Wallachia up to 1456, relations with the Ottoman Empire, on the one hand, and with Transylvania and Hungary, on the other, represented the most important aspects of Vlad III's foreign policy during his principal reign from 1456 to 1462. Like his predecessors, Dracula knew that he needed to preserve the delicate balance of power between his two powerful neighbors if he was to ensure his country's autonomy. Only by engaging in this dangerous policy of playing one off against the other could he ensure a reasonable degree of autonomy for his principality and assure that neither of his neighbors became too powerful so as to further diminish his freedom of action. As a result, Vlad tried to restore something resembling the collective suzerainty of the Hungarian Kingdom and the Ottoman Empire over the principality as it had been established in the treaty of 1451.

Shortly after assuming the throne for the second time, Vlad pledged his allegiance to the Hungarian King Ladislas V and concluded a convention with his Saxon neighbors Braşov and Ţara Bârsei on 6 September 1456:

under oath and with faith in God, we have decided and agreed
that whenever, over the course of time, because of fear of the
Turks or a coup by our enemies, we find ourselves in the lands
of Hungary and amidst those people, that they will take in us
and our followers, take care of us with love, feed us, and be
enemies to our enemies. We in turn have assumed the duty to
defend, with all our forces and power, these lands against the
Turks or the armies of other enemies [of Hungary]. While they
[Braşov and Ţara Bârsei], until we shall be in their midst, have
assumed the duty to defend us against all those who are our
enemies, and if we or one of our men will suffer an injustice in
the midst or within their borders, they will rectify this...

...in addition to the above we add that anyone who is coming
or will come legally to our lands shall not be required to pay
customs taxes and can travel about freely without any impediment.[1]

Clearly, Vlad, who had held the throne for little more than a
month, had not yet had time to establish his relations with the Ottomans. Thus, only four days later, he wrote to Braşov telling them:

Now the time and the appointed hour about which we spoke
has arrived: the Turks intend to put great burdens upon our
shoulders, forcing us to bow down before them... As far as we
ourselves are concerned, we could have made peace, but on
account of you and yours we cannot make peace with the
Turks because they wish to pass through our country to attack
and plunder you... [we ask you to] immediately send, for our
good and for yours, without hesitation, 200 or 100 or 50 chosen men to help us by next Sunday. When the Turks see the
power of the Hungarians they will be softer, and we will tell
them that more men will come. And thus we will be able to

---

[1]Treaty between Vlad Ţepeş and Braşov and Ţara Bârsei, dated 6 September 1456,
doc. 338 in *Documenta Romaniae Historica, D. Relaţii între ţările române*, vol. I,
pp. 456-458; and doc. CCLVII in Bogdan, *Documente privitoare la relaţiile Ţării Româneşti
cu Braşovul şi Ţara Ungurească*, pp. 316-317.

arrange our affairs and yours in a good manner until we receive orders from his majesty, the king.[2]

Although we do not know the details, Dracula succeeded in coming to terms with the sultan and at the same time in preventing an Ottoman attack on Transylvania. Thus, the Ottoman chronicler Sa'adeddin Mehmed Hodja Efendi recorded that:

> Emissaries of Vlad Ţepeş, the Prince of Wallachia, came too, bringing rich gifts. In the days of yore, Dracula [Vlad II Dracul], who was the father of Vlad Ţepeş, had paid tribute and was supported by the Sultan. This is why his son was treated kindly. Whenever his emissary came to the Sublime Porte, bringing abundant gifts to show his master's devotion, he was rewarded with Imperial favors for his loyalty and submission.[3]

From a juridical point of view it would not have been difficult for the Ottomans to consider Dracula's rule as legitimate for he had been installed on the throne in 1448 with the approval of the Porte; thus his second reign could be considered as a continuation of the first, all the more so because the sultan had not ordered his removal from the throne.[4]

In any event, the efforts of Vlad III to reestablish a balance of power in Wallachia between Hungary and the Ottomans soon encountered difficulties. Only three months after making peace with Hungary, the new governor of the kingdom, Ladislas of Hunedoara, wrote to the councilors of Braşov asking them to assist the pretender Dan, the brother of Vladislav II, in his efforts to oust Dracula from the throne:

---

[2]Letter from Vlad III to Braşov, 10 September 1456, in Nicolae Iorga, *Scrisori de boieri, scrisori de domni*, pp. 164-165; and doc. CCLVIII in Bogdan, *Documente privitoare la relaţiile Ţării Româneşti cu Braşovul şi Ţara Ungurească*, pp. 317-318. An English translation of this letter can be found in Appendix I.B.

[3]Sa'adeddin Mehmed Hodja Efendi, "Tadj-ut-Tevarih" in *Cronici turceşti privind ţările române*, vol. I, pp. 317-321. An English translation of the passages from this chronicle referring to Vlad III can be found in Appendix II.E

You do not know all of the difficulties and problems that were created for the kingdom and the Transylvanian lands by the unfaithful Voievod Dracul [Vlad II], and that Vlad, the Prince of Wallachia, when he was outside of his country, promised many things, giving his word both to us and to our Lord, the King. Nevertheless, since he has returned to his country, as I have found out for certain, he has caused many difficulties and problems in those parts, and is not afraid to continue to do so in the future, and he has no intention of remaining faithful to our Lord, the King, and to us, as he promised. Thus, our Lord, the King, desiring to keep those parts protected, has sent Dan voievod against the above-mentioned Vlad voievod, to force him from his country, and to become its Prince, as he [Dan] has promised to remain faithful to our Lord, the King, and the Kingdom. Therefore, we ask you, our good and true friends, through this letter, for our common good, to be so kind as to give the above-mentioned Dan voievod all the help and support that you can, and to provide him with all the men you can spare. We ask you not to do otherwise.[5]

We can only speculate as to the reasons why the relations between Wallachia and Hungary changed so dramatically during this short period of time. The most likely cause, that can be inferred from the above letter, is that Dracula sought to regain the duchies of Amlaş and Făgăraş, traditional domains of the prince of Wallachia in Tran-

---

[4]Such an interpretation helps explain Chalkondyles' account that:

To Vlad... the Emperor [the Sultan] granted the rule of Dacia [Wallachia]; and with the help of the Emperor, Vlad, the son of Drăculea [Vlad II Dracul], invaded and took the throne.

See Chalcocondil, *Expuneri istorice*, p. 283; and an English version of the section relating to Vlad Ţepeş in Appendix III. See also the account of Kritovoulos, *History of Mehmed the Conqueror*, p. 178 [IV.59] who wrote:

the Sultan took this Drakoulis, and at great expense, forcibly set him as ruler over all the country of the Getae.

[5]Doc. 341 in *Documenta Romaniae Historica, D. Relaţii între Ţările Române*, vol. I, pp. 461-462.

sylvania, which John Hunyadi had taken from Vladislav II in 1454. It is possible that Vlad had understood that he would regain these lands upon taking the throne, but that, following Hunyadi's death, King Ladislas decided not to restore these territories to the Wallachian prince. As he grew up, King Ladislas began to resent the fact that Hunyadi was the true leader of the kingdom. The king is known to have been highly critical of the policies of the royal governor following the latter's death in 1456:

> he [John Hunyadi] caused some of our Wallachian and Molda-
> vian princes, faithful to us and to our Kingdom, to be killed,
> and put others in their place...[6]

Thus, it is quite possible that Ladislas V, "desiring to keep those parts [Amlaş and Făgăraş] protected," decided to lend support to the pretender Dan.

Another possible reason for this sudden change is that the Hungarian Court, hoping to put a prince on the throne of Wallachia that would support the interests of the kingdom, was dismayed by the fact that Dracula made peace with the Turks and began to pursue the traditional equilibrium policy of his predecessors. Like his father before him, Vlad had no intention of becoming a pawn of the Hungarian Kingdom. As we have seen, on several occasions during the first half of the fifteenth century attempts by the princes of Wallachia to protect the autonomy of the country led to conflicts with their Catholic neighbor.

All of this helps to explain why the Saxon cities, with the approval of the king of Hungary, broke their initial treaties with the Wallachian prince and began to support pretenders to the throne. We have already mentioned Dan, the brother of Vladislav II, who was organizing against Dracula in Braşov, having received the support of King Ladislas. Meanwhile, the councilors of Sibiu were supporting another pretender to the Wallachian throne, Vlad Călugărul (the

---

[6]Document dated 21 March 1457 in Eudoxiu Hurmuzaki, *Documente privitoare la istoria românilor*, vol. I$_2$ (Bucureşti, 1891), p. 341.

Monk), an illegitimate son of Vlad Dracul. In return for their support, Vlad Călugărul, then organizing against Dracula in the duchy of Amlaş, had promised control of the customs points at Rucăr and Brăila to Petru Gereb and Peterman, two of the leading citizens of Sibiu.[7] This agreement, if implemented, would have had grave economic implications for Wallachia as it would have left Sibiu in control of both ends of the principal trading route linking Transylvania and the Danube.[8]

The ensuing conflict between the Wallachian prince and the Saxon cities of Transylvania in 1457 took place in the context of the power struggle that broke out between members of the Hunyadi family and supporters of King Ladislas V in Transylvania. The king of Hungary, who had grown to resent the leadership of the Hunyadi family in the kingdom, ordered the execution of the royal governor, Ladislas Hunyadi, on 16 March 1457; this led John Hunyadi's brother in law, Mihail Szilagyi, to begin to organize open resistance to the king in Transylvania.[9]

Vlad III attempted to use the situation in neighboring Transylvania, and his good relations with the Ottoman Empire, to assert his autonomy and gain political leverage. His first action was to lend support to his cousin Stephen in his efforts to oust Petru Aron and take the Moldavian throne. The man who would become Moldavia's greatest prince had sought refuge in Wallachia after Vlad had seized the throne in 1456; he may even have fought alongside his cousin against Vladislav II in the summer of 1456. Although few details are

---

[7]This information comes from a letter of Dracula to Sibiu dated 14 March 1457 in which he claims to have respected the terms of the treaty he had concluded with Sibiu, probably similar to those contained in the treaty with Braşov and Ţara Bârsei. See doc. CCLIX in Bogdan, *Documente privitoare la relaţiile Ţării Româneşti cu Braşovul şi Ţara Ungurească*, pp. 318-319.

[8]Gustav Gündisch, "Cu privire la relaţiile lui Vlad Ţepeş cu Transilvania în anii 1456-1458," pp. 681-696, in *Studii. Revista de istorie*, XVI:3 (1963), p. 686.

[9]Nicolae Stoicescu, "Vlad Ţepeş's Relations with Transylvania and Hungary," in Treptow, *Dracula, Essays...*, p. 85.

known about the circumstances that brought Stephen the Great to the throne, the seventeenth century Romanian chronicler Grigore Ureche tells us that:

> This Prince, Ştefan vodă, after two years of the reign of Petru vodă Aron, came from Wallachia with many Wallachian troops and with soldiers from all over the land [Moldavia] and entered the country. Making their way toward the capital of Suceava, they encountered Petru vodă Aron on the Siret river at Doljeşti and they fought on Holy Thursday, 12 April. Ştefan vodă defeated Aron, but the latter did not leave it at this; he tried again and they met for a second time at Orbic where Ştefan vodă won again...[10]

Though he did not participate personally in the invasion of Moldavia,[11] the assistance Vlad lent to Stephen is also acknowledged by contemporary Moldavian chronicles:

> Ştefan voievod, a son of Bogdan voievod, came with a small force of Wallachians and men from the lower country [southern Moldavia], about 6,000 men in all. And they came upon Aron voievod at a small river named Hresca near Doljeşti. There Ştefan voievod defeated Aron voievod and took the country from him...[12]

The Porte, for reasons unknown, looked favorably upon Vlad's support of Stephen in his bid for the throne, most likely approving

---

[10]See the chronicle of Grigore Ureche in *Letopiseţul Ţării Moldovei*, P.P. Panaitescu, ed. (Bucureşti, 1957), p. 83. See also Alexandru Boldur, *Ştefan cel Mare, voievod al Moldovei (1457-1504): Studiu de istorie socială şi politică* (Madrid, 1970), pp. 13-14.

[11]Vlad is known to have been in Târgovişte during this time where he issued a *hrisov* on 16 April, see doc. 115 in *Documenta Romaniae Historica, B. Ţara Românească*, vol. I, pp. 198-200.

[12]See "Cronica moldo-germană," pp. 24-37, in P.P. Panaitescu, ed., *Cronicile slavoromîne*, p. 28. Other mentions of this can be found in "Letopiseţul de la Putna, nr. I," pp. 41-52, in *Ibid.*, p. 49; "Letopiseţul de la Putna, nr. II," pp. 53-66, in *Ibid.*, p. 61; and "Cronica moldo-polonă," pp. 164-187, in *Ibid.*, p. 178. See also Olgierd Górka, *Cronica epocei lui Ştefan cel Mare (1457-1499)* (Bucureşti, 1937), p. 110.

the action beforehand,[13] despite the fact that the previous year Petru Aron had acknowledged Ottoman suzerainty and agreed to pay tribute to the sultan. The relationship between Moldavia and the Porte, as it had been established in 1456, did not change during the early years of Stephen the Great's reign.[14]

After his cousin seized the throne of Moldavia, Vlad took action against Sibiu and Braşov who continued to lend support to the pretenders Vlad Călugărul and Dan. It may be during this time that Vlad led his armies in an attack on the lands surrounding Sibiu, as recounted in the German stories, plundering and burning several villages, including one owned by Petru Gereb and Peterman, before going on to Ţara Bârsei where he did more of the same to punish Braşov for supporting Dan.[15]

This attack was part of the ongoing conflict between King Ladislas and Mihai Szilagyi in Transylvania; Sibiu and Braşov were the strongest centers of opposition to both Szilagyi and the Wallachian prince. To relieve the threat posed by the Saxon cities's support of pretenders to his throne, Vlad allied with Szilagyi against King Ladislas. The conflict extended into the fall of 1457 when the two sides concluded an armistice. On the day the armistice went into effect, 23 November 1457, King Ladislas V died in Prague; news of his death did not reach Transylvania until 9 December.[16] Szilagyi was joined at the peace talks with Braşov by Vlad's representatives, Stoica, Stan, and Dan.[17] Meanwhile, the Wallachian prince awaited the outcome of the negotiations at Rucăr from where he wrote to the councilors of Braşov and Ţara Bârsei on 1 December:

[13]Tursun Beg, "Tarih-i Ebu-l Feth-i Sultan Mehmed-han," in Guboglu and Mehmet, *Cronici turceşti privind ţările române*, vol. I, p. 68.

[14]Ciobanu, "The Equilibrium Policy of the Romanian Principalities," in Treptow, *Dracula: Essays...*, p. 43.

[15]Ioan Bogdan, *Vlad Ţepeş şi naraţiunile germane şi ruseşti asupra lui*, p. 14; Nicolae Stoicescu, "Vlad Ţepeş's Relations with Transylvania and Hungary," in Treptow, *Dracula: Essays...*, p. 85.

[16]Gündisch, "Cu privire la relaţiile lui Vlad Ţepeş cu Transilvania," pp. 690-691.

Let it be known that all which my Lord and elder brother Mihail Szilagyi has ordered I will obey; and I pledge on the faith and soul of my majesty to keep peace with you and let all roads be opened for your people to come to us to buy and to sell freely, without worry and without loss, as they would move about in your own country. In the same way our people will come to you, without any loss, as my Lord and brother Mihail Szilagyi has ordered. But I agree to this only as long as he remains at peace with you, then so will I. And God will be pleased.[18]

In accordance with the terms of the agreement, Braşov expelled the pretender Dan III and paid 10,000 florins to Szilagyi.[19]

Peace had been restored between Wallachia and Transylvania and the Hunyadi family had gained the upper hand in the power struggle in the kingdom. Following the death of Ladislas V, Mihail Szilagyi worked to have his nephew, Matthias [Hunyadi] Corvinus, the young son of John Hunyadi, chosen king; he was elected to the throne on 24 January 1458 and, at the same time, Szilagyi was named royal governor for a period of five years.

With the change in the political situation in Hungary, relations between Wallachia and Transylvania remained good throughout most of 1458. As the conflict of the previous year between Sibiu and Dracula had yet to be settled, in March 1458 Matthias Corvinus, the new king of Hungary, and Mihail Szilagyi, the royal governor, both wrote to the councilors of Sibiu advising them to maintain good relations

---

[17]Stoica is mentioned as *paharnic* in documents from 5 March 1458 and 20 September 1459. Stan perhaps refers to Stan al lui Negre, mentioned in documents from 16 April 1457 and 5 March 1458 and referred to as Stan *vornic* in a document dated 20 September 1459. See docs. 115, 117, and 118 in *Documenta Romaniae Historica, B. Ţara Românească*, vol. I, pp. 198-204.

[18]Doc. LXXI in Bogdan, *Documente privitoare la relaţiile Ţării Româneşti cu Braşovul şi Ţara Ungurească*, p. 93. Bogdan mistakenly dated this letter c. 1458-1459. See also doc. 71 in Tocilescu, *534 documente istorice slavo-române*, p. 68.

[19]Gündisch, "Cu privire la relaţiile lui Vlad Ţepeş cu Transilvania," p. 689.

with the prince of Wallachia, warning them that they would not receive any support if they continued to remain hostile to Vlad:

> You yourselves, through your greed, gave him [Vlad] reason to come against you causing great damage. For this you must bear most of the guilt.[20]

It is also during this time that the duchies of Amlaş and Făgăraş were restored to the prince of Wallachia. In a *hrisov* issued on 20 September 1459, Vlad refers to himself for the first time as "Lord and ruler over all of Wallachia, and the duchies of Amlaş and Făgăraş."[21]

Following Vlad's lead, his cousin Ştefan cel Mare improved relations between Moldavia and Transylvania, renewing the commercial privileges originally accorded by his grandfather, Alexander the Good, to Braşov and Ţara Bârsei.[22] Thus, 1458 marks a period of generally peaceful relations between Wallachia, Moldavia, and Transylvania. Despite these peaceful relations and the fact that they had withdrawn support from the pretenders to the Wallachian throne, the Hunyadi family continued the traditional policy of the Hungarian Kingdom by ordering Sibiu and Braşov, on 28 March 1458, to give shelter to Mihail *logofăt* and other refugees from Wallachia and Moldavia who had fled those countries with their families and belongings.[23] Nevertheless, available documents indicate that normal

[20]See the letter from Matthias Corvinus to the councilors of Sibiu, dated 3 March 1458, doc. 3108 in Gündisch, *Urkundenbuch zur Geschichte der Deutschen in Siebenbürgen*, vol. VI, p. 7; and the letter of Mihail Szilagyi to the councilors of Sibiu, dated 6 March 1458, doc. 3109 in *Ibid.*, p. 7.

[21]Doc. 118 in *Documenta Romaniae Historica, B. Ţara Românească*, vol. I, pp. 203-204. The Transylvanian duchies were restored to Vlad sometime after 5 March 1458 when Vlad refers to himself in a *hrisov* as only *"ruler of all of Wallachia"* (see doc. 117 in *Ibid.*, pp. 201-202). We can assume that this took place before the fall of 1458 when Mihail Szilagyi was arrested by his nephew Matthias Corvinus and Vlad's relations with Hungary turned cool.

[22]Doc. 125 in Ioan Bogdan, *Documentele lui Ştefan cel Mare*, 2 vols. (Bucureşti, 1913), vol. II, p. 261; doc. 486 in Tocilescu, *534 documente istorice slavo-române*, p. 504; and doc. 3115 in Gündisch, *Urkundenbuch zur Geschichte der Deutschen in Siebenbürgen*, vol. VI, pp. 9-10.

relations between Wallachia and Transylvania continued throughout most of 1458.[24]

In the fall of that year, along with the change of seasons, relations between Wallachia and the Hungarian Kingdom again cooled. This happened, in part, because of a change in the internal political situation in Hungary; Matthias Corvinus, wanting to free himself of his uncle's control,

Matthias Corvinus, King of Hungary, 1458-1490
By Octavian Ion Penda

trol, dismissed Mihail Szilagyi as royal governor and imprisoned him in October of 1458.[25] With Vlad's principal ally at the Hungarian court out of the way, closer relations between the king and the Saxon cities of Transylvania followed. The first signs of a deterioration in the relations between Braşov and Wallachia are to be found in a letter Vlad sent to Braşov on 8 December 1458:

[23]Letter from Mihail Szilagyi to Braşov, Sibiu, and the Szeckler lands, dated 28 March 1458, Annex II in Gündisch, "Cu privire la relaţiile lui Vlad Ţepeş cu Transilvania," pp. 692-695. As we have seen, shortly after he sought refuge in Braşov, Mihail *logofăt* was killed by agents of Vlad Ţepeş.

[24]In a letter to Braşov dated 18 May 1458 Vlad III asked Braşov to send some master craftsmen to Wallachia (see doc. 3120 in Gündisch, *Urkundenbuch zur Geschichte der Deutschen in Siebenbürgen*, vol. VI, pp. 12-13; and doc. CCLX in Bogdan, *Documente privitoare la relaţiile Ţării Româneşti cu Braşovul şi Ţara Ungurească*, pp. 319-320). In another letter, dated 13 June 1458, Dracula sends his messenger, Petru Sor, on a mission to Braşov (see doc. 3127 in Gündisch, *ibidem*, p. 18; and doc. CCLXI in Bogdan, *ibidem*, p. 320). This letter is of interest as it was sent from the banks of the Dâmboviţa River, probably a reference to Bucharest that would be mentioned by name for the first time in a document from the following year. In a letter dated 10 September 1458, King Matthias Corvinus ordered the councilors of Braşov to send 48 florins to his messenger at the Wallachian court (see doc. 3141 in Gündisch, *ibidem*, pp. 28-29).

[25]Gündisch, "Cu privire la relaţiile lui Vlad Ţepeş cu Transilvania," p. 691.

I send you news that our man Dumitru bought some steel, and
he bought it fairly, but you did not let him bring the steel back
with him. Therefore, I ask you to either give him the steel or
give him back the ducats; one of the two must be returned as
we cannot accept a loss.[26]

The conflicts erupted into open hostilities during the winter of
1458-1459 and the spring of 1459 as Matthias Corvinus returned the
pretender Dan III to Braşov where he began to organize against Vlad.
Meanwhile, the prince of Wallachia took retaliatory measures against
Saxon merchants in Wallachia. A letter dated 5 April 1459 from the
pretender Dan III to the councilors of Braşov and Ţara Bârsei informs
us:

You know that King Matthias has sent me and when I came to
Ţara Bârsei the officials and councilors of Braşov and the old
men of Ţara Bârsei cried to us with broken hearts about the
things which Dracula, our enemy, did; how he did not remain
faithful to our Lord, the king, and had sided with the Turks.
He did this following the teaching of the Devil. And he captured all the merchants of Braşov and Ţara Bârsei who had
gone in peace to Wallachia and took all their wealth; but he
was not satisfied only with the wealth of these people, but he
imprisoned them and impaled them, 41 in all. Nor were these
people enough; he became even more evil and gathered 300
boys from Braşov and Ţara Bârsei that he found in Târgovişte
and all the markets in Wallachia. Of these he impaled some and
burned others. At the same time he secretly recalled his men
who were in Braşov. Then councilors of Braşov came and told
me that some of the merchants from Wallachia had wealth in
Braşov that they were holding and they asked me to give them
my advice. And when my majesty heard and understood, I discussed it with my boyars and I informed the officials of my
decision: take their [the Wallachian merchants's] wealth and

[26]Doc. LXXII in Bogdan, *Documente privitoare la relaţiile Ţării Româneşti cu
Braşovul şi Ţara Ungurească*, p. 94; and doc. 72 in Tocilescu, *534 documente istorice slavo-
române*, p. 69.

give the money to the families of those who were killed, and this wealth will never be returned to Wallachia and the goods belonging to the merchants from Wallachia shall never be paid for by Braşov.[27]

The accusations, clearly propagandistic in nature, made against Vlad would later be included in the German Stories about Dracula written to discredit the Wallachian prince.[28] A few weeks later, on 23 April 1459, King Matthias ordered the councilors of Braşov to turn over to the Szecklers goods confiscated from the Wallachian merchants.[29]

It seems, however, that the conflict between Wallachia and Braşov was provoked by the court at Buda. Matthias reinstalled the pretender Dan in Braşov and, on 3 April, he ordered the councilors of Braşov to stop exporting arms to Wallachia.[30] It is logical to assume that such an action would have already been taken by Braşov had the conflict started locally. Matthias, probably regretting the loss of the duchies of Amlaş and Făgăraş, also fostered rebellion in those parts during this time.

Another reason for the conflict, as we saw earlier, were abuses committed by Braşov against the free trade agreement concluded with the Wallachian prince. The Saxon cities of Transylvania, which had thriving economies during the previous century, began to experience a

---

[27]Doc. LXXIX in Bogdan, *Documente privitoare la relaţiile Ţării Româneşti cu Braşovul şi Ţara Ungurească*, pp. 101-102; and doc. 75 in Tocilescu, *534 documente istorice slavo-române*, pp. 71-72.

[28]As it was common practice, we can assume that Dan, for political reasons, exaggerated the actions taken by Vlad against the Saxons in Wallachia. By the time the German Stories about Dracula were written the number of merchants from Ţara Bârsei and Braşov killed in Wallachia had grown to 600 and the number of Saxon boys killed had grown to 400 (see Panaitescu, "The German Stories about Vlad Ţepeş," in Treptow, *Dracula: Essays...*, pp. 189-190, and Appendix IV).

[29]Doc. 3179 in Gündisch, *Urkundenbuch zur Geschichte der Deutschen in Siebenbürgen*, vol. VI, pp. 53-54.

[30]Doc. 3177, in Gündisch, *Urkundenbuch zur Geschichte der Deutschen in Siebenbürgen*, vol. VI, pp. 51-52.

decline in commercial activity because Ottoman expansion closed many of the important East-West trade routes.[31] As their livelihood depended largely on commerce they began to take abusive measures against their competitors. When Dracula and other Wallachian princes complained of their unfair actions, they began to lend support to pretenders to the Wallachian throne, such as Dan III and Vlad Călugărul, who promised them economic advantages in return for their support.

Under the communist regime, Romanian historiography suggested another reason for the outbreak of hostilities between Wallachia and Braşov early in 1459. A hypothesis was developed according to which Vlad III would have reacted against the unfair trading practices of the Saxon merchants by forbidding them to enter the country and forcing them to buy and sell at border fairs in specified locations. Shortly after it was developed, this hypothesis began to be accepted as fact in both Romanian and foreign historiography.[32] This theory had been developed by the Marxist historian Barbu T. Câmpina, together with Gustav Gündisch,[33] on the basis of a decree issued by Dracula in Braşov on 7 October 1476 as he prepared to invade Wallachia and take the throne for a third time:

> With faith in our Lord Jesus Christ, I Vlad voievod, by the grace of God Prince of all of Wallachia. My majesty issues this decree to the honest, faithful, and good friends of my majesty, to the county, to the twelve councilors, and to all the other citizens of the great fortress of Braşov, and to all of my good

---

[31]Panaitescu, "Cum au ajuns Bucureştii capitala ţării," in *Interpretări româneşti*, pp. 167-168; and Radu Rosetti, "Stephen the Great of Moldavia and the Turkish Invasion," pp. 86-103, in *The Slavonic Review*, VI:16 (June, 1927), p. 89.

[32]See, for example, Nicolae Stoicescu, "Vlad Ţepeş's Relations with Transylvania and Hungary," in Treptow, *Dracula: Essays...*, pp. 89-91; Ştefan Andreescu, *Vlad Ţepeş (Dracula)*, p. 88; and the American historians Radu R. Florescu and Raymond T. McNally, *Dracula: A Biography of Vlad the Impaler*, p. 73.

[33]See the chapter by Barbu T. Câmpina in *Istoria Romîniei* (Bucureşti, 1962), p. 468; and Gündisch, "Cu privire la relaţiile lui Vlad Ţepeş cu Transilvania," especially pp. 685-686.

Vlad's attack on Brasov in 1459

By Octavian Ion Penda

friends in Țara Bârsei, great and small: they shall benefit, according to the terms of the old agreement, as it was established in earlier days, in the time of the great Prince Mircea voievod, in the days of my majesty's father, the great Vlad voievod, and then also during my reign. In the same manner, my majesty orders that from now on things will be according to the old settlement: that from now on the scale will no longer exist in my country, but every man shall be free and able to trade, to buy, and to sell without a scale. And in addition, regarding wax, my majesty has allowed people the freedom to buy in all the markets, regions, and places in my country, as it was in the old agreement, as well as during my reign, so it will be henceforth, as long as my majesty is alive, they will be free to buy all that they need and want. And, in addition, with regard to customs, as it was in the old agreement, and in the days of my former reign, so it will be now and henceforth in the markets in my country, and in the customs houses in the countryside: they will pay fair customs, as they paid in the beginning and in the days of my reign, and no one shall ever dare to establish higher customs taxes, neither the *pârcălabi* in the cities, nor the *vornici*, nor the customs officials in the cities or the customs houses in the countryside or at the Danube, nor anyone else among my majesty's high officials and servants.[34]

Misusing this document, Câmpina and Gündisch selected certain passages from it to argue that Vlad had taken protectionist measures against the Saxon cities, thereby provoking the hostilities. Using the passages where Vlad decrees that henceforth commerce between Wallachia and Brașov shall be conducted "according to the terms of the old agreement, as it was established in earlier days, in the time of the great Prince Mircea voievod" and that "from now on the scale will no longer exist in my country, but every man shall be free and able to trade, to buy, and to sell without a scale," Câmpina and Gündisch argued that Vlad, during his principal reign, had abandoned the

---

[34]Doc. LXXIV in Bogdan, *Documente privitoare la relațiile Țării Românești cu Brașovul și cu Țara Ungurească*, pp. 95-97.

traditional policy of free trade that had been established during the reign of Mircea the Old and imposed a "scale" on Saxon merchants. This "scale" gave native merchants the right of preemption, forcing the Saxon merchants to sell their goods at a specific time and place. They went so far as to suggest that Saxon commerce in Wallachia may have been limited to the markets at Câmpulung, Târgoviște, and Târgșor because Prince Neagoe Basarab is known to have implemented such a policy in 1517.[35] According to this theory, Brașov would have forced Vlad to abandon the detested "scale" in return for supporting his return to the throne in 1476.[36]

What Câmpina and Gündisch, who never quoted the complete text of the document, failed to mention was that throughout it Vlad refers to the free trade policy practiced during his reign, specifying that henceforth commerce between Wallachia and Brașov shall be carried out "according to the terms of the old agreement, as it was established in earlier days, in the time of the great Prince Mircea voievod, in the days of my majesty's father, the great Vlad voievod, *and then also during my reign.*" After carefully reading the document one may conclude that, perhaps, Radu cel Frumos or his successor Basarab Laiotă, both of whom, like Dracula, had continuing conflicts with the Saxon cities of Transylvania, implemented some sort of protectionist policy against the Saxon merchants,[37] although what exactly is meant by a "scale" remains unclear.

[35]Gündisch, "Cu privire la relațiile lui Vlad Țepeș cu Transilvania," pp. 685-686; and Câmpina in *Istoria Romîniei,* p. 468. On the policy of Neagoe Basarab see Radu Manolescu, "Schimbul de mărfuri între Țara Românească și Brașov în prima jumătate a secolului al XVI-lea," in *Studii și materiale de istorie medie,* vol. II (București, 1957), p. 125.

[36]Gündisch, "Cu privire la relațiile lui Vlad Țepeș cu Transilvania," p. 685.

[37]For example, a letter sent by Radu cel Frumos to the councilors of Brașov, dated 6 March 1470, speaks of punitive measures taken by the prince against Saxon merchants in response to their actions that prohibited Wallachian merchants from trading freely in Transylvania. At the same time Radu asks the councilors of Brașov to abide by the terms of the traditional free trade agreement (see doc. LXXXIII in Bogdan, *Documente privitoare la relațiile Țării Românești cu Brașovul și Țara Ungurească,* pp. 107-109; and doc. 80 in Tocilescu, *534 documente istorice slavo-române,* pp. 76-77.

Although based on a false reading of a single document, the theory that Dracula introduced protectionist economic policies to promote the growth of a native merchant class rapidly took hold in Romanian historiography because it fitted with Marxist ideology. Vlad Țepeş, whom Romanian historiography after World War II had made a hero not only because he fought the Turks, but because he struggled against those eternal villains of Romanian history, the boyars, also became a promoter of economic independence — a goal pursued by the communist regime — even a precursor of centralized economic planning.

It is clear, however, that if Vlad III intended to promote the development of a native merchant class his logical policy would have been to pursue free trade. If he imposed protectionist measures against Transylvanian merchants they certainly would retaliate. Given the lack of urban development in Wallachia the development of commerce in the Romanian principality would depend upon trade with neighboring countries, especially Transylvania, which had a more advanced urban development and thus also the most lucrative markets in the region. What Dracula sought, as emphasized in several of his documents, was free and *fair* trade. The conflict between Vlad and the Saxon cities of Transylvania did not result from any protectionist measures implemented by the Wallachian prince, but rather from the unfair trade practices of Saxon merchants and officials who did not respect the terms of the free trade agreement. In similar circumstances Dracula's brother and successor, Prince Radu cel Frumos, wrote to the councilors of Braşov complaining of their unfair practices, declaring that:

> we have never started any conflict, you have always begun it. Because my poor men [Wallachian merchants] go there with their wealth, and you take their wealth and profits, harming my poor men and not allowing them to go freely with their wealth. Therefore, I did the same to your men... we want things to return to the way they were before: for my poor men to go freely to you and for all of you to go freely everywhere in my country.[38]

In the same spirit, an important document dating from the reign of Basarab cel Tânăr (1477-1481) sheds light on the conflict between Dracula and the Saxons. *Vornic* Neagu wrote to Braşov:

> Remember well who started having people impaled. Again the fugitives [from Wallachia] and you, because you kept Dan among you and thus angered Vlad voievod who did you great wrong and began having people impaled, and came upon you with fire.[39]

One thing is clear: during these conflicts between Wallachia and the Saxon cities of Transylvania trade generally ceased, to the disadvantage of both sides.

As tensions heightened, Dracula led his forces on a raid against Braşov and Ţara Bârsei in late summer or early fall 1459 intended to punish the Saxons for their hostile attitude and for harboring the pretender Dan. The German Stories describe the attack, with due exaggeration and literary embellishment, as follows:

> He invaded Ţara Bârsei and spoiled the rye and ruined all the corn in the fields. And many people were captured outside of Braşov. Dracula went into Braşov as far as the chapel of St. Jakob and ordered that the suburbs of the city should be burned down. And no sooner had he arrived there, when early in the morning he gave orders that the men and women, young and old alike, should be impaled next to the chapel, at the foot of the mountain. He then sat down at a table in their midst and ate his breakfast with great pleasure.[40]

The conflict between Wallachia and Transylvania continued into 1460. At this time a third pretender to Vlad's throne appeared in

---

[38]Doc. LXXXIII in Bogdan, *Documente privitoare la relaţiile Ţării Româneşti cu Braşovul şi Ţara Ungurească*, pp. 107-109; and doc. 80 in Tocilescu, *534 documente istorice slavo-române*, pp. 76-77.

[39]Tocilescu, *534 documente istorice slavo-române*, p. 379.

[40]P.P. Panaitescu, "The German Stories about Vlad Ţepeş," in Treptow, *Dracula: Essays...* p. 189.

Sighişoara, the future Prince Basarab Laiotă, who wrote to Braşov on 21 January 1460 offering to defend them against a new attack by Wallachian troops with a corp of 500-600 men if they can provide them with the necessary material support.[41] The Saxon city, however, continued to pin its hopes on Dan III. As he prepared to invade Wallachia, the pretender declared that Braşov could keep all the wealth and goods confiscated by the Saxon authorities from Wallachian merchants at the beginning of the hostilities as compensation for supporting him.[42] At the same time he issued a decree forbidding those Wallachians who lost their wealth and goods as a result from seeking reparations in the future.[43]

These acts did nothing to garner Dan any support within the country and when he invaded Wallachia in April 1460 he was easily defeated by Dracula. The German Stories recall the fate of the pretender:

> And then he [Vlad] captured Dan cel Tânăr and forced him to dig his own grave and ordered that the funeral service be read according to the Christian rite, and then he had him beheaded next to his tomb.[44]

After failing to oust Vlad and learning of the fate of the pretender Dan the councilors of Braşov, fearing retaliations, sought to come to terms with the prince of Wallachia. This decision was also supported by King Matthias who, faced with a challenge for the throne from Emperor Frederick III, wanted peace in the southeastern part of his kingdom so that he could devote his attention to the threat posed by Vienna. Thus, on 26 May, Nicolae of Ocna Sibiului wrote to

---

[41]Doc. CCLXXIV in Bogdan, *Documente privitoare la relaţiile Ţării Româneşti cu Braşovul şi Ţara Ungurească*, pp. 330-331.

[42]Doc. CCLXIX, dated 2 March 1460, in Bogdan, *Documente privitoare la relaţiile Ţării Româneşti cu Braşovul şi Ţara Ungurească*, pp. 325-327.

[43]Doc. 3206, dated 1 March 1460, in Gündisch, *Urkundenbuch zur Geschichte der Deutschen in Siebenbürgen*, vol. VI, pp. 71-73.

[44]P.P. Panaitescu, "The German Stories about Vlad Ţepeş," in Treptow, *Dracula: Essays...*, p. 189.

The execution of Dan III

By Octavian Ion Penda

the councilors of Braşov that Matthias ordered them not to molest or hinder travelers from Wallachia.[45]

Relations between Dracula and Braşov normalized and an agreement restoring the situation prior to the outbreak of hostilities was negotiated by Vlad's boyar Cârstian; it also specified that the Saxon city would no longer give refuge to enemies of the Wallachian prince. Thus, on 4 June 1460, Vlad III wrote to the councilors of Braşov, informing them that he was sending his representative, the boyar Voico Dobriţa, to them and that, in accordance with the terms of their agreement, they were to send Wallachian exiles back with him or expel them in his presence.[46]

Nevertheless, Vlad's conflicts with Transylvania were not yet ended. He sought to punish the inhabitants of Amlaş and Făgăraş who had rebelled against him during the conflict. While preparing for an attack on his Transylvanian duchies, Ţepeş wrote to Braşov assuring them that he intended to maintain peaceful relations with them, so long as they did not lend assistance to his enemies in southern Transylvania.[47] The German Stories recount this event, exaggerating both the devastation and the horror caused by the attack:

> In the year 1460, on St. Bartholomew's Day [24 August], in the morning, Dracula crossed the forest with his servants and looked for all the Saxons that he could find, of both sexes, around the village of Amlaş. And all those that he could gather together he ordered to be thrown, one on top of the other, like a hill, and to be shredded like cabbage with swords and knives. And their chaplain and the others whom he did not kill imme-

---

[45]Doc. 3215 in Gündisch, *Urkundenbuch zur Geschichte der Deutschen in Siebenbürgen*, vol. VI, p. 77.

[46]Doc. CCLXII in Bogdan, *Documente privitoare la relaţiile Ţării Româneşti cu Braşovul şi Ţara Ungurească*, pp. 320-321; and doc. 3218 in Gündisch, *Urkundenbuch zur Geschichte der Deutschen in Siebenbürgen*, vol. VI, p. 79.

[47]Doc. 3224 in Gündisch, *Urkundenbuch zur Geschichte der Deutschen in Siebenbürgen*, vol. VI, pp. 83-84; and doc. CCLXIII in Bogdan, *Documente privitoare la relaţiile Ţării Româneşti cu Braşovul şi Ţara Ungurească*, p. 321.

diately, he took back to his country, and there he had them hanged. And he ordered the village and everything in it, including the people, who numbered more than 30,000, to be burned.

And then from all the lands that are called Făgăraş he took people and brought them to Wallachia, men, women, and children, and he ordered that all of them be impaled.[48]

The exaggerations are apparent. First, the population of the village of Amlaş could not possibly have been 30,000 or it would have been an important city for its time. Secondly, although he undoubtedly employed terror tactics to suppress the rebellion, Vlad would not have undertaken such wholesale destruction of what were and continued to be his possessions.[49]

After almost two years of hostilities peace was restored between Wallachia and Transylvania, including Braşov, Ţara Bârsei, Sibiu, and the Szeckler lands. An agreement signed on 1 October 1460 established terms similar to those included in the agreement of 6 September 1456:[50] the prince of Wallachia promised not to allow the Turks to attack Transylvania, while they, in turn, promised not to shelter or assist his enemies. In addition, Braşov agreed to pay 15,500 florins in reparations for the goods seized from Wallachian merchants This information comes from an undated letter of Radu cel Frumos to the councilors of Braşov:

> I Radu, Voievod and Prince. My Majesty writes and wishes good health to the good friends of My Majesty, the councilors

---

[48]P.P. Panaitescu, "The German Stories about Vlad Ţepeş," in Treptow, *Dracula: Essays...*, pp. 193-194.

[49]As mentioned earlier, Vlad had regained the duchies in 1458. Internal documents dated 20 September 1459 and 10 February 1461 indicate that they continued to be possessions of the prince of Wallachia throughout the rest of his reign (see docs. 118 and 120 in *Documenta Romaniae Historica, B. Ţara Românească*, vol. I, pp. 203-206).

[50]See Appendix II in Gustav Gündisch, "Vlad Ţepeş und die Sächsischen Selbstverwaltungsgebiete Siebenbürgens," pp. 981-992, in *Revue roumaine d'histoire*, VIII:6 (1969), p. 992.

of Braşov, and I send you news that you have come to me freely on many occasions and I have let you go about freely and make commerce throughout my country. But you know very well that you still have money belonging to my poor men, 15,500 florins of which you paid 4,000 in the time of Vlad voievod, but the rest you were obligated to pay in one year, in three installments. Things happened as they happened, but in the midst of this you remained quiet...[51]

Meanwhile, peaceful relations between the Wallachian prince and the Ottoman Empire continued. Vlad annually sent emissaries to the Porte and continued to pay the tribute to the sultan. The prince of Wallachia may even have concluded a new peace treaty with the sultan in 1460[52] when Mehmed began to consolidate his position in Europe in preparation for a campaign in the Asian portion of his Empire. Although there is some debate as to whether this treaty should be attributed to Vlad or Basarab Laiotă, the terms of the treaty tend to indicate that it probably dates from Dracula's reign:

Article I. The Turks shall not interfere in the affairs of the country, nor rule over it, nor enter the country, except for a single Imperial emissary who shall come with the permission of the Prince. This emissary, when traveling from the Danube to Târgovişte, shall be accompanied by a representative of the Prince and, after receiving the tribute, shall return again with representatives of the Prince up to Giurgiu where he shall again count the money, totalling 10,000 galbens from our treasury, and he shall leave a receipt with the officials of that place. From Giurgiu, crossing to Rusciuc, a receipt shall also be issued

[51]See doc. LXXXII in Bogdan, *Documente privitoare la relaţiile Ţării Româneşti cu Braşovul şi Ţara Ungurească*, pp. 106-107; and doc. 79 in Tocilescu, *534 documente istorice slavo-române*, p. 76.

[52]See the treaty, dated 1460, between the Wallachian prince and the sultan, doc. 2 in Dimitrie A. Sturdza and C. Colescu-Vartic, eds., *Acte şi documente relative la istoria renas-cerei României*, vol. I (1391-1841), pp. 2-4. See also doc. 107 in Ion Ionaşcu, Petre Bărbulescu, and Gheorghe Gheorghe, eds., *Tratatele internaţionale ale României, 1354-1920: Texte rezumate, adnotări, bibliografie* (Bucureşti, 1975), pp. 49-50.

there so that the country shall not be responsible if the money is lost along the way.

Article II. Wallachia shall govern itself according to its own laws and shall have the right to make war with its neighbors or to establish friendly relations with them, and the Prince shall have the power of life and death over his subjects.

Article III. If any Christians shall adopt Islam when they are outside of the country, upon their return they shall once again return to Christianity so that there should be no grievances or conflicts.

Article IV. Those Wallachians who shall travel in the Empire on business shall be exempted from all taxes and shall not be harassed for their dress.

Article V. The Prince shall be chosen by the Metropolitan, the bishops, and the boyars.

Article VI. When a Mohammedan shall have a dispute with a Wallachian, the case shall be judged by the princely council, according to the traditions of the land, and the decision shall be respected.

Article VII. Turkish merchants, who shall come with their goods, shall obtain the permission of the Prince and shall indicate from where they come and without delay they shall sell or buy goods in the cities and then leave the country again. They shall not be allowed to travel about the country freely or to buy and sell in certain places.

Article VIII. These Turkish merchants shall not have the right to take with them Wallachian servants, of either sex, nor shall they be allowed a special place for their prayers.

Article IX. Under no circumstances shall a decree be issued [by the Porte] against a native of the country, nor shall any inhabitants of the country be taken forcibly to Constantinople or other Ottoman possessions.

In preparation for his Asian campaign, Mehmed II also concluded a similar treaty with George Castriota Scanderbeg in Albania, making it plausible that he did the same thing with Vlad. The sultan wanted to consolidate the European portion of his empire before turning his attention to matters in the East.

Nevertheless, the prince of Wallachia would soon radically alter his relations with the Ottoman Empire. Romanian historiography has held that in 1459 Dracula stopped paying tribute to the sultan.[53] This conclusion is based on two sources. First, a passage from the memoirs of the Serbian janissary Konstantin Mihailovic that reads:

> This son of Dracula had come twice in succession to the Emperor's court, but then did not want to come any more for several years, until the Emperor sent after him a lord called Hamzabeg who commanded the Emperor's hawks.[54]

Second, a passage from the chronicle of Giovanni Maria degli Angiolelli that relates:

> At this time the Turkish Emperor sent two of his messengers to Dracula, the prince of Wallachia, asking him to pay the tribute from the past three years.[55]

As Mihailovic tells us that Dracula paid tribute to the sultan during the first two years of his reign, from 1456 to 1458, and Angiolelli states that Vlad had not paid for three years before the sultan's campaign, several historians have concluded that 1459 was the year in which Dracula decided to break off his relations with the Ottomans. This evidence, however, is misleading. Mihailovic, a mere janissary in the sultan's army during the campaign of 1462, and who wrote his account of these events only decades later, cannot be relied upon for

---

[53]See, for example, Nicolae Stoicescu, *Vlad Țepeș*, p. 69; Ștefan Andreescu, *Vlad Țepeș (Dracula)*, p. 84; and *Istoria Romîniei*, vol. II, p. 470. An exception to this is a little known, but valuable study by Sergiu Iosipescu, "Conjunctura și condiționarea internațională politico-militară a celei de a doua domnii a lui Vlad Țepeș (1456-1462)," pp. 175-186, in *Studii și materiale de muzeografie și istorie militară*, no. 11 (1978), who points out the faulty basis of this conclusion.

[54]Mihailovic, *Memoirs of a Janissary*, p. 129.

[55]This chronicle was mistakenly attributed to Donado Da Lezze. See Donado Da Lezze, *Historia Turchesca (1300-1514)*, I. Ursu, ed. (București, 1909), p. 23.

such details. Meanwhile, Angiolelli's chronicle, written in Italy in the early sixteenth century, is not at all a reliable source regarding the events that took place in the Romanian principality more than 50 years before; he places the episode described in the above passage in the year 1458 and the sultan's war against Dracula in 1459.[56]

It seems unlikely that in the midst of a serious conflict with Transylvania and Hungary, and faced with the threat posed by the pretender Dan III, Vlad would have decided to radically alter his relations with the Ottoman Empire.[57] The country could not endure a conflict with two major powers simultaneously. A more likely date is 1461. This would also explain the passage in the chronicle of Tursun Beg, the secretary of the imperial divan during this time and thus a much more reliable source for this piece of information, which reads:

> Thus, finding support in the Sublime Porte, he defeated the Hungarians, killing many of them, as well as other voievozi as powerful as himself [probably referring to the events of 1459-1460]. But victory made him too confident of his own power and, when the Sultan was away on the long expedition in Trebizond [in 1461], driven by his arrogance and his inclination to quarrel, he planned to cause harm to the Ottoman lands.[58]

---

[56]Iosipescu, "Conjunctura şi condiţionarea internaţională politico-militară a celei de a doua domnii a lui Vlad Ţepeş (1456-1462)," pp. 179-180.

[57]It should also be remembered that the Ottomans conquered Serbia in 1459 transforming it into an Ottoman province. Although some historians point to this event as a motive for Vlad to break off relations with the Turks (see, for example, Ştefan Andreescu, *Vlad Ţepeş (Dracula)*, p. 99; and Nicolae Stoicescu, *Vlad Ţepeş*, p. 69), it seems unlikely. If anything, the conquest of Serbia would have made the Wallachian prince even more wary of beginning hostilities with the Porte.

[58]Tursun Beg, "Tarih-i Ebu-l Feth-i Sultan Mehmed-han," in *Cronici turceşti privind ţările române*, vol. I, p. 67. Several other Ottoman chronicles relate a similar story, see Aşik-Pasha-Zade, "Tarih-i al-i Osman," in *ibid*, p. 92; Mehmed Neşri, "Djihannuma, Tarih-i al-i Osman," in *ibid*, p. 125; and Sa'adeddin Mehmed Hodja Efendi, "Tadj-ut-Tevarih," in *ibid*, p. 317. English translations of the portions of relevant Ottoman chronicles concerning Dracula can be found in Appendix II.

In light of the above passage, it is possible that having succeeded in asserting his autonomy and resisting the attempts of Hungary to dominate Wallachia, Vlad now sought to do the same in his relations with the sultan. Several things made it possible for him decide to take this bold move at this time. First of all, the sultan was preoccupied with the Asian portion of his empire, campaigning in Trebizond in 1461. Secondly, the Congress of Mantua, in 1459, under the leadership of Pope Pius II, had supported the idea of a united Christian crusade against the Turks and preparations began to accelerate.[59] Inspired by his successes, Vlad believed the moment to achieve greater independence had arrived. Thus he reoriented his foreign policy away from the Ottoman Empire, allying with his former nemesis, Hungary. Such an alliance had become possible because Vlad had succeeded in asserting his autonomy vis-à-vis the Hungarian king. Likewise, such an alliance would have been to the liking of Matthias Corvinus who had been receiving subsidies from the pope to prepare an anti-Ottoman crusade and had to make some gesture to justify this financial support.[60] The ensuing conflict with the Ottoman Empire is the best documented part of Vlad III's stormy reign as prince of Wallachia.

---

[59]The Venetian ambassador in Buda informed the Senate on 27 November and 15 December 1460 that preparations were being made for a crusade, to be led by Hungarian, Venetian, and papal forces against the Ottomans, planned for 1462. See *Monumenta Hungariae Historica. Acta extera*, vol. IV, pp. 106-110.

[60]In 1460 Matthias had received a subsidy of 40,000 ducats from the Vatican to organize the crusade that had been planned at Mantua the previous year, see *Monumenta Vaticana. Mathiae Corvini Hungariae regis epistolae ad Romanos Pontifices datae et ab eis acceptae* (Budapest, 1891), p. 13.

Chapter VIII

The War with the Ottomans, 1461-1462

The Emperor's soldiers, who caught one of Vlad's men that night, took him to Machmut and they asked him who he was and where he came from. Then, after he talked freely about everything, they asked him if he knew where Vlad, the prince of Dacia, might be at that time. And he replied that he knew very well, but that he dared not speak about it out of fear. Then, when they told him that they would kill him if he did not give the right answers, he kept saying that he was ready to die anytime, but that he would not dare to reveal anything about that. Machmut, in wonder at all of this, would have liked to kill the soldier, but said with some concern for his situation that if he [Vlad] had a large enough army he could achieve great power.

— Laonic Chalkondyles[1]

Jhe conflict between Dracula and the Ottoman Turks began late in 1461 and ended with the campaign against the rebellious prince, personally led by Sultan Mehmed II, the conqueror of Constantinople, in the summer of 1462. Despite the rel-

---

[1]Chalcocondil, *Expuneri istorice*, p. 289.

ative abundance of sources about this campaign, the details of the conflict are unclear and certain myths persist in the historiography concerning the war between the famous Romanian prince and the Ottoman Empire. Some of these have become so widely accepted that they have gone virtually unchallenged in recent studies.

The conflict between Vlad III Dracula and the Turks began during the winter of 1461-1462 when the Romanian prince seized Giurgiu and other Ottoman strongholds along the Danube and plundered northern Bulgaria. This occurred after Dracula captured and killed emissaries sent by Sultan Mehmed II to demand payment of the tribute that the Wallachian prince had withheld after the sultan had set out on his expedition against Trebizond and the Turkoman Emperor Uzun Hasan.[2]

The sultan feared that Dracula's improved relations with the king of Hungary, Matthias Corvinus, which included an agreement to marry a blood relative of the king, would bring Wallachia increasingly into the Hungarian sphere of influence. Vlad described the situation in a letter to Matthias Corvinus:

> In other letters I wrote to your majesty how the Turks, the most cruel enemies of the Cross of Christ, have sent their highest ranking messengers to convince us not to keep the peace and the arrangements that we made with Your Majesty, and not to celebrate the wedding,[3] and to join with them alone and to

---

[2]Doukas, *Decline and Fall of Byzantium to the Ottoman Turks*, pp. 259-260 (XLV.20); Kritovoulos, *History of Mehmed the Conqueror*, p. 178 (IV.60-61); Konstantin Mihailovic, *Memoirs of a Janissary*, p. 129; Tursun Beg, "Tarih-i Ebu-l Feth-i Sultan Mehmed-han," in *Cronici turceşti privind ţările române*, vol. I, Mihail Guboglu and Mustafa Mehmed, eds. (Bucureşti, 1966), p. 67; and Laonic Chalcocondil, *Expuneri istorice*, pp. 283-284.

[3]The alliance between Dracula and Matthias Corvinus was to be cemented by the marriage of the Wallachian prince to the king's sister. This is confirmed by a letter of the Venetian Ambassador to Buda, Petrus de Thomasiis, dated 4 March 1462, that relates news of Dracula's attacks along the Danube. See doc. I in I. Bianu, "Ştefanu celu Mare: Câteva documente din archivulu de statu dela Milanu," in *Columna lui Traianu*, IV:1-2 (Ianuariu-Februariu, 1883), pp. 34-35.

go to the Porte of the Turkish Sultan... They also sent an important advisor of the Turkish Sultan, named Hamza Beg of Nicopolis, to discuss border problems at the Danube, and that if Hamza Beg could bring us, using tricks or promises, to the Porte, fine, but if he could not he was to capture us and bring us there. But, by the grace of God, while we were on our way to that border, we found out about their deceit and trickery, and it was us who captured Hamza Beg...[4]

Writing from the perspective of the Ottoman Porte, the Byzantine chronicler Chalkondyles recorded these events as follows:

when the Emperor [the Sultan] heard that he had evil thoughts on his mind, and that, appealing to the Hungarians, he had entered into some kind of alliance with them, he believed that it was a very serious thing. Sending skillful man from the Porte, a Greek scholar, he called him [Vlad] to Constantinople on the understanding that if he came to the Porte nothing unpleasant would happen to him, but, on the contrary, as he had worked in the interests of the Emperor. With such orders he sent Catavolinos, the messenger of the Porte, to him. And to Chamuza [Hamza Beg]... he sent a secret order that he would be well paid if by some ploy he could capture and bring this man [Vlad] to him, by any means he could, through trickery or another way. Thus, telling the messenger that he wanted to capture this man, they agreed on the arrangements they made for this purpose, namely that when Vlad was coming back with him, he [Hamza Beg] would have a trap already prepared for him... the scholar was supposed to send word to him when they were starting out. The scholar did this and secretly indicated the exact time he was leaving with Vlad, and Chamuza waited at that very spot. But Vlad, with his armed men, on his way back to the leader of the Porte, became aware that it was a

[4]"Letter of Vlad Ţepeş to Matthias Corvinus, 11 February 1462," in Nicolae Iorga, *Scrisori de boieri, scrisori de domni*, pp. 166-170 (for an English translation of this letter see Appendix I.D). The original Latin text can be found in Ioan Bogdan, *Vlad Ţepeş şi naraţiunile germane şi ruseşti asupra lui*, pp. 76-82.

trap and ordered that they [Catavolinos and Hamza Beg]
should be captured, together with their followers. When Chamuza launched his attack, he [Vlad] fought remarkably well
and defeated and captured him, and killed many of those who
had fled. As soon as he captured them he had them taken away
and impaled, after first mutilating them. For Hamza he prepared a higher stake; and to the servants he did the same as to
their masters.[5]

Faced with the sultan's demands that he pay the tribute and
break off his relations with Hungary, including renouncing the proposed marriage, Vlad declared war by attacking Ottoman positions
along the Danube and in northern Bulgaria. In a letter to Matthias
Corvinus dated 11 February 1462, the Romanian prince described the
devastation caused by his attacks along the Danube, giving the precise
number of those killed as being "23,884 Turks and Bulgarians in all,
not including those who were burned in their houses and whose
heads were not presented to our officials."[6] He went on to appeal for
assistance from the Hungarian king against the inevitable Ottoman
counterattack:

Your Majesty should know that we have broken our peace with
them, not for our own benefit, but for the honor of Your Majesty and the Holy Crown of your Majesty, and for the preservation of Christianity and the strengthening of the Catholic
faith... When the weather permits, that is to say in the Spring,
they will come against us with evil intentions and with all their
power. But they have no crossing points because we burned all
of them, except for Vidin, and destroyed them and made them
barren. Because they cannot harm us too much at the crossing
point of Vidin, they should want to bring their ships from Constantinople and Gallipoli, across the sea, to the Danube. Therefore, Your Majesty, Gracious Lord, if it is Your Majesty's desire
to fight against them, then gather all of your country and all of

---

[5]See Chalcocondil, *Expuneri istorice*, pp. 283-284. These events are also described by
Kritovoulos, *History of Mehmed the Conqueror*, p. 178 [IV.60-61].

the fighting men, both cavalry and infantry, and bring them to our Wallachia, and be so kind as to fight against them [the Turks] here.[7]

This conflict culminated in the Ottoman offensive directed against Wallachia, led by the sultan himself, in the summer of 1462. As indicated in his letter to Matthias Corvinus, Vlad clearly anticipated this attack and foresaw the Ottoman military strategy of sending a fleet to the Danube, while at the same time attempting to cross the Danube with an army. By April 1462 he knew well the scope of the sultan's intentions as preparations were being made in the Ottoman capital for the expedition against Wallachia.

Most recent historiography has held that Mehmed II set out to transform Wallachia into a Turkish pashalik, as he had done with Ser-

---

[6]Iorga, *Scrisori de boieri, scrisori de domni*, pp. 166-170. These events are also described in the German Stories about Dracula, emphasizing the excessive cruelty of the Wallachian prince:

> And then in 1462 he went to Sistovul Mare [Nicopolis]. He killed more than five thousand people there of all races, Christians, Jews, and Pagans. Some of them were beautiful women and virgins who were spared by Dracula's servants. They asked him to give them their hands in marriage. Dracula ordered that all of these men, together with their maidens, should be slaughtered with swords and spears, like cabbage. He did this because his country was a tributary state of the Turks and they would often demand he send tribute. He told the Turkish emissaries that he himself would bring the tribute. The people of this country came on horseback and welcomed him, thinking that he had come to pay tribute to the Sultan; one group after another came. When Dracula saw that he had achieved his aim, he killed all those who had come on horseback to greet him, as they had not taken any precautions. Dracula had all of Bulgaria burned down, and he impaled all of the people that he captured. There were 25,000 of them, to say nothing of those who perished in the fires.

See Panaitescu, "The German Stories about Vlad Țepeș," in Treptow, *Dracula: Essays...*, pp. 191-192. The last lines of this story closely resemble the information Vlad sent to Matthias Corvinus; another indication that the German Stories were disseminated as part of a campaign by the Hungarian Court to discredit the Wallachian prince, who had bravely defied the Ottomans, in the eyes of public opinion following his arrest by the king in 1462.

[7]Iorga, *Scrisori de boieri, scrisori de domni*, pp. 166-170; and Treptow, *Dracula: Essays...*, pp. 316-317.

bia in 1459 and Bosnia in the year following this campaign, 1463. It is generally argued that only the determined resistance led by Dracula prevented the sultan from carrying out his plan.[8] For example, in *Istoria militară a poporului român* (*The Military History of the Romanian People*), Mircea Iogaru contends:

> The Ottoman invasion of 1462 ended in a complete military disaster. Mehmed II did not succeed — because of the heroic resistance of the Romanian people led by Prince Vlad Ţepeş — to transform Wallachia into a pashalik and to include the Romanian territory below the Carpathians within the borders of the Ottoman Empire.[9]

This interpretation must be called into question for a number of reasons. First of all, the Ottoman sources clearly state that the sultan's intention was to change the ruling prince, not to transform the country into a pashalik. Tursun-Beg, secretary of the imperial council (the divan) during the time of the expedition, wrote that *before* setting out for Wallachia:

> the conquering Sultan gave the throne of that country to the brother of that wicked man [referring to Vlad], named Radu voievod, who had been accepted by the Porte a long time before and had worked for the Imperial Court for many years.[10]

Being a high official at the Porte during the time of this campaign, Tursun-Beg is a reliable source concerning the intentions of

---

[8]See, for example, Radu Florescu and Raymond T. McNally, *Dracula: A Biography of Vlad the Impaler, 1431-1476*, pp. 109-110; Nicolae Stoicescu, *Vlad Ţepeş, Prince of Wallachia*, p. 96; Barbu T. Câmpina, "Complotul boierilor şi 'răscoala' din Ţara Românească din iulie-noiembrie 1462," in *Studii şi referate privind istoria Romîniei*, p. 609; Vasile Neamţu, *Istoria medie a României* (Iaşi, 1982), p. 160; and Ştefan Andreescu, *Vlad Ţepeş (Dracula)...*, pp. 95-96 and 123.

[9]Mircea Iogaru in *Istoria militară a poporului român*, vol. II (Bucureşti, 1986), p. 281.

[10]Tursun-Beg, "Tarih-i Ebu-l Feth-i Sultan Mehmed-han," in *Cronici turceşti privind ţările române*, vol. I, p. 72.

Mehmed II when he set out against Dracula. It is significant that he gives no indication of any Ottoman plan to transform Wallachia into a pashalik; on the contrary the sultan's investment of Radu as prince before setting out on the campaign against Vlad clearly revealed his intentions for all the world to see.

Tursun-Beg's account is confirmed by other sources. According to the Byzantine chronicler Kritoboulos of Imbros the sultan

> appointed Rados, the brother of Drakoulis, as commander and ruler of the Getae [Wallachians]. This Rados he had with him [on the expedition].[11]

Likewise, the Serbian janissary Konstantin Mihailovic, himself a participant in the campaign, recounted the ceremony in which the sultan invested Radu as prince of Wallachia before setting out on the campaign:

> the Emperor sent for his [Dracula's] brother to come to court, and when he arrived at the Emperor's court, the highest lords, two bassas of the Emperor's council — one of whom they called Machmut-bassa and the other Isakbassa — went to meet him and took him between them and led him to the Emperor, where the Emperor was sitting on his throne. Having risen, the Emperor took him by the hand and seated him alongside himself on the right side in another somewhat lower chair and ordered that a purple garment of gold cloth be brought and placed on him. Then he ordered that a red banner be brought, and he gave it to

Sultan Mehmed II

[11]Kritovoulos, *History of Mehmed the Conqueror*, p. 179 (IV.63).

him and in addition money, horses, and tents, as befit a lord, and he immediately dispatched with him four thousand cavalry horses ahead to Nickopolis, in order that he await him there. And the Emperor having assembled an army without delay, marched after him... we marched forward to the Wallachian land after Dracula, and his brother ahead of us.[12]

From his description it is likely that Mihailovic may have personally participated at the ceremony investing Radu cel Frumos as prince of Wallachia; at the very least he had first-hand details of the investiture. As a result, the Serbian janissary is certainly one of our best-informed sources on these events. Clearly Radu would not have been leading the Ottoman forces into Wallachia at the side of the sultan had he not already been designated as his brother's successor. This is confirmed by the Byz-

Radu cel Frumos
By Octavian Ion Penda

antine chronicler Laonic Chalkondyles who relates that Vlad sent messengers to Matthias Corvinus, asking for assistance and adding that the sultan "has with him our prince's younger brother [Radu cel Frumos] to give him the throne of Wallachia."[13] Thus, the best informed sources about Mehmed's intentions lead us to the conclusion that the sultan set out in the summer of 1462 to remove Vlad III Dracula from the Wallachian throne and to replace him with his brother, Radu cel Frumos. He had no intention of transforming Wallachia into a Turkish pashalik.

Apart from the documentary evidence, there are other factors that corroborate this thesis. In volume IV of his *Istoria românilor*

[12]Mihailovic, *Memoirs of a Janissary*, pp. 132-133. See also Chalcocondil, *Expuneri istorice*, p. 287.

[13]Chalcocondil, *Expuneri istorice*, p. 287.

(*History of the Romanians*), the great Romanian historian Nicolae Iorga argued that the sultan did not intend to turn Wallachia into a pashalik because "There were not here, as in Bosnia and Serbia, or in Byzantium, stone fortresses where the cowardly leader of the country hid," and which, once conquered, the Turks could easily hold. Thus the only solution to the dispute with Dracula, Iorga concluded, was to put a loyal prince on the throne.[14] It must also be remembered that Wallachia and Moldavia were more valuable to the sultan as buffer states. Their conquest would have inevitably brought the Ottoman Empire into conflict with Poland, destroying the basis for the cooperation between the two powers against Hungary that has its origins in this period.[15]

There are other considerations that would also have led Mehmed II to reject the idea of imposing direct Ottoman rule in Wallachia. The natural path of Ottoman expansion in Europe was to the northwest, as evidenced by the attacks on Belgrade in 1456 and 1526, the Otranto Campaign in 1480-1481, the battle of Mohács in 1526, and the sieges of Vienna in 1529 and 1532, among others. The reasons for this are obvious. It was not only the most affluent part of Europe, but also the location of the strongest opponents to Ottoman expansion, most notably the papacy, the kingdom of Hungary and later the Hapsburg Empire. Thus, the desire for material gain and the need to ensure the security of the empire drove Ottoman expansion in this direction in Europe. Of course one must not forget the important Ottoman interests in the Middle East and northern Africa that also drew on the resources of the empire.

---

[14]Nicolae Iorga, *Istoria românilor*, vol. IV (Bucureşti, 1937), p. 140. Iorga, in his vast bibliography, at times contradicted himself from one work to another. Thus, for example, in his *Istoria armatei româneşti* (Vălenii-de-Munte, 1910) he argued that the sultan set out to transform Wallachia into a pashalik (p. 123). Nevertheless, the conclusions presented in his massive ten volume synthesis, published only a few years before his death, should be considered as the definitive results of Iorga's decades of historical research.

[15]See Veniamin Ciobanu, "The Equilibrium Policy of the Romanian Principalities in East-Central Europe, 1444-1485," pp. 29-52, in Treptow, *Dracula: Essays....*

The logical Ottoman objective was to secure this part of the Danube as a line of defense. While the river from Vienna to Belgrade was an important commercial and military route, the river beyond Belgrade could not be used for heavy transport because of the Iron Gates.[16] "Therefore, the Turks did not need the Romanian principalities as a base for their offensive toward Europe," P.P. Panaitescu rightly pointed out. "They could be satisfied with several garrisons at fortified points [along the Danube], at Chilia, Cetatea Albă, Tighina, Brăila, Turnu Măgurele."[17] The need to secure the Danube as a line of defense also helps to explain why the Ottomans, simultaneously with the invasion led by the sultan, launched an attack on Chilia in 1462, and subsequently captured the Danubian fortress in 1484. After all, the principal reason why the Roman Empire abandoned Dacia in 271 A.D. was to shorten the border it had to defend and to use the Danube as a natural line of defense against the barbarian invasions. If the Ottomans had imposed direct rule in the Romanian principalities it would have vastly expanded the border area that needed to be defended and required a much larger commitment of men and resources than was needed to garrison troops in a series of fortresses along the Danube River, apart from the political implications already mentioned. In addition, the system of indirect rule proved to be much more profitable economically, especially in the sixteenth century.[18]

Thus we must conclude that when the sultan led his army into Wallachia in the summer of 1462 it was with the express intention of placing Radu cel Frumos on the throne.

In early June, Mehmed II prepared to cross the Danube at Nicopolis with an army of approximately 60,000 men.[19] According to the

---

[16]Gordon East, *Géographie historique de l'Europe*, I (Paris, 1939), pp. 324-325 and 333-336.

[17]P.P. Panaitescu, "De ce n-au cucerit turcii ţările romane," in *Interpretări româneşti*, p. 118.

[18]Keith Hitchins, "Ottoman Domination of Moldavia and Wallachia in the Sixteenth Century," p. 132. On this problem generally see P.P. Panaitescu, "De ce n-au cucerit turcii ţările romane," in *Interpretări româneşti*, pp. 111-118.

Serbian janissary Konstantin Mihailovic, who participated in this campaign, when the sultan reached Nicopolis:

> on the far side of the Danube Voievod Dracula was encamped with his army so that he guarded against a crossing... And when it was already night we boarded the boats and shoved off downstream in the river so that oars and men would not be heard. And when we reached the other side some furlongs below where the voievod's army lay, and there we dug in having emplaced the cannon and having encircled ourselves with shields and having placed stakes around ourselves so that cavalry could do nothing to us. Then the boats went to the other side until the janissaries had all crossed to us.

> Then having fallen into formation we moved a little toward the army, keeping the stakes, shields, and cannon. And when we approached quite close to them, having halted we emplaced the cannon, for they [Dracula's army] killed two hundred and fifty janissaries with cannon fire... Then, seeing that so many of us were dying, he [the Sultan] quickly prepared, and having one hundred and twenty cannon, immediately began to fire them heavily and thus we drove all the army from the battlefield and established and fortified ourselves... And Dracula, seeing that he could not prevent the crossing, moved away from us.[20]

[19]This is the estimate given by the Venetian ambassador to Buda, Petrus de Thomasiis, in a letter to the doge of Venice dated 14 June 1462, see doc. II in I. Bianu, "Ştefanu celu Mare: Câteva documente din archivulu de statu dela Milanu," p. 37. The Venetian ambassador also informs us that 25,000 of the effective force of 60,000 Ottoman troops were janissaries. As a well-informed diplomat, who watched the events in Wallachia in the summer of 1462 carefully, the troop estimates he gives are probably quite reliable. They seem realistic from what we know of Ottoman resources. Chroniclers of the time did not place importance upon the accuracy of such details, often using exaggerated figures to indicate the importance of a particular campaign; thus we find estimates of 250,000 given by Chalkondyles (see Chalcocondil, *Expuneri istorice*, p. 285) and 300,000 by Tursun Beg (see "Tarih-i Ebu-l Feth-i Sultan Mehmed-han," in *Cronici turceşti privind ţările române*, p. 68).

[20]Mihailovic, *Memoirs of a Janissary*, pp. 130-133.

Vlad, who had gathered an army of approximately 22,000 men,[21] realized that he could not engage the more experienced and numerically superior Ottoman forces in open field combat; under these circumstances he retreated before the enemy, employing a scorched earth policy and using guerilla warfare tactics. After crossing the Danube on 4 June,[22] the sultan proceeded northward in the direction of Târgovişte, the capital of Wallachia at the time, but before reaching it, Dracula launched his famous night attack on the Ottoman camp. The Romanian historian Nicolae Iorga called this assault, "one of the most interesting military episodes in the history of the Ottomans," adding that "until then there did not occur in Turkish history so bold an act as an attack against the person of the sultan himself."[23] It was a brave, desperate effort by the Wallachian prince to turn back the invaders. Chalkondyles related the confusion created by the daring attack:

> he [Vlad] started out at the end of the first night watch and he invaded the Emperor's camp. At first there was a lot of terror in the camp because people thought that a new foreign army had come and attacked them; scared out of their wits by this attack, they considered themselves to be lost as it was being made using torchlight and the sounding of horns to indicate the place to assault... using torchlight, [Vlad] proceeded with his army in closed ranks, and in good order they headed directly for the Emperor's tents. Missing their target, they fell upon the tents of vizier Machmut and Vizier Isaac; and here there was a great battle and they killed the camels, donkeys, and other pack animals. Fighting in closed ranks, they had no losses worth mentioning, but if one of them went astray he was

---

[21]From the letter of Petrus de Thomasiis to the doge of Venice, dated 14 June 1462, doc. II in I. Bianu, "Ştefanu celu Mare: Câteva documente din archivulu de statu dela Milanu," p. 37.

[22]On the chronology of this campaign see Ştefan Andreescu, *Vlad Ţepeş (Dracula)*, p. 119.

[23]Nicolae Iorga, *Istoria armatei româneşti*, vol. I, p. 121.

Vlad's night attack upon the Sultan's camp

By Octavian Ion Penda

immediately killed by the Turks... then, turning back, they headed for the Emperor's court where they found the soldiers around the Emperor's tents in good fighting order. And, after fighting here for a short time, they [Vlad's army] turned back toward the camp market, plundering and killing anyone who came their way. As it was nearly daybreak, they left the camp, having suffered few losses that night. As for the Emperor's armies, they are also said to have suffered few losses.[24]

Vlad hoped to kill the sultan which would almost certainly have caused the Turks to flee in disorder. Indeed, one of the characteristic elements of Dracula's military strategy was his reliance on psychological warfare to compensate for his lack of manpower. Though his daring night assault inflicted some damage on the Turks, the Ottoman forces could not be stopped. Upon reaching Târgovişte, they encountered the gruesome spectacle of impaled bodies vividly described by Chalkondyles:

The Emperor, passing by the city and failing to see any men on the walls, but only some cannon firing at his army, set up no camp, nor did he lay siege to the city. He marched on for about five kilometers when he saw men impaled; the Emperor's army came across a field with stakes, about three kilometers long and one kilometer wide. And there were large stakes upon which he could see the impaled bodies of men, women, and children, about twenty thousand of them, as they said; quite a spectacle for the Turks and the Emperor himself!... And the other Turks, seeing so many people impaled, were scared out of their wits. There were babies clinging to their mothers on the stakes, and birds had made nests in their breasts.[25]

From there the sultan proceeded eastward where he again encountered and defeated Dracula's forces.[26] For all intents and pur-

---

[24]Chalcocondil, *Expuneri istorice*, p. 288. Another account is provided by Kritovoulos, *History of Mehmed the Conqueror*, p. 179 [IV.64-65], who says that the attack was a complete failure and that the Turks killed or captured most of the Wallachian soldiers.

poses, the unsuccessful night attack marked the downfall of Vlad, for after it, as Konstantin Mihailovic recalled:

> The Wallachians, seeing that it was going badly, abandoned him [Vlad] and joined his brother. And he himself rode away to Hungary to King Matthias of glorious memory...[27]

Both the Byzantine chronicler Kritoboulos and the Imperial Secretary Tursun-Beg confirm that Vlad was defeated after this attack.[28] The fact that Dracula would resort to such desperate measures indicates that his forces were no match for the power of the sultan's army.

Meanwhile, an Ottoman fleet, in cooperation with the Moldavian army led by Stephen the Great, had launched an attack against the fortress of Chilia, at the mouth of the Danube, which was a Wallachian possession, probably garrisoned by Hungarian troops.[29] The participation of Stephen the Great alongside the Ottomans in this attack is another of the controversial aspects of this campaign.

Chilia had long been a source of dispute between the princes of Moldavia and Wallachia. As we have seen, the fortress became a Mol-

---

[25]Chalcocondil, *Expuneri istorice*, pp. 288-289. This is probably a highly exaggerated picture of the spectacle Dracula had prepared after the events of the winter of 1462 described in Vlad's letter to Matthias Corvinus, quoted earlier, when, according to the Serbian janissary:

> He had the emissary seized with all his servants — they were thirty in number — and he ordered him to be taken to a very secure stronghold isolated by waters, called Târgoviște. And he had Hamzabeg, the Emperor's emissary, impaled first, and around him all his servants.

See Mihailovic, *Memoirs of a Janissary*, p. 129.

[26]Chalcocondil, *Expuneri istorice*, p. 331.

[27]Mihailovic, *Memoirs of a Janissary*, pp. 132-133.

[28]Kritovoulos, *History of Mehmed the Conqueror*, pp. 179-180 (IV.64, 65, 66); and Tursun Beg, "Tarih-i Ebu-l Feth-i Sultan Mehmed-han," in *Cronici turceşti privind ţările române*, vol. I, pp. 67-73.

[29]It is known that during the reign of Vladislav II Chilia was garrisoned by Hungarian troops, but we have no evidence to tell us whether or not the status of the fortress changed during the reign of Vlad III.

davian possession in 1421 when Alexander the Good, Stephen the Great's grandfather, invaded Wallachia, then in the midst of a dynastic struggle in the wake of Mircea the Old's death, and seized the Danubian stronghold, which was also important economically as a customs point. Despite the efforts of Prince Dan II of Wallachia (1422-1431) to regain the fortress, it remained a possession of Moldavia until 1448 when John Hunyadi intervened in a dynastic conflict in Moldavia and again made Chilia a Wallachian possession, though he garrisoned the fortress with Hungarian troops to ensure it would remain an anti-Ottoman stronghold despite the political vicissitudes in the principality. Thus, it is natural that Chilia became a point of conflict between Stephen the Great and Vlad III Dracula, despite the fact that the latter had helped the former secure the throne of Moldavia only five years earlier.

Much debate has centered on the question of why Stephen the Great cooperated with the Ottomans against his cousin in 1462. At issue is a passage from Chalkondyles that reads:

> [Vlad] divided his army in two, keeping one part with him, and sending the other against the Prince of Black Bogdania [Moldavia], to keep him back if he tried to invade the country. Because this Prince of Black Bogdania had had a misunderstanding with Vlad he was at war with him and, sending messengers to Emperor Mehmed, he said that he was also ready to join him in his war against Vlad. The Emperor was pleased to hear this and urged this prince to have his commanding general join with the commander of his fleet at the river, and that together they should lay siege to the city called Chilia, which belonged to Vlad, at the mouth of the river.[30]

Such active cooperation between Stephen the Great and the Ottomans has generally been rejected by historians. Nicolae Stoicescu, for example, stated that "most historians have generally refuted the idea of such a collaboration, some of them holding, with good reason too, that the prince of Moldavia attempted to get hold of Chilia

[30]Chalcocondil, *Expuneri istorice*, p. 506.

before the Turks did."[31] Because Chalkondyles is one of the few sources of information about this aspect of the campaign of 1462, most historians have found it easy to say, as Ioan Bogdan did, that:

No one, apart from Chalkondyles, speaks of a war between Stephen the Great and Vlad Țepeș in 1462... The common attack of Stephen the Great and Mehmed II [against Vlad] remains, until proven to the contrary, a simple combination of the Byzantine historian, who, knowing that the attack on Chilia and the defeat of Țepeș happened in the same year, connected the two events.[32]

Some historians, guided by misplaced nationalist sentiments, have gone so far as to attempt to completely rewrite history. For example, in his study of Stephen the Great, Nicolae Grigoraș claimed that "detachments of the Moldavian army located near Chilia repelled the Turkish infantry who had disembarked near the fortress. The Turkish attack lasted 8 days, but with help from the Moldavian soldiers the garrison of the fortress repelled them."[33] The interpretation

---

[31]Nicolae Stoicescu, *Vlad Țepeș*, p. 48. See also Ștefan Andreescu, *Vlad Țepeș (Dracula)*, pp. 110-111; Nicolae Iorga, *Istoria românilor*, vol. IV, p. 138; and Nicolae Grigoraș, *Moldova lui Ștefan cel Mare* (Iași, 1982), pp. 59-60.

[32]Ioan Bogdan, *Vlad Țepeș*, pp. 26-27.

[33]Nicolae Grigoraș, *Moldova lui Ștefan cel Mare*, pp. 59-60. Another example of this can be found in *Istoria militară a poporului român*, vol. II, pp. 278-279 where Mircea Iogaru writes:

On the northeastern front, at the mouth of the Danube, the Ottoman fleet, after it plundered both shores, was repelled with great losses in front of Chilia, which it besieged for 8 days, and continually harassed by the corp of soldiers sent by Vlad, was forced to retreat. The decision to retreat was influenced by the defense of the northern shore by the Moldavian cavalry. What happened at Chilia depended, on the strategic level, on the result of the war led by Vlad Țepeș and, having in perspective the independence of Moldavia, Stephen the Great found a solution for intervention in conformity with the secret Moldavian-Wallachian understanding...

This "Moldavian-Wallachian understanding" was so "secret" that no evidence can be found to suggest that it ever existed.

commonly accepted is that of Nicolae Iorga who argued that Stephen did not coordinate a joint offensive with the Ottomans, but "when the sultan's fleet was before Chilia, the Moldavian prince by all means had a duty to be there and to use any means to impede the installation of the Turks in the Lower Danube, which would have been a catastrophe for himself."[34] By joining the attack on Chilia, Stephen the Great clearly hoped to take possession of the fortress for himself, as he was an ally of the sultan at the time and had a legitimate claim to the territory.

The apparent contradiction between the account of Chalkondyles and the interpretation given to these events by contemporary historians certainly gives one cause to reconsider this question. First of all, there is other evidence of a conflict between Stephen the Great and Vlad III Dracula in 1462. The governor of Caffa wrote to King Casimir of Poland on 2 April 1462, asking him to intervene in the conflict between the two Romanian princes:

> I understand that Stephen, prince of Moldavia or Wallachia Minor, is fighting with Vlad voievod who makes happy war with the Turks. This quarrel not only helps the Sultan, but what is more dangerous, if the Turks enter these two Wallachias, it will represent a great danger for us and for other neighboring countries.[35]

When considered together with the account given by Chalkondyles, this is strong evidence of a conflict between Stephen and Vlad prior to the attack on Chilia in June. The reasons for the conflict are also apparent. Although Stephen gained the throne with Vlad's help and, during the early part of his reign, was an ally of the Wallachian prince, he soon began to pursue an independent policy, allying himself with Poland in 1459. Relations between the two

---

[34]Nicolae Iorga, *Istoria românilor*, vol. IV, p. 138. See also Alexandru Boldur, *Ştefan cel Mare, voievod al Moldovei*, p. 178.

[35]Document quoted in Nicolae Iorga, *Studii asupra Chiliei şi Cetăţii-Albe*, (Bucuresci, 1899), pp. 125-126.

Romanian principalities, who were traditional rivals for control of the Danube Delta region, soon turned cool as Vlad was now an ally of Matthias Corvinus and Hungary, while Stephen was allied with Poland and the Ottomans. Moreover, Matthias had given refuge to Stephen's predecessor, Petru Aron, and supported his attempts to regain the Moldavian throne.[36] In addition, in an act issued by Stephen at Suceava on 2 March 1462, which renewed his relations of vassalage with Poland, the Moldavian prince declared:

> we will not give to foreigners any country, land, city or estate without the acceptance and approval of the above-mentioned Prince, our King, and the Crown, by any means; likewise, if some of these have been taken by foreigners, we want to win them back and we will win them.[37]

This is a clear reference to Chilia, the most important Moldavian possession in foreign hands at that time. The available evidence makes it clear that there existed a conflict between Stephen and Vlad in 1462. "The antagonism between the two princes," Nicolae Iorga explained, "is reflected in the political orientation of the two principalities."[38] To this we can add the economic aspect of the struggle for control of Chilia, mentioned earlier.

If we accept that the two Romanian princes were at war, or at the very least on hostile terms prior to the Ottoman campaign against Wallachia, and that Stephen sought to regain possession of Chilia, as indicated in the act of 2 March 1462, then it is logical to accept Chalkondyles' assertion that Stephen made overtures to the sultan. Certainly he did so with the intention that the Turks assist him in taking possession of Chilia and not the other way around. After all, Stephen knew of Ottoman plans to attack Wallachia and he was an

---

[36]Andreescu, *Vlad Țepeș (Dracula)*, p. 98; and Radu Rosetti, "Stephen the Great of Moldavia and the Turkish Invasion," pp. 86-103, in *The Slavonic Review*, VI:16 (June, 1927), pp. 94-95.

[37]Doc. in Ioan Bogdan, *Documentele lui Ștefan cel Mare*, vol. II, p. 287.

[38]Iorga, *Studii asupra Chiliei și Cetății-Albe*, p. 126.

ally of the sultan, as well as a vassal of the Polish king; why should he not try to take advantage of the situation and ask the sultan to help him regain a territory that he believed rightfully belonged to Moldavia? This theory is corroborated by other circumstantial evidence. It is certain that Vlad anticipated a Moldavian attack, in conjunction with the Ottoman offensive, in the summer of 1462. Apart from Chalkondyles, other sources inform us that Vlad had to divide his army in two to defend against a possible attack by Stephen the Great. The Imperial Secretary Tursun-Beg wrote:

> The truth was that the voievod of Wallachia [Dracula] had ordered one of his commanders to be near that place [in the northeast] with 7,000 soldiers chosen to protect the country against his Moldavian enemies.[39]

The existence of a plan for a joint Ottoman-Moldavian attack on Chilia is also implied in a letter of Domenico Balbi, the Venetian representative in Constantinople, who, on 28 July 1462, informed the Senate:

> the naval fleet of the Sultan, together with the Prince of Moldavia, went to attack the fortress of Chilia; they stayed there for eight days but were unable to do anything...[40]

Even Moldavian chronicles recall how Stephen personally participated in the unsuccessful attack on Chilia. For example, the *Moldavian-German Chronicle* reads:

> 6970 [1462]. In the month of June on the 22nd day, Voievod Stephen came in front of Chilia, but he was unable to take it and was shot in the left ankle. Then he left Chilia.[41]

---

[39]Tursun Beg, "Tarih-i Ebu-l Feth-i Sultan Mehmed-han," in *Cronici turceşti privind ţările române*, p. 69.

[40]Quoted in Iorga, *Studii asupra Chiliei şi Cetăţii-Albe*, p. 125; and A.D. Xenopol, "Lupta dintre Dăneşti şi Drăculeşti," p. 22 (204).

[41]P.P. Panaitescu, *Cronicele slavo-romîne*, p. 29. This chronicle, written by a German at the Moldavian court during the reign of Stephen the Great, covers the years 1457-1499.

Stephen the Great
Prince of Moldavia 1457-1504
By Octavian Ion Penda

All of this evidence taken together indicates that the Moldavians cooperated with the Ottomans in the attack on Chilia in 1462.

After carefully examining the available evidence, Chalkondyles's account of Stephen the Great's role in the conflict between Vlad III Dracula and the Turks cannot be so easily rejected as many historians have done in the past. Stephen, knowing of the sultan's upcoming campaign against Wallachia, and himself being in conflict with Vlad, sought to take advantage of the situation and enlist Ottoman support in his efforts to regain possession of Chilia — a fortress of political, military, and economic importance for Moldavia. Certainly he did not intend to help facilitate the Ottoman occupation of this strategic fortress. Although it is usually argued that the Ottomans hoped to conquer Chilia for themselves in 1462,[42] we must admit that helping the Moldavians gain pos-

---

[42]This is based on a passage from the Serbian janissary Konstantin Mihailovic who quotes Mehmed II as saying:

> So long as the Wallachians hold and command Kilia [Chilia] and Belgorod [Cetatea Albă], and the Hungarians, Raskan Belgrade, we will not be able to defeat them.

See Mihailovic, *Memoirs of a Janissary*, p. 133. This passage should not, however, be taken to mean that Mehmed intended to take possession of Chilia in 1462. First of all, Mihailovic wrote his account decades after these events when the Ottomans had only recently gained possession of the fortress (1484). Secondly, Mehmed did not oppose Stephen's taking possession of the fortress after he conquered it in January 1465, nor did he try to capture it again during his reign. Only during the reign of his successor, Bayezid II, did the Ottomans attempt and succeed in taking both Chilia and Cetatea Albă from Moldavia.

session of Chilia would have been an acceptable course of action for the sultan. After all, it probably had a Hungarian garrison, and the combined attack from the south and the northeast forced Vlad to divide his already limited number of troops. In addition, it must be remembered that up to this time Stephen had been a loyal vassal of the sultan.

Less than three years after this campaign, in January 1465, the Moldavian prince achieved his goal and conquered Chilia.[43] Without a doubt, Stephen the Great was one of the shrewdest political figures of fifteenth century Europe. It may be difficult for some to accept that he cooperated with the sultan in the attack on his cousin Vlad III Dracula in the summer of 1462, but it must be remembered that Stephen's interests were to preserve the territorial integrity and autonomy of Moldavia; he had no sense of national consciousness as such a thing did not exist in his time. Stephen's cooperation with the Ottomans to gain possession of Chilia in 1462, though unsuccessful, is characteristic of his political behavior throughout his reign and was aimed at furthering Moldavian interests. Once he had secured himself on the throne, Stephen began to act independently, in accordance with the political, military, and economic interests of his country; as his power grew he would try and exert his influence over the neighboring Romanian principality, attempting to transform it into a buffer state. His policies led to repeated conflicts with the princes of Wallachia; thus Prince Basarab cel Tânăr wrote to Sibiu in 1481, complaining that:

> since Stephen vodă has ruled in Moldavia he has not liked any ruler of Wallachia. He did not wish to live with Radu vodă, nor with Basarab cel Bătrân, nor with me. I don't know who can live with him.[44]

The conflict between Moldavia and Wallachia in 1462, and the cooperation between Stephen the Great and the Ottomans in the

---

[43]Iorga, *Studii istorice asupra Chiliei și Cetății-Albe*, p. 129. Stephen besieged Chilia for three days, from 24 to 26 January 1465, until the heavy bombardment by the Moldavian forces compelled the fortress to capitulate.

attack on Chilia and Vlad, must be viewed in this context. After all, it was his diplomatic skill and political adroitness in balancing his relations with the three major powers — Poland, Hungary, and the Ottoman Empire — that surrounded Moldavia that made Stephen the Great the greatest prince in the history of that Romanian principality.

The sultan's campaign in Wallachia lasted a total of three and a half weeks. After moving north to Târgoviște, the sultan headed east toward Brăila. Before reaching the Danube the Ottoman army was again attacked by Vlad's forces. According to Chalkondyles:

> [Vlad] went against the prince of Black Bogdania [Stephen the Great] who, as stated before, was laying siege to Chilia. He left behind an army of about six thousand men and ordered them to stay in the woods, close to the Emperor, and if anyone went astray they should seize him and kill him. And he himself went against the prince of Black Bogdania; but as the Emperor started to turn back, the army he [Vlad] left behind attacked, thinking theirs would be the glory if they did so... Before long they [the Sultan's troops] defeated the Dacians and chased them away and killed them mercilessly; and they killed about two thousand of them.[45]

After defeating this second attack, the Ottomans reached Brăila where they recrossed the Danube around 29 June. The result of the campaign was the removal of Vlad III Dracula from the Wallachian throne and his replacement by his brother, the sultan's favorite, Radu cel Frumos.

The question of how Dracula was removed from the throne has also been a source of considerable debate. Recent historiography has held that Vlad, in fact, defeated the sultan and forced him to withdraw from Wallachia, and that it was his betrayal by the boyars, who

---

[44]Doc. 8 in Silviu Dragomir, *Documente nouă privitoare la relațiile Țării Românești cu Sibiul*, p. 19. On Stephen's relations with Wallachia, see also Mihai Costăchescu, *Arderea Târgului Floci și a Ialomiței în 1470: Un fapt necunoscut din luptele lui Ștefan cel Mare cu muntenii* (Iași, 1935), especially p. 107.

[45]Chalcocondil, *Expuneri istorice*, p. 290.

defected to Radu cel Frumos *after* Dracula's victory over the sultan, that led to his downfall. This idea, initially suggested by Gh. Ghibănescu at the end of the nineteenth century,[46] was developed by Barbu T. Câmpina who, as Ştefan Andreescu observed, "imposed it as a definitive conclusion in recent Romanian historiography."[47] Many historians have analyzed the events of 1462 and declared, as Nicolae Stoicescu did, that "Vlad Ţepeş was victorious and the sultan was compelled to leave Wallachia without having attained the goal he had set — to subdue the country and replace Ţepeş."[48] This interpretation of the outcome of the campaign of 1462 and its corresponding explanation for the removal of Dracula from the Wallachian throne must also be called into question.

The theory that Vlad had driven the sultan from his country and was then overthrown by his own boyars does not stand up to a careful examination of the evidence. As we discussed previously, Dracula pursued a conscious policy designed to break the power of recalcitrant boyars from the beginning of his reign. It seems incredible to believe that a prince who had so carefully rooted out his domestic opposition and replaced them with others who owed their wealth and status to

---

[46]Gh. Ghibănescu, "Vlad Ţepeş (studiu critic)," in *Arhiva. Organul societăţii ştiinţifice şi literare din Iaşi*, VIII:7-8 (1897), pp. 373-417; and *ibid*. VIII:9-10, pp. 497-520. Ghibănescu tried to prove that Dracula lost the throne due to a revolt of the boyars by pointing out that Dragomir Udrişte, a boyar in the *sfatul domnesc* of Vladislav II, who is again found in the council during the reign of Radu cel Frumos, is not to be found in documents from the reign of Vlad III. This is not, however, a unique case in fifteenth century Wallachian politics. We can assume that he was an enemy of Vlad and lived in exile during his reign. This cannot be seen as evidence of a revolt by the boyars.

[47]Andreescu, *Vlad Ţepeş (Dracula)*, p. 8. See Câmpina, "Complotul boierilor...," and Barbu T. Câmpina, "Victoria oştii lui Ţepeş asupra sultanului Mehmed al II-lea," pp. 533-555.

[48]Stoicescu, *Vlad Ţepeş*, p. 95. Vlad Georgescu's *The Romanians: A History*, Matei Călinescu, ed., trans. Alexandra Bley-Vroman (Columbus, 1991), p. 54, is an example of how such theories are transformed into simple fact in works of synthesis. The author simply states that "The Wallachians led by Vlad the Impaler (r. 1456-1462) vanquished sultan Mehmed II in 1462." For an accurate presentation of these events in the overall context of Romanian history see Kurt W. Treptow, ed., *A History of Romania* (Iaşi, 1997), pp. 113-114.

him, and who had just succeeded in humiliating the mighty conqueror of Constantinople, could then be so quickly and easily overthrown by his own people. Constantin C. Giurescu correctly observed that "If Dracula had defeated the Turkish army... his authority and prestige would have been so great that any uprising by the boyars would have been impossible."[49] Though several sources proclaim Vlad as the victor in his confrontation with the sultan,[50] many others support the conclusion that he was defeated and driven from the throne by the Ottoman army, aided by Stephen the Great.[51]

Following the ill-fated night attack and the loss of Târgovişte, Bucharest, Brăila, and other important localities it undoubtedly became clear to many boyars and others that their interests lay in joining with Radu cel Frumos, to whom the sultan had granted the Wallachian throne. As Constantin C. Giurescu stated, these boyars "deserted the loser and sided with the man who accompanied the vic-

---

[49]Constantin C. Giurescu, "The Historical Dracula," pp. 13-27, in Treptow, *Dracula, Essays...*, p. 20.

[50]See, for example, Doukas, *Decline and Fall of Byzantium to the Ottoman Turks*, pp. 260-261. See also the list of sources in Barbu T. Câmpina, "Victoria oştii lui Ţepeş asupra sultanului Mehmed al II-lea (cu prilejul împlinirii a 500 de ani)," p. 541. Câmpina relies mainly on Venetian chronicles from the late fifteenth and early sixteenth centuries to make his argument, such as D. Malipiero and St. Magno, who were far from the events of 1462 in the Romanian principality (for these Venetian chronicles see Nicolae Iorga, *Acte şi fragmente cu privire la istoria romînilor*, vol. III (Bucureşti, 1897), pp. 39 and 84-86). Venetian sources must be read with some caution as the Republic of St. Mark was preparing to go to war with the Ottomans and, for political purposes, wanted to portray the Ottomans as *defeatable*. Much of this confusion is the result of Christian zeal and the desire to portray the Ottomans in a negative light. The Slavic Stories also make mention of a victory over the Turks (see Olteanu, *Limba povestirilor slave despre Vlad Ţepeş*, p. 356; and Panaitescu, *Cronicile slavo-romîne*, pp. 207-208), but they are of little value as a historical source for they borrowed heavily from the German Stories. In addition, they were written more than 20 years after the events of 1462 and were not intended as a chronicle of historical events. Another source often used (see, for example, Andreescu, *Vlad Ţepeş (Dracula)*, pp. 124-125) is Michael Bocignoli from Ragusa, a visitor to the Romanian principality in June, 1524, and, as such, cannot be considered as a primary source on the events of 1462 in Wallachia (see Michael Bocignoli, "Descrierea Ţării Româneşti," in Holban, *Călători străini despre ţările române*, pp. 176-177).

torious army of Mehmed the Conqueror."[52] In the same manner Chalkondyles related that:

> they knew that the young man [Radu] was better for them than Prince Vlad, and they crossed over to him little by little.[53]

The confusion about the outcome of the campaign of 1462 is understandable. First of all, Vlad Ţepeş had not been captured, only driven from the throne. With his whereabouts unknown, it is under-

---

[51]In this regard, special importance should be given to the account of the Serbian janissary Konstantin Mihailovic, a participant in the campaign and our only eyewitness account of these events. In addition, although he served in the sultan's army, he cannot be accused of pro-Ottoman sympathies for he later defected from the Ottoman army and wrote his memoirs in Poland, decades after the events (see Mihailovic, *Memoirs of a Janissary*, pp. 128-133).

The Ottoman chronicles are unanimous in declaring the sultan's victory over Vlad through the installation of Radu cel Frumos on the throne. See, for example, Hodja Husein who declares that the Turks "made slaves of the Wallachians... and the sultan gave [their country] to the brother of Ţepeş," quoted in Keith Hitchins, "Ottoman Domination of Moldavia and Wallachia in the Sixteenth Century," p. 125. Numerous other examples can be found in *Cronici turceşti privind ţările române*, vol. I, and, in English translation, the chronicles of Tursun Beg, Aşik-paşa-zade, Mehmed Neşri, Anonymous, and Sa'adeddin Mehmed Hodja Efendi in Appendix II.

In addition to Ottoman sources there are the Byzantine chroniclers, such as Sphrantzes, who writes that:

In the spring of the year 6970 [1462], the Sultan moved against Greater Wallachia and put a stop to the plots that were being formed against him.

See Georges Sphrantzes, *The Fall of the Byzantine Empire*, trans. Marios Philippides (Amherst, 1980), p. 86 [XLII.3]. See also Kritovoulos, *History of Mehmed the Conqueror*, p. 179 [IV.62-63], who relates that:

[the Sultan] overran in a few days practically the whole country... He captured fortresses, pillaged towns, and carried off immense booty... [then] he appointed Rados, the brother of Drakoulis, as commander and ruler of the Getae. This Rados he had with him.

The Venetian chronicler Marino Sanudo who compiled *La progenia della cassa de'Octomani* recounted the victory of Mehmed II over Dracula, but he incorrectly places these events in the year 1459 (see Nicolae Iorga, *Acte şi fragmente cu privire la istoria romînilor*, vol. III, pp. 12-15).

[52]Giurescu, "The Historical Dracula," in Treptow, *Dracula: Essays...*, p. 20.

standable that many observers might interpret this as an Ottoman defeat. Secondly, it had been a very difficult campaign. The Turkish chronicler Tursun Beg recalled the difficulties faced by the sultan's army:

> the front lines of the army announced that there was not a drop of water to quench their thirst. All the carts and animals stopped there. The heat of the sun was so great that one could cook kebabs on the mail shirts of the gazis.[54]

With this in mind we can understand the report of the Venetian rector in Candia who wrote that an Albanian slave who had fled from Adrianople came to him and said that:

> two days before his flight, the Sultan arrived in Adrianople with his army in great disorder and without any sign of victory... [the Turks] returned by land suffering from a lack of food for the army and their horses...[55]

The thesis developed by Barbu Câmpina about the boyars betraying the victorious Vlad Ţepeş is a classic example of molding the facts to fit Marxist-Leninist dogma. The Marxist historian asserted that the lower classes formed the bulk of Dracula's army, as he had been abandoned by the boyars, thus, "the victory of the armies of Ţepeş, by the social base itself, placed in front of the boyars a fearful prospect for the whole system of class relations on which their domination was founded."[56] We have already seen that Vlad III had no intention of altering socio-economic relations in Wallachia. In

---

[53]Chalcocondil, *Expuneri istorice*, p. 291.

[54]Tursun Beg, "Tarih-i Ebu-l Feth-i Sultan Mehmed-han," in *Cronici turceşti privind ţările române*, vol. I, p. 69.

[55]Letter of Alois Gabriel, Venetian rector of Candia, dated 12 August 1462, in doc. IV in Bianu, "Ştefanu celu Mare: Câteva documente din archivulu de statu dela Milanu," pp. 40-41. See also the letter of the same rector to Antonio Loredano, captain of Modena, dated 3 August 1462, in which he relays similar information received from Constantinople, doc. III in *Ibidem*, p. 39.

[56]Câmpina, "Complotul boierilor şi răscoala din Ţara Românească din iulie-noiembrie 1462," p. 606.

addition, there exists no real evidence that the social composition of his military forces differed from those led by other Wallachian princes in the fifteenth century.

How could Dracula have lost the throne after achieving a feat of arms so great as the defeat of the conqueror of Constantinople? At the end of the nineteenth century Ioan Bogdan pointed out the absurdity of such a scenario when he wrote:

> if the Turks had been defeated by Țepeș, he would have remained as prince in Muntenia [Wallachia], he would have impaled all of them, and he probably would have put his brother Radu on the highest stake.[57]

As for Vlad's alleged betrayal by his boyars, the documentary evidence does not support this thesis. In fact, it seems that the powerful Wallachian boyars remained unusually loyal to him. A strong indication of this is that of those present on the final list of members of the *sfatul domnesc* which we possess from Dracula's reign, there is not a single name to be found on the first one that we possess from the reign of Radu cel Frumos, dated 12 November 1463.[58] This is the only incident during the entire fifteenth century when no boyar serving on the council during the reign of the former prince is to be found on the *sfatul domnesc* at the beginning of the reign of the new prince, thus indicating a high degree of loyalty on the part of Dracula's boyars. It also substantiates the theory that the sultan forcibly installed Radu cel Frumos on the Wallachian throne in the summer of 1462, probably accompanied by a court of exiled boyars. It should be remembered that even after Dracula's victory over Vladislav II in 1456 he had retained at least three of his predecessor's boyars on the *sfatul domnesc*.[59]

---

[57]Bogdan, *Vlad Țepeș*, p. 27.

[58]See docs. 120 and 122 in *Documenta Romaniae Historica, B. Țara Românească*, vol. I, pp. 205-208. The only carryover from Țepeș's last *sfatul domnesc* is the scribe who recorded the document, Constandin — himself a court servant, neither a member of the council nor a leading boyar.

There is no evidence to indicate that Vlad's boyars helped Radu cel Frumos attain the throne. It is only in the summer of 1464 that one of his boyars, Voico Dobriţa, is reconciled with the new prince and again joins the *sfatul domnesc*.[60] The loyalty of Dracula's boyars is also confirmed by letters of Radu cel Frumos to Braşov and Sibiu, complaining that they were harboring boyars, loyal to his brother, who had taken refuge there.[61] Likewise, it appears that some of the boyars loyal to Vlad during his second reign can also be identified among his supporters in 1476 when he prepared to take the throne for a third time. Thus, we find Basarab Laiotă, in a letter dated 9 May 1476, complaining to Braşov that they were supporting his enemies, especially Oprea *logofăt*, a member of Vlad's *sfatul domnesc*, 1456-1462.[62] There is also a letter from Cârstian, *pârcălab* of Târgovişte, announcing the victory of Dracula over Basarab Laiotă in 1476 to the citizens of Braşov.[63] This is the same Cârstian referred to in the letter of Dracula to Braşov, dated 4 June 1460, mentioned earlier.

---

[59]See docs. 113 and 115 in *Documenta Romaniae Historica, B. Ţara Românească*, vol. I, pp. 196-200.

[60]Doc. 124 in *Documenta Romaniae Historica, B. Ţara Românească*, vol. I, pp. 209-213, dated 10 July 1464.

[61]See doc. LXXXI in Bogdan, *Documente privitoare la relaţiile Ţării Româneşti...*, pp. 104-106; doc. 77 in Tocilescu, *534 documente istorice slavo-române*, pp. 73-74; and doc. 4 in Dragomir, *Documente nouă privitoare la relaţiile Ţării Româneşti cu Sibiul*, p. 13.

[62]Doc. CCLXXVIII in Bogdan, *Documente privitoare la relaţiile Ţării Româneşti cu Braşovul şi Ţara Ungurească*, p. 333. The document also mentions Voico al lui Tatu who is not identified in the existent documents from Dracula's second reign, but whose father, Tatu Sârbul, was among the loyal supporters of Vlad's father, Vlad Dracul. See Stoicescu, *Dicţionar al marilor dregători*, pp. 25, 28. There is also a similar letter dated 28 February 1476 in which Basarab Laiotă calls on Braşov to expel his enemies, see doc. CI in Bogdan, *Documente privitoare la relaţiile Ţării Româneşti cu Braşovul şi Ţara Ungurească*, pp. 126-127.

[63]Doc. CCCXII in Bogdan, *Documente privitoare la relaţiile Ţării Româneşti cu Braşovul şi Ţara Ungurească*, pp. 357-358. The same Cârstian is also referred to in a letter of Dracula to Sibiu dated 4 August 1475, see doc. CCLXV in Bogdan, *Documente privitoare la relaţiile Ţării Româneşti cu Braşovul şi Ţara Ungurească*, pp. 322-323.

An alternative explanation why many people — boyars, town dwellers, and peasants alike — may have abandoned Dracula during the sultan's campaign in Wallachia is that they may have feared what they perceived as the growing influence of Catholic Hungary in Wallachia, especially in light of the proposed marriage between Vlad and the king's sister.[64] Radu cel Frumos, although installed on the throne by Ottoman forces, as had been the case with several of his predecessors, represented a continuation of Romanian traditions, while Vlad III, after allying with Hungary, may have been viewed as betraying Orthodoxy. While we usually speak of a conflict between Christianity and Islam, the conflict within Christianity itself should not be forgotten. Evidence of this outlook can be inferred from the German Stories about Dracula that, after relating the many evils and misdeeds done by the Wallachian prince against the Saxons, end with the following passage:

> And then, soon after, the King of Hungary caught him and put him in prison for a long time. Later, he was baptized at Buda and showed great repentance. Therefore, the King of Hungary made this Dracula a great prince again, as before. And it is said that he did a multitude of good deeds, because he became a Christian [Catholic].[65]

The conflict between Catholicism and Orthodoxy, demonstrated by the violent reaction against the Union of Florence in the Orthodox lands, must be taken into consideration when trying to understand the foreign relations of Wallachia and Moldavia during this period.

Therefore, the little information that the documents provide clearly contradicts the theory too often put forward that Dracula's

---

[64]This would more likely have been an important consideration for the lesser boyars, townspeople, and peasants — whose mentality was more profoundly influenced by religious ideals — than for the great boyars who had a greater understanding of political considerations. Thus, as we have seen, Dracula's great boyars seem to have been exceptionally loyal to their prince during the events of 1462.

[65]P.P. Panaitescu, "The German Stories about Vlad Țepeș," in Treptow, *Dracula: Essays...*, p. 193.

downfall in the summer of 1462 was caused by the opposition of the boyars as a social group. Although Vlad tried to strengthen his authority, this cannot be construed as an attack on the privileges of the boyars; after all, the prince and the boyars had essentially the same interest — the consolidation and strengthening of the power of the state as it protected their status and privileges. It is better to view Dracula's policy as being one aimed at strengthening and securing the positions of his family and friends — typical behavior for his time — instead of being one directed against the boyars as a social class. Dracula's boyars on the whole appear to have remained remarkably loyal to him, even during the great Ottoman invasion in the summer of 1462.

In the final analysis we must admit that it was the power of the sultan's armies that led to his downfall and brought his brother, Radu cel Frumos, to the Wallachian throne in 1462. Nicolae Iorga aptly summed up the campaign of 1462 when he wrote:

> Suffering from hunger in a country that had been systematically devastated, and having completely achieved his goal of placing Radu, the Sultan's favorite, on the throne in place of his brother who had fled, Mehmed II again crossed the Danube.[66]

This, of course, does not imply that all fighting ceased at the end of June. Evidence indicates that Dracula continued to harass the Ottoman army and, later, the forces of his brother,[67] while he waited in the mountains bordering Transylvania for the long anticipated arrival of Matthias Corvinus,[68] his ally, who he hoped would help restore him to the throne. His hopes would not be fulfilled. Matthias did not even leave Buda until the sultan had departed from Wallachia,[69] and it was early November before he reached Braşov.[70] Clearly he had no serious intentions of going to war with the Ottomans. Already in August the king's subjects in Transylvania were making peace with the new prince of Wallachia, Radu cel Frumos; on 15 August 1462 the *vicecomitele*

---

[66]Nicolae Iorga, *Studii istorice asupra Chiliei şi Cetăţii-Albe*, p. 123.

of the Szecklers wrote to the councilors of Braşov, telling them to respect the peace treaty concluded with the new prince of Wallachia, adding that:

> You should not fear what the king, the governor or the noble-men of the Kingdom might do since they are preoccupied with other things.[71]

Matthias's dispute with the Holy Roman Emperor Frederick III of Hapsburg over the Hungarian crown is one of the reasons for his

---

[67]The chronicle of the English pilgrim William Wey makes mention of news about conflicts in Wallachia after the departure of the sultan from Wallachia and the installation of Radu cel Frumos on the throne. See William Wey, *The Itineraries of William Wey, Fellow of Eton College, Published from the Bodleian Manuscript for the Roxburghe Club* (London, 1857), pp. 100-101. See also Francisc Pall, "Notes du pèlerin William Wey à propos des opérations militaires des Turcs en 1462," pp. 264-266, in *Revue historique du sud-est européen*, XXII (1945); and "Iunie 1462. Biruinţa lui Vlad Ţepeş," pp. 28-29, in *Magazin istoric*, XXI:2 (Noiembrie, 1987), pp. 28-29. Marxist Romanian historiography has given special attention to this source which also speaks of a victory of Vlad Ţepeş over the Turks. Wey, a pilgrim on his way to the holy land, heard of events in Wallachia during a stop over in Rhodes. His account of the events in the Romanian principality during that summer is confused and cannot be relied upon as a source for the campaign of 1462 as he merely recorded rumors that circulated at the time.

[68]In his letter of 14 June 1462 the Venetian ambassador in Buda, Petrus de Thomasiis, reports to the doge of Venice about the preparations being made in Transylvania to assist Dracula. See doc. II in I. Bianu, "Ştefanu celu Mare: Câteva documente din archivulu de statu dela Milanu," pp. 36-38.

[69]Although he knew of Ottoman military plans for months, on 11 June 1462, when the sultan was making his way from the Danube to Târgovişte, Matthias Corvinus was still in Buda (see doc. 3280 in Gündisch, *Urkundenbuch zur Geschichte der Deutschen in Siebenbürgen*, vol. VI, p. 117). On 2 July, after the sultan had installed Radu cel Frumos on the throne and recrossed the Danube, Matthias, then at Pressburg, announced that in a few days he would set out against the Turks (see Iorga, *Studii istorice asupra Chiliei şi Cetăţii-Albe*, p. 123).

[70]On 12 August Matthias was in Seghedin (see doc. 3284 in Gündisch, *Urkundenbuch zur Geschichte der Deutschen in Siebenbürgen*, vol. VI, p. 121), while on 26 September the king is known to have been in Sibiu where he accorded privileges to St. Michael's Church in Cluj (see doc. 3291 in Gündisch, *op. cit.*, p. 124). He showed no signs of beginning a campaign against the Ottomans, and it is more than a month later, on 4 November 1462, that we find him in Braşov (see doc. 3295 in Gündisch, *op. cit.*, pp. 126-127).

apparent lack of enthusiasm for a campaign in the southeast.[72] Nevertheless, the Hungarian king, who had received substantial financial support as part of Pope Pius II's plan for a crusade to liberate the Balkans from the Turkish infidels elaborated at the Congress of Mantua in 1459, had to make a gesture to justify his use of these funds.[73] Thus, he began a slow march into Transylvania on the pretext of aiding Vlad against the Ottomans. Yet, as the Polish chronicler Jan

Pope Pius II

By Octavian Ion Penda

Dlugosz remarked, it seemed as if Matthias "were in league with the Turks."[74] Once the king reached Braşov in November, however, he ordered the arrest of Vlad. Toward the end of November Dracula was taken prisoner by the king's Czech General Jan Jiskra von Brandeis at Piatra Craiului, near Rucăr.[75] Forged letters were created in order to

---

[71]See the letter of the vicecomitele of the Szecklers to the councilors of Braşov, dated 15 August 1462, doc. 3285 in Gündisch, *Urkundenbuch zur Geschichte der Deutschen in Siebenbürgen*, vol. VI, pp. 121-122; and Eudoxiu Hurmuzaki and Nicolae Iorga, *Documente privitoare la istoria românilor*, vol. XV₁ (Bucureşti, 1911), p. 58.

[72]Stoicescu, *Vlad Ţepeş*, pp. 102-103.

[73]Pius II eagerly awaited Matthias to come to the assistance of Vlad and begin the long awaited crusade against the Turkish Infidels. On 15 June 1462 the pope issued a bull granting indulgences to all visitors of churches in Alba Iulia who made contributions to the war against the Ottomans, see doc. 3281 in Gündisch, *Urkundenbuch zur Geschichte der Deutschen in Siebenbürgen*, vol. VI, pp. 118-119.

[74]Minea, *Informaţiile româneşti ale cronicii lui Ian Dlugosz*, and Ioannis Dlugossi, *Historia Poloniae*, vol. II (Leipzig, 1712), p. 344 (Book XIII).

[75]See Michel Beheim, "Von ainem wutrich der Hiess Trakle Waida," in Cazacu, *L'histoire du prince Dracula*, pp. 150-153. Piatra Craiului was located six kilometers from Rucăr, see Ştefan Andreescu and Raymond T. McNally, "Exactly Where Was Dracula Captured in 1462?," pp. 269-281, in *East European Quarterly*, XXIII:3 (September, 1989), p. 271.

Vlad's arrest at the order of Matthias Corvinus
at Piatra Craiului in 1462

By Octavian Ion Penda

justify Matthias's actions, in which the Wallachian prince purportedly promised to Sultan Mehmed II that:

> in atonement for my sin, [I can] hand over to you all Transylvania, the possession of which will enable you to bring all Hungary under your power.[76]

Though this explanation for Dracula's imprisonment was accepted in some official circles, its absurdity is clear. Even Matthias's chronicler, Antonius Bonfinius, wrote:

> On his way there, I do not know the reason why because this was never understood clearly by anyone, he [Matthias] captured Dracula in Transylvania, but the other Dracula[77] [Radu cel Frumos], whom the Turks had appointed prince of that province [Wallachia], he approved of, against all expectations.[78]

So ended Dracula's hopes of regaining his throne in 1462. As the Ottoman chronicler Tursun Beg commented, with some irony:

> In their despair they [Vlad and his followers] took refuge in the land of the Hungarians. He had caused many disasters for the Hungarian king, and now he had brought about his own

---

[76]Pius II, "The Commentaries of Pius II, Books X-XIII," trans. Florence Alden Gragg, in *Smith College Studies in History*, vol. XLIII (Northhampton, MA, 1957), p. 739 (Book XI). On the authenticity of this letter, that unfortunately does not exist in an original copy, see Bogdan, *Vlad Țepeș*, pp. 29-30. Romanian and foreign historiography has almost unanimously considered this letter to be a forgery to compromise Dracula in the eyes of King Matthias or to justify the king's failure to undertake an anti-Ottoman crusade in 1462. The latter seems the most likely explanation. Such letters are not unknown in Romanian history, a similar forgery having been used to justify the assassination of the Wallachian Prince Mihai Viteazul (*Michael the Brave*, 1593-1601) by Hapsburg troops.

[77]Further proof that, at this time, the name *Dracula* simply meant "son of Dracul."

[78]See the translation of Antonius Bonfinius's remarks in P.P. Panaitescu, "The German Stories about Vlad Țepeș," pp. 185-196, in Treptow, *Dracula: Essays...*, pp. 195-196. The complete chronicle is published in Antonius Bonfinius, *Rerum Ungaricum Decades*, I. Fogel, B. Ivanyi, and L. Juhasz, eds. (Leipzig, 1936). The relevant section concerning Dracula can be found in vol. III, p. 243.

destruction. Trying to escape from the lion's claws, he had chosen the claws of a bird of prey.[79] The Hungarian King took him prisoner."[80]

He was imprisoned briefly at Alba Iulia[81] and then taken to Hungary where he spent many years imprisoned in the castle of Visegrad near Buda.[82] It would be fourteen long years before he would have the chance to regain his throne.

---

[79]The "lion's claws" refers to the sultan, while the "claws of a bird of prey" is an allusion to the name Corvinus, derived from the Latin for 'raven.' The raven was also portrayed on the family seal.

[80]Tursun Beg, "Tarih-i Ebu-l Feth-i Sultan Mehmed-han," in *Cronici turceşti privind ţările române*, vol. I, p. 73.

[81]Chalcocondil, *Expuneri istorice*, p. 293.

[82]See "Viaţa lui Vlad Ţepeş: Povestire despre Dracula voievod," in *Cronicele slavo-romîne*, P.P. Panaitescu, ed., p. 212; Olteanu, *Limba povestirilor slave despre Vlad Ţepeş*, p. 363; and Bonfinius in P.P. Panaitescu, "The German Stories about Vlad Ţepeş," in Treptow, *Dracula: Essays...*, p. 195. See also appendix V.

Chapter IX

Epilogue: The Imprisonment and Final Reign of Dracula

We have faith in God that we shall again be that which we once were, and much more.

— Petru Rareş, 1540[1]

After his arrest and imprisonment in 1462, Dracula would not be heard from again for thirteen years. During this time, a legend was born which over the centuries would be transformed into the vampire myth of today. The forged letter used to justify Matthias Corvinus's imprisonment of the brave prince who defied the sultan was only the beginning; the Hungarian court, aided by Vlad's Saxon enemies, promoted the spread of legends about the evil deeds of the prince. They were aided in their efforts by a new technological development of the fifteenth century, the invention of moveable type.

---

[1]Letter of Petru Rareş, prince of Moldavia (1527-1528 and 1541-1546), as he prepared to take the throne of Moldavia for a second time, see Iorga, *Scrisori de boieri, scrisori de domni*, p. 201.

As a result, these stories were published in a variety of editions and spread throughout the German speaking world during the late fifteenth and early sixteenth centuries;[2] first as political propaganda against the Wallachian prince to justify the actions of Matthias Corvinus, and later as popular literature that would be among the first best-sellers in Europe. These stories would also form the basis for a similar set of tales that circulated in the Slavic world, first appearing in 1486.[3] These tales all helped to create the image of the ruthless and bloody tyrant that centuries later would be transformed into a diabolical vampire; the nature of these tales and the purpose for which they were written demand that they be used with great caution by historians. In this way the legend of Dracula was born even before the death of the Wallachian prince.

During this missing period in the career of Vlad III Dracula he was held prisoner at the castle of Visegrad, near Buda. Meanwhile, his brother, Radu cel Frumos, enjoyed relatively good relations with both the Ottoman Empire and Hungary, apart from the usual conflicts with the Saxon cities of Transylvania. The greatest threat faced by Wallachia during his reign came from Stephen the Great, who, as he began to assert his independence more and more, tried to dominate the neighboring Romanian principality. The first conflict between the two occurred in 1465 when Stephen succeeded in seizing Chilia.[4] After

---

[2]On the German Stories about Dracula see P.P. Panaitescu, "The German Stories about Vlad Țepeș," pp. 185-196, in Treptow, *Dracula: Essays...* See appendix IV which contains a complete English translation of the tales; and Anton Balotă, "An Analysis of the Dracula Tales," in *Ibidem*, pp. 153-184. See also the long poem of the court bard Michel Beheim, "Von Ainem Wutrich der Hiess Trakle Waida," pp. 104-153, in Cazacu, *L'histoire du prince Dracula*. These tales present an extremely negative image of Dracula in order to justify Saxon political opposition to the prince, as well as his arrest and imprisonment by Matthias Corvinus.

[3]See P.P. Panaitescu, "Viața lui Vlad Țepeș: Povestire despre Dracula voievod," pp. 195-214, in *Cronicile slavo-romîne*; Pandele Olteanu, *Limba povestirilor slave despre Vlad Țepeș*; and Balotă, "An Analysis of the Dracula Tales," pp. 153-184, in Treptow, *Dracula: Essays....* The Slavic Stories present the image of a cruel but just prince, unlike the German tales that stress his excessive cruelty. Some have gone so far as to suggest that these stories could be considered as a Slavic version of Machiavelli's *The Prince*.

this attack, peaceful relations between Moldavia and Wallachia resumed,[5] until Stephen again launched an attack on his neighbor, pillaging and burning Brăila, Târgul Floci, and Ialomiţa in 1470.[6] These attacks had an economic character as the localities pillaged and burned were important commercial centers of eastern Wallachia, and craftsmen and Gypsy slaves were taken in the raids. The Moldavian prince hoped to destroy Wallachian commerce in the Danube region in favor of his principality.[7] This marked the beginning of a series of border wars between the two Romanian states.

During this period Stephen the Great began to support Basarab Laiotă, a pretender to the Wallachian throne.[8] At the end of 1473 Stephen invaded Wallachia and installed Laiotă on the throne, capturing part of the princely treasure along with Radu's wife and his young daughter, Maria Voichiţa, who would later become his wife. Less than a month later, Radu, with Ottoman assistance, would regain the throne.[9] The throne would alternate a number of times over the next year between Radu cel Frumos and Basarab Laiotă, until Stephen finally succeeded in establishing his protege on the Wallachian throne at the beginning of 1475. At the same time, Stephen broke off relations with the Ottomans in 1474, refusing to pay tribute any longer. The Ottomans responded by invading Moldavia early in 1475, but

---

[4]"Cronica moldo-germană," in Panaitescu, *Cronicile slavo-romîne*, p. 29.

[5]See the treaty between Moldavia and Poland from 1468 in which Stephen the Great does not list Wallachia among his enemies. See Bogdan, *Documentele lui Ştefan cel Mare*, vol. II, pp. 300-304.

[6]Costăchescu, *Arderea Târgului Floci şi a Ialomiţei în 1470*, pp. 1-3.

[7]Panaitescu, "Comunele medievale în principatele române," in *Interpretări româneşti*, pp. 151-152.

[8]See Costăchescu, *Arderea Târgului Floci şi a Ialomiţei în 1470*, pp. 99-105. This is the same pretender that had established himself in Sighişoara in 1459-1460 during the reign of Dracula.

[9]"Letopiseţul anonim al Moldovei," p. 17, and "Letopiseţul de la Putna II," p. 63, in Panaitescu, *Cronicile slavo-romîne.*

suffered a great defeat at the hands of the Moldavian army at Podul Înalt near Vaslui on 10 January.[10]

It is during this period that we again hear news of Dracula. Stephen's ally, Basarab Laiotă, after seizing the throne from Radu cel Frumos, turned his back on the Moldavian prince and cooperated with the Turks during their invasion of Moldavia. The Moldavian prince knew that the sultan would not be content to leave the humiliating defeat of his forces at Vaslui unpunished, and that he would soon prepare a campaign against Moldavia. Under these circumstances Stephen now entered into an alliance with his former enemy, Matthias Corvinus,[11] and looked for a new pretender to the throne of Wallachia:

> I asked that Prince Basarab be removed from the other Romanian land and that another Christian prince be put on its throne, Dracula by name, with whom we can cooperate; I requested of His Majesty, the king of Hungary to allow Vlad Dracula to become prince.[12]

It is reasonable that Stephen would ask for Vlad's restoration to the throne at this time. Like Dracula in 1462, the Moldavian prince was now an ally of the Hungarian king and at war with the Ottomans. Under these circumstances Matthias Corvinus released Vlad from prison. The Slavic Stories about Vlad Ţepeş, which contain information about his imprisonment at Buda, relate that:

> the king sent a messenger to him in prison, telling him that if he wished to again be prince of Wallachia, as before, then he must accept the Latin faith [Catholicism]. If he refused he

---

[10]This event is mentioned in all the Moldavian chronicles of the time, see Panaitescu, *Cronicile slavo-romîne*, pp. 18, 33, 50, 63, and 72. News of this remarkable victory circulated throughout Europe. See, for example, the letter of the rector of Raguza to the doge of Venice, dated 12 February 1475, doc. V in Bianu, "Ştefanu cel Mare: Câteva documente din archivulu de statu dela Milanu," pp. 41-42.

[11]Bogdan, *Documentele lui Ştefan cel Mare*, vol. II, p. 332.

[12]Bogdan, *Documentele lui Ştefan cel Mare*, vol. II, p. 349.

would die in prison. Dracula preferred the sweetness of temporal life more than eternal life, and he abandoned Orthodoxy and the truth, and left light for darkness. He did not have the patience to endure the passing hardships of prison and he prepared himself for eternal suffering by abandoning our Orthodox faith and receiving the Latin heresy. The king not only made him prince of Wallachia, but he also gave his sister to him to be his wife.[13]

Essentially, in return for his release from prison, Vlad was required to accept the terms of the agreement he concluded with Matthias at the end of 1461. Dracula accepted these terms and was released from prison in 1475; he then prepared to take the throne of Wallachia for the third time.

In August, 1475, Matthias Corvinus sought to reconcile the two princes who had been enemies in 1462, announcing that:

we bring about an agreement between the two princes, Stephen of Moldavia and Vlad of Wallachia, based upon the agreements that had been concluded between Alexander the Good and Mircea the Old, princes of these two countries.[14]

It would still be some time, however, before Vlad would be allowed to reclaim his heritage. As usual, Matthias Corvinus was indecisive. Being occupied during this time with affairs in Serbia and Bosnia, he delayed preparations for an attack on Wallachia. Meanwhile, Vlad served as a commander in the royal army; together with the Serbian Prince Vuk Brankovic, he led an attack on the Ottomans in Bosnia in February-March, 1476, seizing Srebrenica and other towns, capturing great booty, and spreading terror among the Turks.[15]

---

[13]"Viaţa lui Vlad Ţepeş," in Panaitescu, *Cronicele slavo-romîne*, p. 212; and Olteanu, *Limba povestirile slave despre Vlad Ţepeş*, p. 363.

[14]Bogdan, *Documentele lui Ştefan cel Mare*, vol. II, pp. 334-335.

[15]Ştefan Andreescu, "Military Actions of Vlad Ţepeş in Southeastern Europe in 1476," in Treptow, *Dracula: Essays...*, pp. 139-140.

In the summer of 1476 the sultan, accompanied by Basarab Laiotă, personally led an expedition against the prince of Moldavia. The Ottoman forces plundered Moldavia, reaching as far as the capital of Suceava. The two armies met in a great battle at Războieni on 26 July where the Moldavian army was defeated, but Stephen the Great escaped. The sultan then besieged the fortress of Neamţ, an important Moldavian stronghold, but he was unable to capture it. The Ottomans, suffering from a lack of provisions and an outbreak of the plague, were forced to retreat; a German chronicler, Jakob Unrest, recalls that, around the time of the sultan's retreat from Moldavia, Stephen was joined by forces commanded by Dracula and Vuk Brankovic who helped him regain control of Moldavia.[16] As they withdrew from the country, the Ottoman troops were harassed all along their way by the regrouped Moldavian forces.[17] Thus, the Byzantine chronicler George Sphrantzes recorded:

> In the summer of 6984 [1476] the Sultan advanced against Greater Wallachia [Moldavia] with all his forces. He returned in September... he had suffered more defeats than victories.[18]

After the failure of the Ottomans to remove Stephen from the throne of Moldavia, both the Hungarian king and the Moldavian prince began to make preparations to oust Basarab Laiotă and return Vlad III Dracula to the throne of Wallachia. On 7 October 1476 he was in Braşov where he emitted the decree previously discussed, reestablishing economic relations between Wallachia and the Saxon lands,

---

[16]Jakob Unrest, "Osterreichische Chronik," in Karl Grossman, ed., *Monumenta Germaniae Historica, Scriptores Rerum Germanicarum, Nova Series*, XI (Weimar, 1957), p. 68. On this question see Andreescu, "Military Actions of Vlad Ţepeş in Southeastern Europe in 1476," in Treptow, *Dracula: Essays...*, pp. 145-146.

[17]See the Moldavian chronicles from the time contained in Panaitescu, *Cronicile slavo-romîne*, pp. 18, 33-34, 50, 63, and 72; Nicolae Iorga, *Istoria lui Ştefan cel Mare povestită neamului românesc* (Bucureşti, 1904), pp. 174-181; Ion Ursu, *Ştefan cel Mare şi turcii* (Bucureşti, 1914), pp. 71-72; and Ilie Minea, *Cetatea Neamţului* (Iaşi, 1943), p. 8.

[18]Sphrantzes, *The Fall of the Byzantine Empire*, p. 94 [XLVII.6].

as it was in earlier days, in the time of the great Mircea voievod, until the days of My Majesty's father, the great Vlad voievod, and then also during my reign.[19]

By early November preparations for the invasion of Wallachia had been completed. Vlad, aided by Hungarian troops, set out from Braşov, while Stephen the Great simultaneously launched an invasion from the northeast. Victory came swiftly for the invading forces led by Dracula, who, on 8 November, wrote to the councilors of Braşov announcing:

> Herewith I give you news that I have overthrown our foe Laiotă, who fled to the Turks. Thus, God has given you a free path. Come with bread and goods, and you will eat now that God has given us a single country.[20]

After having captured the capital of Wallachia, the next important objective was the fortress of Bucharest; here troops led by Stephen the Great would join Vlad's army in their attack on this key fortress. News of this battle reached Braşov in a letter sent by Cârstian, the *pârcălab* of Târgovişte, on 17 November:

> I send you news that the fortress of Bucharest was won this past Saturday [16 November]. Therefore, I ask you to give praise to the Almighty God with organs, songs, and bells, as we have done in our country which is also yours. And you must know that all the boyars of the country have sworn allegiance to Vlad vodă.[21]

Vlad III Dracula had succeeded in gaining the throne of Wallachia for a third time. In a report sent to the duke of Milan by Giustin-

---

[19]Doc. LXXIV in Bogdan, *Documente privitoare la relaţiile Ţării Româneşti cu Braşovul şi Ţara Ungurească*, pp. 95-97; doc. 100 in Tocilescu, *534 documente istorice slavo-române*, pp. 95-97.

[20]Doc. LXXV in Bogdan, *Documente privitoare la relaţiile Ţării Româneşti cu Braşovul şi Ţara Ungurească*, pp. 97-98; and doc. 101 in Tocilescu, *534 documente istorice slavo-române*, p. 97.

14 The Life and Times of the Historical Dracula

iano Cavitello, his representative in Buda, dated 4 December 1476,
we learn that:

> the people [the assembly of boyars that proclaimed Dracula as
> prince] asked both of the voievods [Vlad and Stephen] to swear
> love and allegiance to one another so that all of the country
> could be certain that the Turks would no longer harm them.[22]

Although we have little information about his third reign, we do
know that Vlad respected the promises contained in his decree of 7
October and restored free trade between Wallachia and the Saxon
lands. Shortly after regaining the throne for a third time, Dracula
informed the officials and councilors of Braşov and Ţara Bârsei:

> My Majesty gives you news that, with the help of God, all of
> Wallachia and its boyars have submitted to me; and God has
> opened the roads to you everywhere, to Rucăr, Prahova,
> Teleajin, and Buzău. Therefore go now freely where you like
> and feed yourselves. And God will be pleased.[23]

---

[21]Doc. CCCXII in Bogdan, *Documente privitoare la relaţiile Ţării Româneşti cu
Braşovul şi Ţara Ungurească*, pp. 357-358. In a letter to the pope, dated 8 December 1476,
Matthias Corvinus wrote:

> My army, which numbered 60,000 men, besieged the fortress [Bucharest] and
> conquered it, taking control of the country through which the Turks had easy
> entry into Moldavia, while Vlad Dracula, my captain, a fierce warrior... in
> accordance with my wishes and desire was received as prince by the inhabitants
> of the country.

See Hurmuzaki, *Documente*, vol. VIII, pp. 22-23. The Hungarian king's estimation
of the size of his forces is an exaggeration, probably to impress upon the pope the great
expense he incurred, as diplomatic sources indicate that Vlad had 25,000 troops, while
Stephen led a force of 15,000 (see the letter of Giustiniano Cavitello to the Duke of Milan,
dated 4 December 1476, in Iorga, *Acte şi fragmente cu privire la istoria romînilor*,
pp. 58-59).

[22]Iorga, *Acte şi fragmente cu privire la istoria romînilor*, pp. 58-59.

[23]Doc. LXXVI in Bogdan, *Documente privitoare la relaţiile Ţării Româneşti cu
Braşovul şi Ţara Ungurească*, p. 98; and doc. 102 in Tocilescu, *534 documente istorice
slavo-române*, pp. 97-98.

Vlad III Dracula and Stephen the Great
entering Wallachia in 1476

By Octavian Ion Penda

Although it seemed as if his former power and glory had been restored to him, Dracula's reign would come to an abrupt end. Little over a month after his third reign began, Basarab Laiotă, joined by an Ottoman army, invaded Wallachia and seized the throne from Vlad III who perished in the fighting. In early January, 1477, news of Vlad's death reached Moldavia. In a letter dated 10 January, Stephen recounted that:

> the disloyal Basarab returned, and finding Vlad voievod alone, killed him along with all my men; only ten of them escaped with their lives.[24]

Additional information is provided in a letter, dated 1 February 1477, to the duke of Milan from his ambassador to Buda, Leonardo Botta:

> the Turks entered Wallachia and again conquered the country and cut to pieces Dracula, the captain of the king of Hungary, with approximately 4,000 of his men.[25]

Thus the life of Vlad III Dracula came to an end. The legend surrounding this enigmatic figure, however, would continue to grow, making him one of the most famous Romanian princes in all of history. While many consider him a villainous tyrant or a heroic crusader for the cause of Christianity against the Turkish Infidels, what can be said of Dracula for certain is that he was a prince driven by the desire to strengthen and protect his country's independence. "We do not want to leave unfinished that which we began," he wrote to Matthias Corvinus in 1462, "but to follow it through to the end."[26] His failure to do so would be symbolic of the fate of the Romanian principalities that would endure centuries of foreign domination.

---

[24]See doc. CLIV in Bogdan, *Documentele lui Ştefan cel Mare*, vol. II, p. 345. At Vlad's request, Stephen had left a guard of 200 Moldavian troops to help protect the Wallachian prince.

[25]Quoted in Xenopol, "Lupta dintre Dăneşti şi Drăculeşti," p. 33 (215).

[26]Iorga, *Scrisori de boieri, scrisori de domni*, pp. 166-170.

Conclusion

Thou, O Padishah, knowest well the great dissensions that are raging in Italy especially, and in all Frankistan [Christian Europe] generally. In consequence of these dissensions the Gaiours [Infidels] are incapable of united action against us. The Christian potentates will never unite together. When after protracted efforts they conclude something like a peace among themselves, it never lasts long. Even when they are bound by treaties of alliance, they are not prevented from seizing territories from each other. They always stand in fear of each other, and are busily occupied in intriguing against each other. No doubt they think much, speak much, and explain much, but after all they do very little. When they decide to do anything, they waste much time before they begin to act. Suppose they have even commenced something. They cannot progress very far with it because they are sure to disagree amongst themselves how to proceed...

— Zagan Pasha to Mehmed the Conqueror, 27 May 1453[1]

Zagan Pasha's speech before the walls of Constantinople, encouraging the sultan to order an all out assault on the city, provides an apt description of the situation confronting Vlad III Dracula and the princes of Wallachia and Moldavia during the fif-

---

[1]Quoted in L.S. Stavrianos, *The Balkans since 1453*, p. 58.

teenth century. His struggle against the Turks would be the defining moment in Vlad's career. Likewise, the ultimate failure of his efforts would symbolize the fate of this region of Europe. Nearly half a millennium of Ottoman domination would leave its mark on Romanian society — the results of which are still evident today.

Vlad III Dracula would be among the first generation of leaders in the Romanian lands to have been educated at the Ottoman Porte. Sultan Murad II had granted Vlad Dracula his first leadership role when he gained the throne of Wallachia for the first time in 1448 with direct Ottoman military assistance. This fact would be of vital importance for his later career; as the Serbian janissary, Konstantin Mihailovic, observed:

> it is far easier for one to defend himself against the Turks who is familiar with them than for one who does not know their customs.[2]

The driving force behind Vlad's domestic and foreign policies was the desire to defend the independence of his lands. In this respect he was a worthy successor of his predecessors, such as his grandfather Mircea the Old and his father Vlad II Dracul. The political and military decisions he took were dictated by this consideration above all else. To this end Vlad sought to strengthen his authority internally.

Although Vlad, like his cousin Stephen the Great and his Albanian counterpart George Castriota Scanderbeg, would become renowned for his fierce resistance to Ottoman expansion, his foreign policy, aimed at protecting the autonomy of Wallachia, led him into conflict with Christian powers as well, as can be seen in Vlad's conflicts with Hungary, and especially with the Hungarian king's Saxon subjects in southern Transylvania.

These conflicts illustrate the fact that Dracula was not primarily motivated by religious considerations in pursuing his struggle against Ottoman expansion. Wallachia was on the border of the Catholic and Orthodox worlds; it had a very profound impact on life in Wallachia.

---

[2]Mihailovic, *Memoirs of a Janissary*, p. 135.

Nevertheless, Vlad placed the interests of the state before religious considerations. When considering the question of the struggle of Christianity against Islam, it is essential to remember that the Union proclaimed by the Council of Florence in 1439 failed, like similar attempts before it, to resolve the deep rupture between the Catholic and Orthodox worlds. As L.S. Stavrianos observed, "each agreement for union proved meaningless in the face of the undying hatred of the Orthodox Greeks for the Catholic Latins — a hatred intensified by the barbarities of the Fourth Crusade and the merciless stranglehold of the Italian merchants."[3] For peoples throughout the Orthodox world the cry "Better Islam than the Pope!" was more than just a slogan.

This is not to underestimate the importance of religion in the system of international relations of the time. Religion served as an important instrument of diplomacy. Thus, Vlad wrote to Matthias Corvinus in 1462, explaining to the king that:

> we have broken our peace with them, not for our own benefit, but for the honor of Your Majesty and the Holy Crown of Your Majesty, and for the preservation of Christianity and the strengthening of the Catholic faith.[4]

Religion affected every aspect of life in medieval times and this is no less true of diplomacy; thus, religion, as a diplomatic instrument, would be utilized by Vlad, the ruler of an Orthodox land, in his dealings with the Catholic powers of Europe, especially when trying to obtain material support for their resistance to Ottoman expansion.

Ultimately the anti-Ottoman resistance led by Vlad failed. The reasons for this failure are complex. One cause was the failure of strong state institutions to develop in this part of Europe for reasons we suggested earlier in our study. Wallachia was not prepared to face the threat posed by Ottoman expansion. Interference from neighboring powers, who sought to preserve these weak institutions, both to

---

[3]Stavrianos, *The Balkans since 1453*, p. 56.

[4]Iorga, *Scrisori de boieri, scrisori de domni*, pp. 166-170.

protect their own interests in the region, as well as to use Wallachia and Moldavia as buffer states to stave off the threat posed by the extension of Islam into Southeastern Europe, further inhibited the creation of strong state formations. The problem of foreign interference, however, is a double-edged sword. On the one hand, outside threats helped to promote the consolidation of state formations, as was true, for example, in the case of Wallachia and Moldavia during the first half of the fifteenth century when both states formed in response to the threat posed by the kingdom of Hungary to the pre-existing smaller state formations on those territories. On the other hand, if the threat was too great it could stifle the development of native institutions. The important elements in this calculation are the degree of the threat and at what point in the development of the state it appeared.

An additional reason for the failure of strong state institutions to develop in this region of Europe was the relative strength of peasant organization in the Balkans. The basically agricultural communities of Southeastern Europe had a long tradition of communal organization, as we saw in the example of the Slavic *zadruga*. These were, in essence, extended family organizations whose way of life was based on ancient customs and traditions. While it would be a strong, effective form of social organization for Balkan society during the early Middle Ages, it would also inhibit the development of the strong state institutions necessary to confront the Ottoman threat and have serious consequences for the future social and economic development of the region.

Although the Romanians are not a Slavic people, the impact of Slavic culture on all aspects of life in the Romanian lands was significant. In this respect, one of the most important aspects was the Slavic customary law of equal division of inheritances among male offspring and the lack of primogeniture. As Philip Longworth pointed out, when analyzing the causes for the underdevelopment of Eastern Europe, "These arrangements were conducive to the maintenance of peace within the family, the village, and the clan, but their effectiveness was predicated on a low population and relatively plentiful

resources, conditions that were not to last. In the long term the consequences of these customary understandings were profound and
largely adverse; and they took political and cultural, as well as economic forms."[5] The lack of primogeniture would have a serious
impact upon the development of state institutions and, in later centuries, for village life as well. Its most serious political consequence during the period that we have studied is that it prevented the
establishment of a system of orderly succession to the throne in Wallachia, creating conditions for incessant internal political struggles that
were utilized by foreign powers in their attempts to assert their hege-
mony over the Romanian principality.

Another aspect of Slavic customary law that had a negative
impact on state development was the principle that a ruler was not
bound by the acts of his predecessors. This is evidenced in several *hrisoave* issued by the princes of Wallachia during the fifteenth century
that merely confirm donations made by their predecessors; for example, Prince Alexandru Aldea issued a *hrisov* on 25 June 1436 to confirm the lands and privileges that had previously been granted to the
Monastery of Cozia,[6] an act repeated by Basarab II in 1443[7] and
Vladislav II in 1451.[8] In addition, most deeds contain a formula that
reflects this problem; thus, in a *hrisov* through which Vlad III Dracula
granted the lands of Poiana of Stev and Ponor to Andrei and his sons
we find the following clause:

> after my death, whoever the Lord God grants the throne of
> Wallachia, whether it be one of my sons or relatives, or, for our
> sins, one of another family, if he will strengthen, protect, and

---

[5]See Philip Longworth, *The Making of Eastern Europe* (London: The MacMillan
Press, 1992), p. 300.

[6]Doc. 77 in *Documenta Romaniae Historica, B. Ţara Românească*, vol. I, pp. 138-
140.

[7]Doc. 96 in *Documenta Romaniae Historica, B. Ţara Românească*, vol. I, pp. 167-
168.

[8]Doc. 107 in *Documenta Romaniae Historica, B. Ţara Românească*, vol. I, pp. 187-
188.

renew this deed of mine, may God grant him His support; but if he will not renew and strengthen it and ruins and destroys it, let God destroy and kill him, in the body in this world, and in spirit in the hereafter he will be in the company of Judas and Cain, and of all the others to whom it was said: his blood be on them and on their children, as it is and will be, forever and ever, Amen.[9]

Nevertheless, the lack of internal documents for Wallachia makes it difficult to estimate the impact this had on political and social life. We can, however, deduce that it prevented the development of a civic society, based on law, and created anxiety and instability in political and social life. In addition, it would have serious economic consequences as property rights failed to be established on any sort of legal, contractual basis; an essential element for the evolution of a mercantile or capitalist system of economic relations.

Thus, we can conclude that the weakness of institutional development is directly responsible for the failure to organize a strong defense against the Ottoman threat, making it a principal cause for the failure of the resistance in Wallachia. Neither Vlad nor any of his successors could remedy this defect. Nor has the situation improved much over the centuries as these developmental problems continue to confront political leaders in Southeastern Europe today.

Another cause would be the failure of the Christian states of Europe to organize effectively against the Ottoman threat. The analysis of Mehmed's general, Zagan Pasha, is valid for the situation all throughout this period. Every effort at organizing a Christian offensive to halt the expansion of Ottoman power would be doomed to failure for the reasons cited by Zagan Pasha as he urged Mehmed to order the final, decisive assault on the walls of the Byzantine capital in May, 1453. Meanwhile, the centralized political and military organization of the Ottomans, based on a militant religious ideology, would propel the expansion of the empire into Europe.

---

[9] Doc. 118 in *Documenta Romaniae Historica, B. Ţara Românească*, vol. I, pp. 203-204.

In Wallachia agricultural life was essentially independent and, due to the low level of urban development, little economic activity was devoted to the creation of goods for export. The urban economy in the Romanian principality was geared almost exclusively to commerce.[10] As a result, the resistance to the Ottomans led by Dracula in Wallachia was a movement conceived of and created by the state; it lacked a popular basis as the Ottoman danger had not yet seriously threatened the traditional way of life in the Romanian lands and would do so only indirectly during this century.

In Wallachia, a state had come into being at the beginning of the fourteenth century. Vlad confronted the Ottomans not as the leader of a popular uprising opposing foreign domination of his land, but as a head of state seeking to protect the independence of his country. Thus, our study of Dracula's reign and his confrontation with the Ottoman Empire is supplemented by internal documents generated by the state bureaucracy that, although sparse, are revealing about the internal situation in the Romanian principality.

Wallachia was located on the margins of the main path of Ottoman expansion. As land transport and travel were quicker and more practical than by river or sea,[11] the Romanian principalities bordering the Danube were merely intended as buffer states to protect the Ottoman flank. For this reason the sultan would not seriously consider the complete transformation of the Romanian principalities into pashaliks. In the following century this reason would be supplemented by an economic motive as it proved more profitable for the Ottomans to exploit the resources of the Romanian lands indirectly rather than to rule them directly.[12]

---

[10]P.P. Panaitescu, "Comunele medievale în principatele române," in *Interpretări românești*, pp. 152-153.

[11]Kurt W. Treptow, "Distance and Communications in Southeastern Europe," in *From Zalmoxis to Jan Palach*, pp. 76-78.

[12]On this question see Keith Hitchins, "Ottoman Domination of Moldavia and Wallachia in the Sixteenth Century," pp. 140-141; and P.P. Panaitescu, "De ce n-au cucerit turcii țările române," in *Interpretări românești*, pp. 114-116.

The establishment of Ottoman rule in Southeastern Europe would have a decisive impact on the future social and economic development of this region. The Ottoman system of economic exploitation would establish a feudal-military economic system in this region, while in the Romanian principalities, where native institutions resisted, Ottoman political and economic domination would promote the extension and strengthening of a feudal social and economic system — a process completed by the end of the sixteenth century. Thus, while feudalism was breaking down in Western Europe, it emerged from the turmoil of the fifteenth century, aided by the installation of Ottoman rule in the region, and persisted throughout the following centuries.

The installation of Ottoman rule in Southeastern Europe also had another consequence; it closed off prosperous trading routes between East and West. Instead of being located along important commercial routes that brought with them a certain degree of prosperity, the lands of Southeastern Europe became marginalized in the world economy. As an iron curtain between the Christian and Islamic worlds was erected, commerce came to a halt. Trade with the Orient would henceforth be conducted over sea routes; a change symbolically marked by the discovery of America at the end of the fifteenth century. Thus, the installation of the Ottoman regime would be decisive for the future social and economic development of this region of Europe.

We must, however, avoid any deterministic view of these events. Despite the conditions that facilitated their establishment in this region, including the existence of numerous elements that created a political vacuum in Southeastern Europe prior to their arrival, the Ottoman conquest was not inevitable. Had the Christian states of Europe been able to make a concerted effort, they could have halted the Ottoman advance. Had the unification of the Polish and Hungarian crowns, realized for a brief time (1440-1444) under King Ladislas, continued it could have led to other results. Had the Ottomans not succeeded in overcoming its own internal conflicts at the beginning of the century, the empire could very well have faded away like the

Vlad III Dracula

(Fifteenth century portrait from Ambras Castle in Austria)

Mongol Empire before it. Had not the Ottoman royal family been able to produce several capable and determined leaders, it would have failed to assert its dominance in this region. These speculations all pose questions outside of the scope of historical study where we are obliged to concentrate on what happened and why. We only mention these things here to remind us that in our analyses of why things happened the way they did, and the impact they had on the future, it is necessary to remember that the resistance to Ottoman expansion in Southeastern Europe was not futile and that things could have had another outcome.

The reign of Vlad III Dracula and his defiance of Ottoman suzerainty would be an event of great historical importance. His defiance would also help keep alive the spirit of independence in the Romanian principality. At the same time, the failure of Matthias Corvinus to come to the aid of the Wallachian prince in the summer of 1462 revealed the hopelessness of efforts to organize the united Christian effort against the Ottomans discussed at the Congress of Mantua in 1459. The age of crusading had come to an end.

Despite the failure of his efforts against the Turks, Vlad would not be forgotten. A legend would be born that circulated throughout Europe and later worldwide. Still, he would never achieve the historical stature of some of his contemporaries; Dracula's reign would never become a point of reference in the history of his principality, such as that of his grandfather Mircea the Old. Nor would he achieve the stature of his cousin, Stephen the Great, whom he helped to place on the throne in 1457. Nevertheless, the legends and myths created about him as a result of his conflicts with the Saxons would make him internationally by far the best-known personality of the Romanian Middle Ages.

Vlad's fame was in large measure due to the fact that he was a contemporary of Johann Gutenburg. The invention of moveable type marked the beginning of the widespread dissemination of printed materials and its propaganda value was quickly realized. First as political propaganda and then as popular literature, the German Stories about Dracula would become one of the first best-sellers in Europe.

Had he lived a century earlier he probably would never have achieved the international fame he enjoys today.

Despite his notoriety, Vlad ultimately failed to maintain the delicate balance between his neighboring powers necessary to defend the autonomy of his principality. His remarkable successes against Hungary perhaps made him too over-confident when trying to gain the same measure of independence vis-à-vis the Ottoman Empire. He would thus be left by his unfaithful ally to confront the sultan's armies alone. In this respect Dracula lacked a certain quality that led to the success of Stephen the Great in Moldavia who, as the Romanian historian Radu Rosetti has correctly argued, managed to maintain the autonomy of his principality throughout his forty-seven year reign due to his "judicious appreciation of situations and possibilities, his ability in diplomatic negotiations."[13] In fairness to Vlad, however, it must be pointed out that, for geopolitical reasons, "The voievod of this province [Moldavia] is less exposed to dangerous changes than the one in Wallachia."[14]

Vlad III Dracula lived in a moment of great importance for the future of the Romanian people. It was a crossroads in history that would influence the historical development of Southeastern Europe for almost the next five hundred years. From the images of saint and sinner that we discussed at the outset of our work, the examination of the life and times of Dracula leads us back again to George Bernard Shaw's observation that "hunger and cold and thirst, age and decay and disease, death above all, make them slaves of reality." Vlad was neither a saint nor a sinner, neither the maniacal degenerate tyrant that was later transformed into a vampire nor a selfless hero defending his nation, merely a human being confronted with the task of dealing with the realities he faced. The decisions he made, and the motivations for these, have been the object of our study.

---

[13]Radu Rosetti, "Stephen the Great of Moldavia and the Turkish Invasion," p. 91.

[14]Quote from the chronicle of Oláh in Johann Christian Engel, *Geschichte der Moldau und Walachey* (Halle, 1804), p. 151.

Vlad was a man of his times — a capable leader, driven by clear objectives, yet flawed, as men are. Had he been the degenerate, inhuman creature that some have transformed him into, Dracula would never have regained his throne in 1476, supported by the Christian leaders of Southeastern Europe. Unfortunately, the propaganda of the time distorted the image of this brave prince whose role in history deserves reconsideration. This book has been a first step in attempting to remove the veil of myth surrounding the man who proudly signed his name, Dracula.

Selected Documents and Letters concerning Vlad III Dracula

A. Letter of Vlad III Dracula to Brasov, 31 October 1448.
B. Letter of Vlad III Dracula to Brasov, 10 September 1456.
C. Deed issued by Vlad III Dracula, 20 September 1456.
D. Letter of Vlad III Dracula to Matthias Corvinus,
　　11 February 1462.
E. Decree of Vlad III Dracula in Brasov, 7 October 1476.
F. Letter of Vlad III Dracula to Brasov, 8 November 1476.
G. Letter of Cârstian, Pârcălab of Târgoviste, to Brasov,
　　17 November 1476.
H. Deed issued by Mircea Ciobanul, 1 April 1551.

A. Letter of Vlad III Dracula to Brasov, 31 October 1448.

31 October 1448, Târgovişte

Vlad Dracula, prince of Wallachia, to the officials of Braşov.

We give you news that Mr. Nicolae from Ocna of Sibiu writes to us and asks us to be so kind as to come to him until John [Hunyadi], the Royal Governor of Hungary, returns from the war. We are unable to do this because an emissary from Nicopolis came to us this past Tuesday [29 October] and said with great certainty that Murad, the Turkish Sultan, made war for three days against John [Hunyadi] the Governor, and that on the last day he [Hunyadi] formed a circle with his caravan, then the Sultan himself went down among the janissaries and they attacked this caravan, broke through the lines, and defeated and killed them. If we come now to him, the Turks could come and kill both you and us. Therefore, we ask you to have patience until we see what has happened to John [Hunyadi]. We don't even know if he is alive. If he returns from the war, we will meet him and we will make peace with him. But if you will be our enemies now, and if something happens, you will have sinned and you will have to answer for it before God. Written at Târgovişte the day before All Saints' Day [31 October] in the year of our Lord 1448.

Vlad, voievod of Wallachia, your brother in all.

To the officials of Braşov, our most loved brothers and friends.

Source: *Nicolae Iorga, Scrisori de boieri, scrisori de domni,* 3rd ed. (Vălenii de Munte, 1931), pp. 160-161. Iorga mistakenly attributes this letter to Vladislav II.

B. Letter of Vlad III Dracula to Brasov, 10 September 1456.

10 September 1456, Târgovişte

Vlad Dracula, prince of Wallachia, to the officials of Braşov.

You brethren, friends, and neighbors who are truly loved. Herewith we let you know, aş we did before, that a messenger from the Turks has now come to us. You should understand well and keep in mind our former agreements for brotherhood and peace; what we said at that time, now and always from the depth of our heart, we will adhere to. As we do our best and work hard on our behalf, even more so we want to work hard on your behalf. Now the time and the appointed hour about which we spoke before has arrived: the Turks intend to put great burdens, almost impossible to bear, upon our shoulders, forcing us to bow down before them. It is not for us or ours that they put such a great burden, but for you and yours; the Turks do this to humiliate us. As far as we ourselves are concerned, we could have made peace, but on account of you and your we cannot make peace with the Turks because they wish to pass through our country to attack and plunder you; in addition, they force us to work against the Catholic faith and against you. But our strong desire is never to do anything bad against you and we will never be separated from you willingly, as we have told you, as we are sworn to be your faithful brothers and friends. This is why we have retained the Turkish messenger until you receive this news. You can judge for yourselves that when a man or a Prince is strong and powerful, he can make peace as he wants to; but when he is weak, a stronger one will come and do what wants to him. This is why, herewith, we ask all of you, with sincerity, that when you read this, immediately send, for our good and for yours, without hesitation, 200 or 100 or 50 chosen men to help us by next Sunday. When the Turks see the power of the Hungarians they will be softer and we will tell them that more men will come. And thus we will be able to arrange our affairs and yours on a good manner, until we receive orders from his majesty, the King. As I have told you, for your and our well being and defense, hurry as quickly as you can because, we swear before God, that we are thinking more of your welfare and security than of ours. And you should think about what we and ours deserve in fairness and in honor, as there may be some people who think badly of us and who are working against is [referring to exiles, especially Dan, brother of Vladislav II, who was plotting against Dracula]. You should be enemies of such men, as we are towards your enemies; do to them what we are now doing for you. Târgoviște, the Friday after St. Mary's Day [10 September], in the year of our Lord 1456.

Vlad, prince of Wallachia, and ruler of Făgăraş.
Your brother and friend in all.

Source: Nicolae Iorga, *Scrisori de boieri, scrisori de domni*, 2nd ed. (Vălenii de Munte, 1925), pp. 164-165.

C. Deed issued by Vlad III Dracula, 20 September 1459.

20 September 1459 (6968), Bucharest

Vlad III Dracula, prince of Wallachia grants Andrei and his sons lands in Poiana of Stev and in Ponor, exempting them from taxes and special services. This is the first document known to have been issued in Bucharest.

By the grace of God, I Vlad, voievod and prince, son of the great Vlad voievod, ruler and lord of all Wallachia, and of Amlaş and Făgăraş, by my grace, willingly, with a pure hart, I have granted this most beautiful and honest gift, this deed by my authority, to Andrei and his sons to have as theirs Poiana of Stev, and of Iova, and of Drag, and of..., and to have the third of Ponor which used to belong to Sipin, and the third of Ponor and the estate of Petre of Ponor because they brought the third from Petre for 12 florins. And they gave to my court a horse.

And if one of them will die, the land will remain with the others, without any taxes. And again to Andrei and his children over a fourth of Ponor.

All of this is to be their land and to be inherited by heir children, grandchildren, and great-grandchildren, without any taxes such as for sheep, pigs, water, and wine, or any special services, such as cutting hay, trees, etc., that is to say all great and small services. And no one should dare cause any trouble for them, no clerk or tax collector, and none of the boyars or servants of my realm, because whoever dares to harm them will be severely punished.

In addition, after my death, whoever the Lord god grants the throne of Wallachia, whether it be one of my sons or relatives, or for our sins, one of another family, if he will strengthen, protect, and renew this deed of mine, may God grant him His support; but if he will not renew and strengthen it and ruins and destroys it, let God destroy and kill him, in body in this world, and in spirit in the hereafter he will be in the company of Judas and of Cain, and of all the others to whom it was said: his blood be on them and on their children, as it is and will be, forever and ever, Amen.

Witnesses: jupan Dragomir Ţacal, jupan Voico Dobriţa, jupan Stan vornic, jupan Stepan Turcul, jupan Oprea, jupan... and Bratul from Milcov, and Moldovean spătar, and Iova vistier, and ...spătar, and Tocsaba stolnic, Stoica paharnic, Gherghina comis...

Written in the fortress of Bucharest on 20 September 1459 (6968).

I Vlad voievod, by the grace of God, Prince.

Source: *Documenta Romaniae Historica, B. Ţara Românească, Volumul I (1247-1500)*. Bucureşti: Editura Academiei Republicii Socialiste România, 1966. Doc. 118, pp. 203-204.

D. Letter of Vlad III Dracula to Matthias Corvinus, 11 February 1462

11 February 1462, Giurgiu

Vlad Dracula, prince of Wallachia, to Matthias Corvinus, king of Hungary

Your Royal Highness and our most gracious Lord. In other letter I wrote to Your Majesty how the Turks, the most cruel enemies of the Cross of Christ, have sent their highest ranking messengers to convince us not to keep the peace and the agreements that we made with Your Majesty, and not to celebrate the wedding [Vlad had agreed to marry a relative of Matthias Corvinus], and to join with them alone and to go to the Porte of the Turkish Sultan, that is to say to his Court. And if we fail to give up the peace, the agreements, and the wedding with Your Majesty, the Turks will not keep the peace with us either. They also sent an important advisor of the Turkish Sultan, named Hamza-beg of Nicopolis, to settle border questions at the Danube, but with the intent that, if that Hamza-beg could bring us, by using tricks or promises, or some other means, to the Porte, fine, but if he could not, he was to capture us and bring us there. But, by the grace of God, while we were going to that border, we found out about their deceit, and trickery, and it was us who captured that Hamza-beg, in the Land and in the Turkish Country, near the fortress that is called Giurgiu; the Turks opened the gates of the fortress at the shouts of our men, thinking that only their men would get inside, but ours, mixing together with them, entered and conquered the fortress, which we burned down immediately. And we killed the men and women, old and young, who lived from the area of Oblucița and Novoselo, where the Danube flows into the sea, to Rahova, which is near Chilia, down to the villages of Samovit and Ghigen [the Bulgarian Ghighiul], 23,884 Turks and Bulgarians in all, not including who were burned in their houses and whose heads were not presented to our officials. Your Majesty should know that we have done all we could, for the time being, to harm those who kept urging us to leave the Christians and to take their side. Therefore, Your Majesty should know that we have broken our peace with them, not for our own benefit, but for the honor of Your Majesty and the Holy Crown of Your Majesty, and for the preservation of Christianity and the strengthening of the Catholic faith. Seeing what we did to them, they left the quarrels and fights they had up to now in other places, including the country and Holy Crown of Your Majesty, as well as all other places, and they threw all of their strength against us. When the weather permits, that is to say in the spring, they will come with evil intentions and with all their power. But they have no crossing points, because we burned all of them, except for Vidin, and destroyed them, and made them barren. Because they cannot harm us too much at the crossing point at Vidin, they should want to bring their ships from Constantinople and Galipoli, across the sea, to the Danube. Therefore, Your Majesty, gracious lord, if it is Your Majesty's desire to fight against them, then gather all of your country and all of the fighting men, both cavalry and infantry, and bring them to our Wallachia, and be so kind as to fight against them [the Turks] here. But Your Majesty, if you don't want to come yourself, then please send your whole army to Your Majesty's Transylvanian lands, beginning with St. George's Day

[23 April]. If Your Majesty does not want to give your whole army, then send only what you desire, at least from Tranyslvania and the Saxons. But, if Your Majesty wants to give us assistance, then please do not delay, but tell us truly the thoughts of Your Majesty. Our man, who brings you this letter, this time do not detain him, please, Your Majesty, but send him back to me soon and quickly. Because by no means do we want to leave unfinished what we began, but to follow this through to the end. Because we will not flee before their savagery, but by all of the Christians, and if he will kindly lend his ear to the prayers of his poor subjects and grants us victory over the Infidels, the enemies of the Cross of Christ, it will be the greatest honor, benefit, and spiritual help for Your Majesty, the Holy Crown of Your Majesty, and for all true Christians. Because we will not flee before their savagery, but by all means we will fight with them. And if, God forbid, it ends badly for us, and our little country is lost, Your Majesty will not benefit from this either, because it will be a loss for all Christianity. And so, you must believe what our man, Radu Farmă, will tell you, just as if we were speaking directly to Your Majesty. From the fortress of Giurgiu, 11 February 1462.

[There follows a list of the places and number of people killed in Dracula's attack against the Turks during the winter of 1461-1462]

First, in the places called Obluciţa and Novoselo there were killed 1,350; and 6,840 at Dârstor, Cartal, and Dridopotrom (?); likewise 343 at Orşova, and 840 were killed at Vectrem (?); 630 were killed at Turtucaia; likewise 210 were killed at Marotin; 6,414 were killed at Giurgiu on both sides of the river, and the fortress on the Danube was conquered and taken. The commander of the fortress [the subaşa] was killed, and Hamza-beg was captured there, and the commander of Nicopolis, the son of Firuz-beg, was also captured and beheaded; and of the Turks stationed at Nicopolis, all of the most important were killed with him. Likewise, 384 were killed at Turnu, Batin, and Novigrad; at Şiştov and in two other villages near it 410 were killed; likewise, the crossing point at Nicopolis was burned and completely destroyed, the same at Samnovit; and at Ghighen 1,138 were killed; at Rahova 1,460 were killed, and, likewise, the crossing point was completely burned, and Neagoe was appointed captain there by Prince Vlad. Likewise, at the above places where there were crossing points, they were burned and destroyed, the people, men, women, children, and babies were all killed, and in all these places nothing remained. And in the above are included only those whose heads or signs were brought to our officials who were everywhere; but those who were not presented to them, or who were burned in their houses, could not be counted, because there were so many.

Source: *Nicolae Iorga, Scrisori de boieri, scrisori de domni*, 2nd ed. (Vălenii de Munte, 1925), pp. 166-170; and Ioan Bogdan, *Vlad Ţepeş şi naraţiunile germane şi ruseşti asupra lui* (Bucureşti, 1896), pp. 76-82.

E. Decree of Vlad III Dracula in Brasov, 7 October 1476.

7 October 1476 (6985), Braşov

Vlad Dracula to the officials of Braşov.

With faith in the Lord Jesus Christ, I Vlad voievod, by the grace of God, Prince of all Wallachia, My Majesty gives this order to the honest, faithful, and good friends of My Majesty, to the county, to the twelve councilors, and to all other citizens of the great fortress of Braşov, and to all of my good friends in all of Bârsa County, great and small: that they should benefit according to the old settlement, as it was in earlier days, in the time of the great Mircea voievod, until the days of My Majesty's father, the great Vlad voievod, and then also during my reign. In the same manner, My Majesty orders that from now on things will be according to the old settlement; that from now on the scale that was will no longer be in my country, but every man will be free and able to trade, to buy, and to sell without a scale. And again, regarding wax, My Majesty has allowed people to be free to buy in all the markets, regions, and places in my country, as it was in the old agreement, as well as during my reign, so it will be hence-forth, as long as My Majesty is alive, they will be free to buy all that they need and want. And again, with regard to customs, as it was in the old settlement, and in the days of my former reign, so it will be now and henceforth, in the markets in my country, and in the customs houses in the countryside: they will pay fair customs, as they paid in the beginning and in the days of my reign, and no one should ever dare to establish higher customs taxes, neither the governors in the cities, nor the vornics [administrative officials for domestic affairs], nor the customs officials in the cities, or in the customs houses in the countryside, or at the Danube, nor anyone else among My Majesty's high officials and servants. If anyone should not respect the old settle-ment and would take more than what is written in this decree of My Majesty, they will receive the wrath of My Majesty. It cannot be dif-ferent, according to the order of My Majesty. Written on 7 October, in the great fortress of Braşov, in the year 1476 (6985).

Source: Ioan Bogdan, ed., *Documente privitoare la relaţiile Ţării Româneşti cu Braşovul şi cu Ţara Ungurească în sec. XV şi XVI* (Bucureşti, 1905), pp. 95-97.

F. Letter of Vlad III Dracula to Brasov, 8 November 1476.

8 November 1476, Târgovişte

Vlad Dracula, Prince of Wallachia, to the officials of Braşov.

I Vlad, voievod and Prince. My Majesty writes to my faithful and good, sweet, and honest friends of My Majesty to the county and the councilors of Braşov. Herewith I give you news that I have over-thrown our foe Laiotă, who fled to the Turks. Thus, God has given you a free path. Come with bread and goods, and you will eat, now that God has given us a single country. And all that the servant of My Majesty, jupan [Lord] Ratundul, tells you, you must believe, as they are the true words of My Majesty. They are no different. Written on 8 November at Târgovişte.

Source: Ioan Bogdan, ed., *Documente privitoare la relaţiile Ţării Româneşti cu Braşovul şi cu Ţara Ungurească în sec. XV şi XVI* (Bucureşti, 1905), pp. 97-98.

G. Letter of Cârstian, Pârcălab of Târgoviste, to Brasov.

17 November 1476, Târgovişte

Cârstian, pârcălab [governor] of Târgovişte, to the officials of Braşov.

To you my beloved friends, I give news that the fortress of Bucharest was won this past Saturday [16 November]. Therefore, I ask you to give praise to the Almighty God with organs, songs, and bells, as we have done in our country which is also yours. And you must know that the boyars of all the country have sworn allegiance to Vlad vodă [Dracula]. Also, I ask you to send to us two carpenters, and each of them must have three apprentices who can help them. And they will be given a sum of money and they will be treated well with food and drink; as a matter of fact they will come only to Târgovişte to build a house. I have written this letter at the request of Vlad vodă and all of you must trust the messenger who brings this letter. Written at Târgovişte, the Sunday after this victory, in the year of our Lord 1476.

Cârstian, pârcălab [governor] of Târgovişte.

Your faithful servant in all.

Source: Ioan Bogdan, ed., *Documente privitoare la relaţiile Ţării Româneşti şi cu Braşovul şi cu Ţara Ungurească în sec. XV şi XVI* (Bucureşti, 1905), pp. 357-358.

H. Deed issued by Mircea Ciobanul, 1 April 1551.

1 April 1551 (7059), Bucharest

Mircea Ciobanul, Prince of Wallachia, confirms possession of the villages of Glodul and Hinţea to the monastery of Govora (extract).

...In the time of Vlad voievod Ţepeş there was a boyar called Albu cel Mare who took the above mentioned villages [Glodul and Hinţea] by force, and also devastated the holy monastery [Govora]. It remained so devastated until the time when the Lord God gave the throne to my father Radu voievod cel Bun, the son of Vlad voievod Călugărul [the document later describes the gifts bestowed to the monastery of Govora by Radu cel Bun]. In the days of Vlad voievod Ţepeş, this boyar, Albu cel Mare, tried to take the throne from him, but Vlad voievod went with his army against him and caught him, together with his whole family. When Vlad Voievod saw the holy monastery devastated, he granted these villages, Glodul and Hinţea, to it...

Source: *Documente privind istoria României, veacul XVI, B. Ţara Românească, vol. III (1551-1570)*. Bucureşti: Editura Academiei Republicii Populare Române, 1952, p. 4.

Appendix II

Ottoman Chronicles concerning
Vlad III Dracula

A. Tursun Beg — Tarih-i Ebu-l Feth-i Sultan Mehmed-han
B. As'k-pasa-zade — Tarih-i al-i Osman
C. Mehmed Nesri — Djihannuma, Tarih-i al-i Osman
D. Anonymous Chronicle — Tevarih-i al-i Osman
E. Sa'adeddin Mehmed Hodja Efendi — Tadj-üt Tevarih

A. Tursun Beg
Tarih-i Ebu-l Feth-i Sultan Mehmed-han
(written c. 1497-1500)

The Description of the Expedition against the Voievod Vlad Țepeș, [*Kazîklî*, the Impaler] the Disobedient Ruler of the Infidels of Wallachia. The Destruction of this Voievod and his country, as well as his replacement by his brother, Radu cel Frumos.

When the bloody tyrant and merciless Infidel [Vlad III Dracula] became the ruler of Wallachia, the Sublime Porte obliged him to pay a great tribute. Every year he would come himself to the Porte, bringing the tribute and many gifts and he would renew his princely rights.

The Sultan would send him back to his country, offering him precious clothes, the red gown and other princely presents. But Vlad Țepeș was a merciless tyrant for the Infidels. His cruelty was so great that if someone in a village committed some unlawful act, he could impale all the inhabitants of that village, including women and children. In front of the wooden fortress where he had his princely residence, Vlad Țepeș ordered two rows of fences, protected by brambles, to be built for six miles, saying that he wanted to make a garden. Then he filled up the area between the two fences with impaled Hungarians, Moldavians, and Wallachians. Beside the fortress, which was surrounded by woods, on every branch of the trees many people were hanged and Vlad Țepeș ordered that anyone who would take down one of the hanged men be hanged in his place on the same tree.

Thus, finding support in the Sublime Porte, he defeated the Hungarians, killing many of them, as well as other voievods as powerful as himself. But victory made him too confident of his own power and when the Sultan was away on the long expedition in Trebizond, driven by his arrogance and his inclination to quarrel, he planned to cause damage to the Ottoman countries. As he had reached the throne with the help of the Sublime Porte, this deed could not go unpunished.

...Putting him to the test, they asked him to give the proper tribute and he was ordered to come himself to the Sublime Porte. But this wicked, cowardly man withdrew his submission, concocting different pretexts and excuses.

He said he had no more resources to pay the tribute, for the Hungarian enemy was strong and represented an obstacle in his way. He also said that the Sublime Porte was too far for him to come and that he had spent everything he had in battles that year in order to defend himself against his enemies.

...He neither came nor paid the tribute. Then he had to be punished and destroyed. When the spring of the year 866 [October 1461 to 25 September 1462] came, the colors of triumph waved on their way to Wallachia. An army of about 30 tümen (300,000 men) crossed the Danube; the land of Wallachia shone in the presence of the Sultan. The Turkish army boldly started fighting and destroying.

...The truth is that one day Mahmud Pasha, one of the wisest viziers, sent scouts ahead and ordered them to gather reliable information about those places. He also sent reconnaissance troops in front of the glorious tent [of the Sultan].

Verses:
On one sunny morning
The Sultan became the ruler of the victorious army.

The whole sky seemed to move. The army looked like powerful waves on the sea. When they got closer to the established place, the front lines of the army announced that there was not a drop of water to quench their thirst. All the carts and animals stopped there. The heat of the sun was so great that one could cook kebabs on the mail shirts of the gazis. This is why the angry Sultan accused the commanders of carelessness. At the same time the scouts were scolded and punished. As there was no water in that place, they had to advance. After thousands of difficulties and troubles they reached the next locality and they pitched the Sultan's tent and the tents of the soldiers. But hardly had they dismounted and put down their swords and spears, when they found out that the enemy was coming. The truth was that the voievod of Wallachia [Vlad Ţepeş] had ordered one of his commanders to be near that place with 7,000 soldiers chosen to protect the country against his Moldavian enemies. The victorious one [the Sultan] had sent Ali-bey to make an incursion into those parts. The Infidels, hearing the noise of his horses and being eager [to destroy] his tired soldiers, had hidden in the pass.

Vlad Ţepeş was thinking that the brave soldiers would be very tired on their way back and that he would defeat them by blocking their path. But, just like [the Koran] verse says: "The Alimighty Allah helps the believers." Allah's help was evident as something unexpected happened to the Infidels. Finding no water, the army was led towards that band of wicked Infidels. Because of the woods and high weeds, the Infidels knew nothing about the arrival of the victorious army. As the corps of scouts advanced in scattered little groups, the Infidels knew nothing about the arrival of the victorious army, divided their army into ten units and attacked the army of Rumelia. When it was announced that the enemy had arrived, the army, as vast as the sea, was ordered to remain silent; the janissaries and the army of Anatolia remained still, ready to fight. His Highness, the Sultan, ordered to Mehmed-Pasha to meet the enemies. To obey the instructions he was chosen to carry out, he put in good order his soldiers and strengthened both of his flanks.

Turhan-bey-oglu, Omer-bey, Ali-bey-oglu, Ahmed-bey, Mihalogly Ali-bey, and Malkoci-oglu Bali-bey, as well as many other famous beys, were on the right flank of the army. Nasuh-bey of Arnavut [Albania], Deli-oglu Urmur-bey of Iania, and Mihal-oglu Iskender-bey, along with other emirs of their rank, were on the left flank of the army. Thus protected, he advanced towards the enemy. When the Infidels left the shelter of the woods and saw them, as well as their banners waving in the wind, they realized immediately that they were defeated and terror seized their hearts.

Verses:
They couldn't fight for a minute the powerful swords ready
to shed blood
And then they bowed their heads and bodies to the blows
of swords and spears.

Being devastated, the Infidels fled. The victorious gazis slaughtered the Infidels with their bloody swords as if they had cut cucumbers, and also took prisoners. A troop of horsemen which had fled from the battlefield met Evrenos-bey-oglu's troops in the steep valleys. The Turks had taken many prisoners and much plunder and most of them were tired and had dismounted from their horses. They were walking, knowing nothing of what had happened. Suddenly, the Turks saw a troop of Infidels coming towards them and thought that they would not be able to resist. Yet, trusting themselves to Allah's help, they decided to fight the enemy. The Infidels were defeated and fled in all directions. When they found out that the Infidels were vanquished, they started pursuing them, destroying what was left of them. Of 7,000 Infidels only 700 escaped. When, with Allah's help, this great and holy expedition was finished, they loaded the heads of the Infidels on their camels and mules. Besides this, each soldier put on top of his sword the head of an Infidel; their swords looked like snakes with the heads of men. The sky was an amazing sight. Hundreds and thousands of Infidels were brought in chains to the victorious Court. After the evening service, torches were lighted and the triumphant Sultan sat on his chair. Then the Infidels, resembling dragons and as evil as Ahriman [God of Evil in Persian mythology], were brought to him.

The janissaries and the army of the Sublime Porte killed the Infidels in a second with their blood thirsty swords.

...When this Happy feast ended, the Sultan and his army, as numerous as the stars in the sky, thanked the omnipotent Allah for this joy. He [the Sultan] also made presents to his beys and soldiers.

...With Allah's help, for almost 30 days the glorious army moved like the waves on the sea through Wallachia. Plunder, as well as young prisoners, both boys and girls, were taken by the Imperial army. But all of a sudden, Vlad Ţepeş left his peaceful shelter in the east and headed towards the west. It was a dark night when he planned his deception. The wicked horseman [Vlad Ţepeş], an evil man, planned to fight with his army against the powerful victorious Imperial army. He knew that Allah helps the just, but as a verse from the Koran says, the Infidels didn't know that they could only end up being destroyed if they came against an ocean [of armies]. Then he tried to execute his plan. One night [the Sultan] received news about this wicked man and thoroughly examined the situation of the Turkish soldiers in the clear light of the moon. The soldiers of the Infidel, having gathered, attacked the Imperial army, but it was as if a drop of water fell into the ocean. They first encountered the army from Anatolia and they read verses of welcome and death to them, as they deserved. They could not pass quickly through the tents of the victorious army of the Sublime Porte and the tents of the janissaries, but they found what they were looking for. They were adequately welcomed; their mouths were filled with spears.

Verses:
So much enemy blood was shed that the black sky became as red as a tulip,
And the brilliance of the swords in the dark night made it look a blossomed flower.

Most of them were wounded or killed while they were trying to run away. In the confusion of the darkness they advanced towards the center of the army, thinking that it was the way out and that they would be saved. In fact, they came across the soldiers from Rumelia and they were responsible for their own destruction. When numerous candles and torches were lit in each tent and when the shouts of the brave soldiers ready to fight were heard here and there, the mean Infidels lost their heads and scattered, having lost all presence of mind, like a bird which, blinded by the light, throws itself right into the fire. Most of them, leaving their horses and trying to escape, entered the Turkish tents and fought against the brave troops. Their defeat was so great that even ten-year old children, who were apprentices and servants in the army, killed many Infidels twice as powerful as themselves. It was all the fault of that wicked man with broken wings and a heart pierced by the spears and swords of the brave soldiers. He finally found a safe place, left the battle, and ran away severely wounded, almost dead, accompanied by a few of his men.

Verse:
It was his desire to come and to flee in a hurry as well.

Not even a quarter of his army survived. The captured were divided into three groups. The heads of those belonging to the first were cut off to nourish the swords, and then were placed on top of the spears... A second group of soldiers were taken prisoner. They had chosen the path of deception, and they tried to look friendly while they behaved as enemies; they proved to be treacherous. This is why, as the Koran says, the powerful sword must fall upon them and split them in two, 3,700 Infidels were brought to the Sultan alive and then cut in two. A third group was formed of those who had left the battlefield wounded, nearly dead. Those whose chests were pierced by swords died and their abject souls flew through the woods towards the Valley of Hell. Thus, they were saved from the torments of their serious wounds. A few Infidels, but not many, saved themselves by fleeing with Vlad Țepeș. In their despair they took refuge in the land of the Hungarians. He had caused many disasters for the Hungarian King, and now he had brought about his own destruction. Trying to escape from the lion's claws, he had chosen the claws of a bird of prey. The Hungarian King took him prisoner. And there he sent his soul to Hell.

Verses:
You must never believe that a bad man will do any good;
His head must be cut off or he be hanged.

...The revenge being over, the conquering Sultan gave the throne of that country to the brother of that wicked man, named Radu voievod, who had been accepted by the Porte a long time before and had worked for the Imperial Court for many years. The Sultan gave him the decorated flag, the sword, and the symbols of power. The Turkish army, which had taken abundant plunder, prepared for feasts and each victorious soldier returned to his home. The Sultan, the conqueror of the world, started, with Allah's permission, on his way towards Adrianople, accompanied by the dignitaries of his court.

Source: *Cronici turcești privind țările române, extrase, vol. I, sec. XV-mijlocul sec. XVII.* Mihail Guboglu and Mustafa Mehmet, eds. (București, 1966), pp. 67-73.

B. Asik-Pasa-Zade
Tarih-i Al-i Osman
(written late 15th century)

How Mehmed II went to Wallachia and what he did there.

You should understand that when the Sultan came back to Istanbul from the expedition in Trebizond, Ishak Pasha who had remained in Rumelia, also came to Istanbul. Emissaries also arrived from the neighboring areas. An emissary from Wallachia also came. This emissary was accompanied back to Wallachia by a messenger sent to call the Prince of Wallachia to the Porte.

When this messenger arrived, he delivered his message to the Prince of Wallachia. The Prince told the messenger: "My people are not faithful to me. If I leave my country and go there they will bring a Hungarian and give him the throne. I hope that the Sultan will immediately send one of the beys from the neighboring regions to the Danube so that he can protect my country while I go and pay homage to the Sultan."

The Sultan believed the words of this Infidel and sent the bey, Hamza Ceakirdjiba, to him. This bey went and remained at the border of the Danube. The Turks then went about their own business. The Danube was frozen solid at that time.

The bey of Wallachia, that damned son of a bitch, attacked Hamza bey about midnight. He killed many Turks and took Hamza bey prisoner. The Infidels crossed the Danube at several places and made an incursion into the regions neighboring Wallachia and plundered, causing much damage in that vilayet.

He [Vlad III Dracula] cut off the head of Hamza bey, which he sent, together with the heads of other Muslims, to the Hungarian King with the message: "I am now an enemy of the Turks." All the Infidel rulers heard this and believed that this Infidel had indeed become an enemy of the Sultan...

When the Sultan found out that this damned Infidel uses such deception, he gathered his army and advanced with it, announcing that he had planned an expedition against him. He crossed the Danube after an initial attack and he entered Wallachia. All the inhabitants of Wallachia came and surrendered to the Sultan, only Țepeș voievod did not. For a while the Sultan wandered all over Wallachia. One night he was unexpectedly attached, but his brave soldiers were ready to fight. When they realized that the attack was made by the devilish Ţepeş and that he himself led it, the soldiers remained still, allowing him to get closer to the Turkish army. When he was right in the middle of the army, the soldiers shouted "Allah be blessed!" and slaughtered them so badly that more than half of the Infidels were killed. The slaughter lasted until dawn and Ţepeş voievod barely got away alive. In the morning Ali-bey was sent to pursue him. The soldiers who had accompanied Ţepeş were disloyal boyars. They all gathered and went to beg the forgiveness of the Sultan, kneeling down in front of him and submitting themselves to him.

Ţepeş had a younger brother who was in the Sultan's Court where he was working. The Sultan gave the throne of Wallachia to him asking the nobles to accompany him. After he plundered the country, the Sultan went back triumphantly to his throne.

This expedition against the Infidels took place in the year 866 [6 October 1461 to 25 September 1462], being led by Sultan Mehmed-Han.

Source: *Cronici turceşti privind ţările române, extrase, vol. I, sec. XV-mijlocul sec. XVII.* Mihail Guboglu and Mustafa Mehmet, eds. (Bucureşti, 1966), pp. 92-94.

C. Mehmed Nesri

Djihannuma, Tarih-i al-i Osman

(written c. 1512-1520)

The Holy Expedition in Wallachia

When the Sultan Mehmed came back to Istanbul from the expedition in Trebizond, Ishak-Pasha also came to Istanbul from Adrianople. Emissaries from everywhere arrived. There was also an emissary from Vlad Ţepeş. The Sultan ordered a messenger to accompany his emissary, and this messenger asked Vlad Ţepeş to come to the Porte. The voievod said to the messenger: "My country is not faithful to me. If I leave and go to the Porte, my subjects will bring a Hungarian and make him Prince and my country will not obey me any longer. I hope the Sultan will send one of his beys, a neighbor of ours, on the border of the Danube, who can protect the country so I'll be free to go and bow to the Sublime Porte." The Sultan believed his words and sent Hamza-bey. Meanwhile, the Danube had completely frozen, Hamza bey made his camp on the shore of the Danube. While his soldiers spent their time leisurely, this wicked man, called Ţepeş Voievod, son of Dracul, crossed the frozen Danube at midnight and attacked Hamza bey, killing many Moslems. He took Hamza bey prisoner and killed Iunus-bey who died like a martyr. The Infidels crossed the Danube in several places and attacked those regions causing much damage. Afterwards he cut off the head of Hamza-bey and sent it to the Hungarian King, with the message: "I am now an enemy of the Turks." Everybody found out that he was an enemy of the Sultan. To put it briefly, when the Sultan was told about the treachery that damned Infidel had planned, he gathered the Turkish army and announced he was undertaking a holy expedition. They advanced and crossed the Danube and invaded Wallachia. All the inhabitants of Wallachia came and bowed to him, only Ţepeş voievod had disappeared without a trace. The Sultan traveled all over Wallachia for a time; one night he was unexpectedly attacked. Being forewarned, his soldiers got ready to fight. When they realized that Ţepeş voievod was attacking them at night, they [the Turks] remained still, until his [Dracula's] soldiers scattered among them. The Turkish soldiers then shouted Allah's name and fought against the Infidels. They slaughtered so many of them that not even half of the Infidels survived. Ţepeş barely escaped with life. In the morning they sent Ali-bey to pursue him. The remainder of Ţepeş' army surrendered and knelt in front of the Sultan, accepting slavery. Ţepeş had a younger brother [Radu cel Frumos], who was in the Sultan's court. The latter gave him the throne of Wallachia and an entourage to accompany him. Afterwards, the Sultan took great plunder from Wallachia and went back to

his glorious throne. This holy expedition took place in the year 866
[6 October 1461 to 25 September 1462].

Source: *Cronici turceşti privind ţările române, extrase, vol. I, sec. XV-mijlocul
sec. XVII.* Mihail Guboglu and Mustafa Mehmet, eds. (Bucureşti, 1966),
pp. 125-127.

D. Anonymous Chronicle
Tevrih-i Al-i Osman
(written c. mid-sixteenth century)

In the year 865 [17 October 1460 to 5 October 1461], Sultan
Mehmed ordered a new expedition in Wallachia and crossed the
Danube. Ţepeş attacked them one night. He was defeated, so he ran
away. All his army was killed and he was alone. He left his country
and throne and went to Hungary. In the end the Hungarian King
killed Ţepeş. Sultan Mehmed named the brother of Ţepeş [Radu cel
Frumos] Prince of Wallachia. Afterwards, Sultan Mehmed, having
obtained the complete submission of Wallachia, sent ships on the sea
and he conquered by battles on land and sea the Island and the city of
Mitilene. Wallachia and the Island of Mitilene were both conquered
in the same year, 866 [6 October 1461 to 25 September 1462].

Source: *Cronici turceşti privind ţările române, extrase, vol. I, sec. XV-mijlocul
sec. XVII.* Mihail Guboglu and Mustafa Mehmet, eds. (Bucureşti, 1966),
p. 186.

E. Sa'Adeddin Mehmed Hodja Efendi
Tadj-Ut-Tevarih
(written c. 1584)

The Expedition of the Sultan (Mehmed II) in Wallachia

...Emissaries came and brought gifts after the conquest of Constantinople, showing the Sublime Porte the submission of those who
had sent them. Emissaries of Vlad Ţepeş, the Prince of Wallachia,
came too, bringing rich gifts. In days of yore Dracul, who was the

father of Vlad Ţepeş, had paid tribute and was supported by the Sultan. This is why his son was treated kindly. Whenever his emissary came to the Sublime Porte, bringing abundant gifts to show his master's devotion, he was rewarded with Imperial favors for his loyalty and submission. But the wickedness of his abject character was revealed by treachery; he considered that the expedition of the Sultan in Trebizond would be a good opportunity to fulfill his evil plans.

Ishak-Pasha had been given the task of defending Rumelia, and during his governorship the region had flourished. Ishak-Pasha came to the Sublime Porte and, after the ceremony of kissing the Sultan's hand, he revealed the bad deeds and the disloyal behavior of Ţepeş voievod. He told the all conquering Sultan about the troubles caused by Vlad Ţepeş to the inhabitants of the Turkish countries, as well as about the borders he had established.

...His conduct was revealed to the Sultan.

(Vlad Dracula will be punished for he is considered a rebel.)

The commanders and great emirs received orders to prepare the victorious army.

But before this, the black-hearted one [Vlad Ţepeş] was called to the Sublime Porte to kneel before the Sultan. That malicious man pretended to submit and invented the following excuse: "My people are rash and my boyars and high officials are treacherous. If I go to kneel down the Sublime Porte which protects me, then they would submit to the Hungarian, put him in my place, and give him my throne and my wealth. I am always trying to find some opportunity to kiss the feet of the throne and to wipe away the dust from the Imperial horse to show my submission and devotion. All these thoughts have been present in my mind since long ago, but for the reasons already explained, my desire could not be fulfilled. If this is thought wise, let one of the emirs ruling the neighboring parts come to protect my country. Then I am sure to go and kneel to the Sublime Porte and to dust with my eyelashes the throne of the Empire."

The Prince of Wallachia succeeded in hiding his hostility and persuaded the great Sultan to listen to his request. His false words piercing the Sultan's heart, a firman was issued for Hamza-bey, the bey of Nicopolis, to go to Wallachia and defend it, together with other emirs, until Vlad Țepeș would be back from the Sublime Porte. Hamza-bey obeyed the orders written in the firman and advanced, although the weather was horrible, because of the ruthless winter.

(The bad weather is described.)

The Danube was frozen. Hamza-bey, together with his companions, made his camp on the river banks, where death came upon those brave soldiers. While the Turkish army was carefully crossing the frozen Danube, Țepeș voievod attacked it late at night and defeated it, killing most of the Turkish soldiers. [Vlad Țepeș] took vengeance on Iunus-bey, and killed him, along with Hamza-bey, whose head was sent to the Hungarian King.

Turning away from the rightful submission to the Sultan, [Vlad Țepeș] declared that he rejected it. This abject fraud of Țepeș was announced to the Grand Divan and the army was prepared. In accordance with the firman, it began to conquer Wallachia in the spring of the year 866 [6 October 1461 to 25 September 1462].

Shouting "Allah, lead us to victory!" the soldiers passed through many places, with their numerous flags waving in the wind. One bright day they reached the borders of Wallachia; Mahmud-Pasha, being the ruler of the victorious army, was the first to cross the Danube. He was followed by the Great Sultan with the rest of the glorious army; they inflicted such a merciless punishment on Wallachia that it seemed as if the end of the world had come, shedding much blood with their terrifying swords. [Vlad Țepeș], unable to fight against the brave army, fled and hid in places too difficult to reach.

Mevlana Idris[1] said that Ali-bey Evrenos-oglu had been appointed commander of an army that was sent to plunder Wallachia, while Mahmud-Pasha's troops formed the advanced detachment of the Imperial army... [Mahmud-Pasha] arrived at a place where it was impossible to find a single drop of water for a great distance.

(The suffering from thirst the Turks had to endure is poetically described.)

...While the Turkish army was still searching for water, a large troop of Infidels was seen. As [Vlad] Ţepeş was an old enemy of the Prince of Moldavia, the latter had considered the victorious arrival of the Sultan to be a good opportunity, and was ready to devastate Wallachia. When he found it out, [Vlad Ţepeş] sent a troop of villains to prevent an invasion by the Moldavians.

Being told that Ali-bey and his soldiers had taken as much plunder as they wanted, the Wallachians attacked the victorious soldiers of the Almighty Sultan which they mistook for the soldiers of Ali-bey. They drew their swords out of their sheaths and they mounted big and restless horses, attacking the brave soldiers of Rum [the army of Anatolia].

The triumphant Sultan, realizing that the vile Infidels advanced towards the victorious army, remained in the middle of his army, shining like the north star. He ordered his viziers and emirs to surround him and sent famous warriors to different places.

He asked Turhan-oglu Omer-bey, Evrenos-oglu Ahmed-bey, Mihail-oglu Ali-bey, Malkoci-oglu Bali-bey, and others to be on his right flank, and Nasuh-bey, the ruler of Albania, Deli-oglu Urmur-bey, Mihail-oglu Iskender and other renowned beys, full of glory, to be on his left flank, ordering them to fight against the hateful enemy. When the Infidels were in front of the Turks, it was suddenly dark because of the heavy swords of the angels helping the Turkish army.

---

[1]Hakimeddin Idris bin Husameddin Ali el-Bitlisi, Turkish historian (died in 1520), the author of a chronicle in Persian which describes events up to the reign of Bayezid II.

...Seven thousand Infidels were slaughtered, and the others were taken prisoner and put in chains. After this brilliant deed, the brave Sultan stayed for a month in Wallachia and enjoyed himself.

Being told about the defeat of his army which he had sent to prevent the Moldavians attack, [Vlad] Ţepeş found nothing better to do than to attack the mighty Sultan [Mehmed II]. On a dark night, his heart full of wickedness and accompanied by his Infidel army, he flew like a black cloud towards the army of the wise Sultan, attacking him. The all conquering Sultan knew about the vile enemy's attack and all his troops were on the watch. They were ready to fight and he was careful that everything should be prepared. At midnight, the army of Wallachia started like a torrent towards the Imperial camp and made their way on horse into the middle of the triumphant army. The Turkish soldiers thrust their fiery swords deep into their black hearts. The heaps of corpses which poisoned [the earth] were so high that the victims of the slaughter could be easily seen even on such a dark night. With Allah's help, the lives of the Turkish soldiers were protected from the numerous attacks of the abject enemy. The soldiers gathered their courage and were quick in stabbing and cutting off the hands of the enemies. They surrounded the vile troops, attacked them from one side and killed numerous Infidels with their swords. They surrounded them in the middle of the battlefield, leaving no escape for the Infidels.

(The description of the battle until dawn is given in prose and verse.)

...Although [Vlad] Ţepeş fought bravely, he decided to run away with a few of his men, for he was no longer as powerful as he had been before. An ocean of blood had covered the earth in those places so that no matter what direction his horse took he had to walk in blood and on wounded bodies. Seeing the dead everywhere and believing that he was followed by the ghosts of Akbekir,[2] he [Vlad

---

[2]A hero in the Persian mythology.

Țepeș] was terrified, Mihail-oglu Ali-bey obeyed the Sultan's orders and, accompanied by his courageous soldiers, he started pursuing Vlad Țepeș. Finally, being too frightened by the defeat the Great Sultan, he fled to the Hungarian lands. The Conquering Sultan killed all those who still resisted him in various places throughout the country and became the master of the wealth and people of Wallachia, so that the plunder of the Turkish army was very great.

The Wallachian throne, being under the suzerainty of the Great Sultan, was given to Radu voievod, who was the brother of Vlad Țepeș. As he had worked at the Sublime Porte, he was faithful and loyal. After Wallachia was subjugated in that year, the Sultan discharged the victorious army.

Source: *Cronici turcești privind țările române, extrase, vol. I, sec. XV-mijlocul sec. XVII*, Mihail Guboglu and Mustafa Mehmet, eds. (București, 1966), pp. 317-321.

Extracts from the Chronicle of Laonic Chalkondyles concerning Vlad III Dracula

Book IX

...To Vlad [Dracula]... the Emperor [Sultan Mehmed II] granted the rule of Dacia [Wallachia]; and with the help of the Emperor, Vlad, the son of Drăculea [Vlad II Dracul], invaded and took the throne. Soon after he began his rule he created a personal guard which he always kept by his side; after this, he sent for some of his boyars, one by one, whom be thought might be treasonous and plot to overthrow him, and he had them mutilated and impaled, together with their wives, children, and servants, so that we heard that he alone among the men, about whom we know, killed the most people. To strengthen his power, he killed, in a short time, twenty thousand men, women, and children; he surrounded himself with a number of distinguished and devoted soldiers and servants to whom he gave the money, wealth, and social positions of those he killed, so that in a short time he brought about a radical change, and this man completely altered the organization of Dacia. And the Hungarians, not a small number, who thought that they might play a role in public affairs, he spared none of them, and had them killed in great numbers. And when he had consolidated his rule over Dacia, the thought occurred to him to get rid of the Emperor. But these people he had killed with the consent of the Emperor to strengthen his rule, unless he would have trouble with the leading citizens of Dacia who might take up arms and appeal to their Hungarian allies for assistance.

...And then, in the winter, when the Emperor heard that he had evil thoughts on his mind, and that, appealing to the Hungarians, he entered into some kind of alliance with them, he believed that it was a very serious thing. Sending a skillful man from the Porte, a Greek scholar, he called him to Constantinople, on the understanding that if he came to the Porte nothing unpleasant would happen to him, but on the contrary, as he had worked in the interests of the Emperor, he would receive favors and rewards in excess of the good he had done for the Emperor. With such orders he sent Catavolinos, the messenger of the Porte, to him. And to Chamuza [Hamza-beg], appointed the hawk-keeper, who had been given the task of ruling a large land at the Istru [Danube] and was made governor of Vidin [Nicopolis], he sent a secret order that he would be well paid if by some ploy he could capture and bring this man [Vlad] to him, by any means he could, through trickery or in another way. Thus, telling to the messenger that he wanted to capture this man, they agreed on the arrangements they made for this purpose, namely that when Vlad was coming back with him, he [Chamuza] would have a trap already prepared for him in great secret in his own country and that they could capture him; the scholar was supposed to send word to him when they were starting out. The scholar did this and secretly indicated the exact time he was leaving with Vlad, and Chamuza waited at that very spot. But Vlad, with his armed men, on his way back to the leader of the Porte, became aware that it was a trap and ordered that they [Catavolinos and Chamuza] should be captured, together with their followers. When Chamuza launched his attack, he [Vlad] fought remarkably well and defeated and captured him, and killed many of those who fled. As soon as he captured them, he had them taken away and impaled, after first mutilating them. For Hamza he prepared a higher stake; and to the servants he did the same as to their masters. And after this, he immediately prepared, as best he could, a large army and started directly for the Istru, and passing through the places along the Istru to the lands of the Emperor, he slaughtered all of the inhabitants, with women and children, and set fire to the houses, burning everything where he went. And after having killed a great many he returned to Dacia.

When Emperor Mehmed was informed about this, that his messengers had been killed by Vlad, Prince of Dacia, along with Chamuza, a high official at the Porte, who was put to death without any negotiation, as was usual, he became very angry, quite understandably, and thought that he could not just ignore the killing of such people and be slow to punish the impudence of this man, who went so far as to kill his emissaries. He did not ask the Prince of Dacia for any explanations for their deaths. He was also angry that he [Vlad] had crossed the Istru with many soldiers, and that after he had killed many of his subjects, he had returned home unharmed. But of all this, he considered what he had done to his messengers to be the most serious. That is why he sent word to his high officials everywhere, and told others to come to his Court, armed and in good order, because he was going to war with his armies. Thus, he prepared the expedition against the Dacians...

After his armies were prepared for war, the Emperor immediately started out for Dacia in the early spring. People say that this army was very large, second only to the one the Emperor took against Byzantium. This camp is said to have been more beautiful than other camps, and to have been well supplied with weapons and equipment, the army being as large as two hundred and fifty thousand men. And this can be learned easily from the bankers who worked at the crossing point of the Istru, and who had bought the rights to cross the river from the Emperor for 300,000 galbens, and it is said that they made a lot of money. On land, the army started out from Philippopolis, while on the sea twenty-five triremes and one hundred and fifty boats also set out towards the Istru, with the idea of crossing at Vidin. And he ordered that these ships should sail up the Black Sea to the Istru. And the fleet, following the orders of the Emperor, set out on the Black Sea to the mouth of the Istru; as soon as they reached the mouth, they went up the river to Vidin. And wherever the fleet stopped they burned the houses, and setting fire, they burned down Brăila, the Dacian's city, where there is more trade than in all the other cities of the country. Because, almost everywhere the houses are made of wood. But the Dacians, when they heard that the Emperor was coming there, put their women and children in hiding places, some of them on the mountain of Braşov, others in a city named... [omitted in text], around which there was a swamp, so that they could strengthen and defend it naturally and protect it very well. And some others they sheltered in oak forests, hard to cross for a man who had just come and who was not a resident, as they are so thick with trees that one can barely enter them. Thus, they hid their women and children in his manner, and they, gathering together, followed Prince Vlad. He divided his army in two, keeping one part with him, and sending the other against the Prince of Black Bogdania [Moldavia], to keep him back if he tried to invade the country. Because this Prince of Black Bogdania had had a misunderstanding with Vlad, he was at war with him and, sending messengers to Emperor Mehmed, he said that he was ready to join him in his war against Vlad. The Emperor was pleased to hear this and urged this Prince to have his commanding general join with the commander of his fleet at the river, and that together they should lay siege to the city called Chilia, which belonged to Vlad, at the mouth of the river. Thus, this man gathered up the army of his country and hurried to join with the Emperor's fleet at Chilia. When he arrived there, they both laid siege to the city and bombarded it for several days, but they were repelled and lost several men. As they could not conquer the city, they both retreated. And then Black Bogdan [the Moldavian, i.e., Stephen the Great] invaded the country of the Dacians, but he was stopped by one of the armies which was sent there to defend the country. And, Vlad with the larger part of his army with him, stayed in the forest, waiting to see which way the Emperor's army was headed. But the Emperor, after his armies crossed the Istru, headed directly for Dacia, not allowing his soldiers to wander of in search of plunder. He went straight for the city in which the Dacians had put their women and children, while they [Vlad's army] remained in the woods, always close to the Emperor; and if a detachment [of the Turkish army] happened to go astray, it was immediately destroyed by them. And so the Emperor, when he found that they would not come out in the open to fight him, and that the Hungarians had not come to help Vlad, he worried little about the safety of the camp; they made their camp in an open area. But Vlad, as soon as he found out about the invasion by his enemies, sent messengers to the Hungarians who said the following: "Hungarians, you know that we are your neighbors and that both our countries are next to the Istru. You have probably heard by now that the Emperor of the Turks is currently waging a terrible war against us, with a large army. And if he conquers Dacia, you know very well that he will not sit still, but will wage war against you, and your countrymen will suffer greatly at their hands. So it is time now that you should give us assistance and defend yourselves as well by keeping their army as far as possible from your country; please don't let them spoil our country and ruin and conquer our people. He [Mehmed II] also has with him our Prince's younger brother [Radu cel Frumos] to give him the throne of Wallachia. We hope that nothing comes of their intentions! When he began the war against Dacia he gave Vlad's younger brother high honors and money and many fine clothes, and he had him send word to Dacia, to the most influential boyars in the country. With this money he sent people as the Emperor urged him to do. But sending these people and things before him did him no good." Now the Hungarians, hearing such words from the messengers, considered these statements and felt obliged to help and defend them as best they could. And they began to gather an army.

As they were busy doing this, the Emperor proceeded with his army, setting fire to villages and taking any cattle he happened to find. His light cavalry brought very few slaves into camp and suffered severe losses whenever a part of it went astray. As to Vlad, it is said that he entered the Emperor's camp as a spy, and that, going around, he found out how the camp was set up. But I cannot believe that Vlad himself would take such a great risk, having so many spies at his disposal; I think this is an invention to accentuate his courage. He would also come in the daytime close to the camp and watch the Emperor's tents, Machmut's tent, and the market. Having less than 10,000 cavalrymen, some say he had no more than 2,000 cavalrymen with him, he started out at the end of the first night watch and he invaded the Emperor's camp. At first there was a lot of terror in the camp because people thought that a new foreign army had come and attacked them; scared out of their wits by this attack, they considered themselves to be lost as it was being made using torch-light and the sound of horns to indicate the place to assault. But the camp, truth to say, stayed in place without moving; the armies of these people are in the habit of never moving at night, even if a thief got inside or some trouble had started. And then the Turks, though seized with fear, stood their ground and sent word around that no one should move or they would be put to death on the orders of the Emperor. The Emperor's heralds encouraged them in this manner and urged them to stay in the places where they had been assigned, telling them the following words: "Muslims, be calm! You will soon see that the camp is under our control and that the Emperor's enemy is being punished for his daring behavior towards the Emperor." They would repeat such things often because if the army stood its ground the enemy would soon be defeated, but if they moved about all of them would certainly be killed because the Emperor would put them to death if they fled. When Vlad invaded the camp so quickly, the Asian army was the first to meet him and, after a short battle, they fled, trying to save their lives. But he [Vlad], using torch-light, proceeded with his army in closed ranks, and in good order they headed directly for the Emperor's tents. Missing their target, they fell upon the tents of Vizier Machmut and Vizier Isaac; and here there was a great battle and they killed the camels, donkeys, and other pack animals. Fighting in closed ranks, they had no losses worth mentioning, but if one of them went astray he was immediately killed by the Turks. The men around

Machmut, being brave, fought remarkably well, all of them being
infantrymen. The men in the camp also mounted their horses, except
for the soldiers in the Emperor's Court. They fought here for a long
time, but then, turning back, they headed for the Emperor's Court
where they found the soldiers around the Emperor's tents in good
fighting order. And, after fighting here for a short time, they [Vlad's
army] turned back towards the camp market, plundering, and killing
anyone who came their way. As it was nearly daybreak, they left the
camp, having suffered few losses that night. As for the Emperor's
armies, they are also said to have suffered few losses. At daybreak, the
Emperor summoned the best soldiers of the governors, and placing
them under the command of Ali, Michael's son, he ordered them to
pursue the Dacians as quickly as they could. So Ali took this army and
immediately led it against Vlad; after learning of his whereabouts, he
rode fast and caught up with Vlad's army and attacked it, killing
many of them. Capturing about 1,000 Dacians, he took them to the
camp of the Emperor. The Emperor had them all taken away and
killed.

And the Emperor's soliders, who caught one of Vlad's men that
night, took him to Machmut and they asked him who he was and
where he came from. Then, after he talked freely about everything,
they asked him if he knew where Vlad, the prince of Dacia, might be
at that time. And he replied that he knew very well, but that he dared
not speak about it out of fear. Then, when they told him that they
would kill him if he did not give the right answers, he kept saying that
he was ready to die anytime, but that he would not dare to reveal anything about that. Machmut, in wonder at all of this, would have liked
to kill the soldier, but said with some concern for his situation that if
he [Vlad] had a large enough army he could obtain great power.

All of this happened then as follows: after the Emperor entered
the country he was in a hurry to go directly to the city where Vlad
had his residence [Târgovişte]. And each night, wherever he stopped,
he put palisades all around his camp and strengthened it inside; he
kept it closed and put many guards on duty, as usual, and gave orders
that the soldiers should be armed day and night. Thus, advancing

with his army in serried lines further into Dacia, he arrived at the city in which Vlad had his princely residence. And the Dacians, who were prepared to fight the Emperor, opened the gates and were ready to fight the Emperor himself who was coming towards them with his army. The Emperor, passing by the city and failing to see any men on the walls, but only some cannon firing at his army, set up no camp, nor did he lay siege to the city. He marched on for about five kilometers when he saw his men impaled; the Emperor's army came across a field with stakes, about three kilometers long and one kilometer wide. And there were large stakes on which they could see the impaled bodies of men, women, and children, about twenty thousand of them, as they said; quite a spectacle for the Turks and the Emperor himself! The Emperor himself, in wonder, kept saying that he could not conquer the country of a man who could do such terrible and unnatural things, and put his power and his subjects to such use. He also used to say that this man who did such things would be worthy of more. And the other Turks, seeing so many people impaled, were scared out of their wits. There were babies clinging to their mothers on the stakes, and birds had made nests in their breasts. After Vlad had stayed close to the Emperor's armies, killing anyone who dared to go astray, either cavalryman or infantryman, he himself went against the prince of Black Bogdania who, as stated before, was laying siege to Chilia. He left behind an army of about six thousand men and ordered them to stay in the woods, close to the Emperor, and that if anyone went astray they should seize him and kill him. And he himself went after the prince of Black Bogdania; but as the Emperor started to turn back, the army he left behind attacked, thinking that theirs would be the glory if they did so. When news arrived that the enemy was attacking, everyone, except for the Emperor's Court, rose arms; Machmut ordered Iosuf to come out and meet the enemies. And Machmut himself stood beside his men in arms. But Iosuf, after he started out and engaged in battle, was defeated and fled to the Emperor's camp. But Omar, son of Turachan, who had also been ordered by Machmut to attack the enemies, met Iosuf on the way, pursued by the foes, and he began to scold him and told him the following: "Wretched man, where are you going? Don't you know the Emperor? How is he going to trust you when you are running away! Won't the Emperor himself treat you worse than he treats his enemies and soon give you an evil death if he sees that you have run away." With such words he cheered the man up, and returning with Omar, son of Turachan, they together fought the enemy, and they fought remarkably well. Before long they defeated the Dacians and chased them away and killed mercilessly; and they killed about two thousand of them. And placing their heads on spears they returned to the camp. He [the Emperor] appointed Omar governor of Thessaly; he was a former official at the time and having brave men he again joined the Emperor.

And so it happened to the second bold attack of the Dacians on the Emperor's army; and the Emperor took many slaves from the country because he gave a free hand to the light cavalry which rode all over the land and, bringing slaves back to their country, they made a lot of money. And driving cattle along as well, over two hundred thousand horses, oxen, and cows, the Emperor's armies came to the Istru River. They were scared, truth to say, of the Dacians who were by no means less courageous then before and continued to harass them on and off, so the Turks crossed the Istru in a great hurry. And the Emperor ordered Ali, son of Michael, to protect the rear; and when he came to the Istru he left Dracula [Radu cel Frumos], brother of Prince Vlad, inside the country to make a deal with the Dacians and bring the country under his control; and he ordered the governor of the land to be of assistance, while he himself went straight to his royal residence.

So the young Dracula [Radu cel Frumos] called each and every one to him and told him, "Dacians, what do you think will become of you in the future? Don't you know what great power the Emperor possesses, and that in a short while the armies of the Emperor will come upon you, plundering the land, and we will be deprived of everything that is left to us? Why should you not be the Emperor's friends? Then you will have peace in the country and in your homes. You know only too well that there are no cattle left. Look at all the great suffering you had to go through because of my brother, because you had sided with the heathen who brought such misfortune upon Dacia, the kind of which I have never seen before." Telling such things to the Dacians who had come to pay ransom for their relatives who were now slaves, he enticed and urged them to pass the word to others to come to him and trust him. So they came together; they knew that the young man was better for them than Prince Vlad, and they crossed over to him little by little. And the other Dacians, as soon as they realized it, deserted Vlad and sided with his brother. And as soon as he had an army ready he attacked and took the throne, and together with an army of the Emperor he conquered the country. Then his brother [Vlad], when the Dacians deserted him for his brother [Radu], realized that his killings were of no avail and he left for the Hungarians.

Book X

The Emperor's campaign against the Dacians unfolded this way, but Vlad, as soon as his brother attacked and conquered the country of Dacia, he himself, truth to say, went to the Hungarians. But the Hungarians, whose relatives he had killed in Dacia, brought the case to the Hungarian Emperor [Matthias Corvinus], son of Choniat [John Hunyadi], and, punishing him [Vlad] severely, the way a man who unjustly kills people deserves, put him in prison in the city of Belograd [Alba Iulia]...

Source: Laonic Chalcocondil, *Expuneri istorice*, trans. in Romanian by Vasile Grecu (Bucureşti, 1958), pp. 283-293.

The German Stories about Vlad III Dracula

About a mischievous tyrant called Dracula vodă

In the year of our Lord 1456 this Dracula vodă did and threatened to do terrible things in Wallachia, as well as in Hungary.

1. And the former governor [John Hunyadi] had the old Dracul [Vlad II Dracul, the father of Dracula] killed. And Dracula and his brother gave up their religion [Orthodoxy] and took an oath to defend the Christian [Catholic] faith.

2. In that same year he was anointed Prince of Wallachia. He immediately had Vladislav vodă [Vladislav II, Prince of Wallachia, 1448-1456], the former prince of that land, killed.

3. And then he invaded Transylvania and Țara Bârsei, namely Beckendorf [perhaps Brenndorf, i.e. Bod, near Brașov], which he burned. He captured many of the men and women, both young and old, and took them back to Wallachia, and when he got there he had them all impaled.

4. And then the young people, who were learning the language in his country, he had locked in a room and then burned it down. There were four hundred of them.

5. Then he held a great feast in his country where he ordered that the merchants and the leading citizens of Țara Bârsei should be impaled.

6. And then he had the people surrounded and impaled each and every one of them, both young and old.

7. And then he captured Dan cel Tânăr [Dan III, brother of Vladislav II] and forced him to dig his own grave and ordered that the funeral service be read according to the Christian ritual, and then he had him beheaded next to his tomb.

8. And then the King of Hungary and the Saxons of Transylvania sent messengers to him in Wallachia. There were 55 of them. Dracula entertained them as guests for five weeks and then ordered that stakes should be erected in front of their rooms. Thus, the messengers were very worried. He did this because he was afraid of treachery. In the meantime, he invaded Țara Bârsei and spoiled the rye and ruined all the corn in the fields. And the people were all captured outside of Brașov. Dracula went into Brașov as far as the chapel of St. Jakob and ordered that the suburbs of the city should be burned down. And no sooner had he arrived there, when early in the morning he gave orders that the men and women, young and old alike, should be impaled next to the chapel, at the foot of the mountain. He then sat down at a table in their midst and ate his breakfast with great pleasure.

9. And then, on St. Bartholomew's day, he ordered that two churches be burned down and plundered of their riches and holy vessels.

10. And then he sent his captain into a large village, named Codlea [a suburb of Brașov where St. Bartholomew's Church is located] and ordered his soldiers to set fire to it. And when his captain could not burn the village because of the resistance offered by the inhabitants, and returned to Dracula and told him, "I could not do what you asked me to do," he had the captain impaled.

11. And then the merchants and their entourage went with their goods from Ţara Bârsei to Brăila on the Danube; there were 600 of them. Dracula captured and impaled all of them on stakes, and took their goods by force.

12. And then he had a big copper cauldron built and put a lid made of wood with holes in it on top. He put the people in the cauldron and put their heads in the holes and fastened them there; then he filled it with water and set a fire under it and let the people cry their eyes out until they were boiled to death.

13. And then he invented frightening, terrible, unheard of tortures. He ordered that women be impaled together with their suckling babies on the same stake. The babies fought for their lives at their mother's breasts until they died. Then he had the women's breasts cut off and put the babies inside head first; thus he had them impaled together.

14. And then he ordered that many people should be impaled; all kinds of people, whether Christians, Jews, or Pagans, struggled and came whirling down like frogs. Then he had their hands and legs pinned down. And he would often say in his own language, "What a nuisance they are!" This was his way of having a good time.

15. And then he caught a Tartar who had stolen something. Then the other Tartars came and asked Dracula to set him free. He answered them by saying, "he must be hanged and you ought to do it yourselves." They responded that this was not their custom. Then Dracula had the Tartar boiled to death in a cauldron and forced the other Tartars to eat him, flesh and bones.

16. And then a high-ranking official came to him, to the very place where he had been impaling people. Dracula went there and looked at the stakes with the impaled corpses which looked like a vast forest. Then the official asked Dracula why he was walking around amidst the stinking smell. Dracula asked him, "Does it smell badly?" The man answered, "Yes, it does." Then the Dracula ordered that the man be put on a stake higher than the others so that he wouldn't smell anything.

17. And then one day a priest from his country gave a sermon saying that sins would not be forgiven unless goods that had not been lawfully acquired were returned to their rightful owner. Dracula asked the priest to came to his house for dinner. Dracula cut a slice of bread that he was about to eat. Meanwhile, the priest had taken a slice of bread and ate it. Then Dracula said to him, "Haven't you preached that sins will not be forgiven unless thing which have been taken are returned?" The priest said, "Yes, I have." Then Dracula asked him, "Why are you eating my bread which I myself have cut in slices?" Then he quickly had the priest impaled.

18. And then Dracula went to Transylvania, to Tâlmaci, and he had people shredded like cabbage and took others away to his country where he had them impaled.

19. Also, he asked his boyars to came to his house for a feast. When the feast was over, Dracula went to the oldest of them and asked him how many princes he thought the country had? And then he asked the others, one by one, the same question. They all said what they knew; one answered fifty, another thirty, but none of them answered that there had been seven of them, so he had them all impaled. There were five hundred of them altogether.

20. And then he put many people on spinning wheels and killed them. And he also did many other such inhuman cruelties that were talked about in many countries.

21. And then he had a mistress. She meant to make him happy and told him that she was pregnant with his child. Then Dracula asked nurses to see her and they told him that she was not pregnant, so he cut his mistress open, saying that he wanted to see where the baby was, or if there was one.

22. And then messengers from Sibiu came to Wallachia. When they returned home they told stories about the misfortune they had seen there, including impaled bodies, like a great forest.

23. And then in 1462 he went to Sistovul Mare [Nicopolis]. He killed more than five thousand people there of all races, Christians, Jews, and Pagans. Some of them were beautiful women and virgins

who were spared by Dracula's servants. They asked him to give them their hands in marriage. Dracula ordered that all of these men, together with their maidens, should be slaughtered with swords and spears, like cabbage. He did this because his country was a tributary state of the Turks and they would often demand he sent tribute. He told the Turkish emissaries that he himself would bring the tribute. The people of this country came on horseback and welcomed him, thinking that he had come to play tribute to the Sultan; one group after another came. When Dracula saw that he had achieved his aim, he killed all those who had come on horseback to greet him, as they had not taken any precautions. Dracula had all of Bulgaria burned down, and he impaled all of the people that he captured. There were 25.000 of them, to say nothing of those who perished in fires.

24. And then Dracula saw a man who was working, dressed in a short sleeve shirt. He asked the man if he had a wife. The man answered, "Yes, I have." Then Dracula ordered that she should be brought to him and he asked her what she did for a living. She replied, "I wash, cook, and weave." Then he ordered that she should be impaled because she had not made a long sleeve shirt for her husband. Then he [Dracula] gave him another woman and told her that she should make a long sleeve shirt for her man, unless she also wanted to be impaled.

25. And then about three hundred Tartars came to his country. He took three of the best of them and had them roasted whole, and then he obliged the others to eat them. And he told them, "You must eat each other, the lot of you, or else you must attack the Turks." And all of the Tartars were glad to start fighting against the Turks. Then Dracula had the men and their horses covered with cow hides. And the Turks' horses were scared by the smell of the cow hide and they began to run away. And while they were fleeing they entered a river, and many Turks were drowned. Then the Tartars returned again.

26. And then on a trip he met a monk of the barefooted [Franciscan] order who was traveling on a donkey. Then Dracula ordered that the monk and his donkey be impaled, one on top of the other.

27. And then one time some Saxons were sent to him. When they came to him, he asked them why they did not take off their caps. They replied and said that it was not their custom to take them off, even in front of their emperor. Then he ordered that their caps should be nailed to their heads, so that they would not fall off, so as to continue their custom and to strengthen it.

28. And then one time two monks came to his country. He ordered that they should come to him. And so they did. When they came to him, he called one of the monks over to him and asked him what was being said in the country about him. The monk was very scared of him and said: "They say many good things about you and that you are a Prince full of virtue and piety. The same things that I say about you." Then he put this monk under guard. And then they brought before him the other monk and he asked him the same question as the first. The other monk thought: "everyone must die, so I will only speak the truth," and he said, "you are the worst and greatest tyrant in the whole world, and I have never seen or heard of a man who has something good to say about you... And this I know to be the truth from many people." Then Dracula said, "You have told me the truth. For this reason I will let you live." And he set him free. Then he sent for the other and asked him to tell him the truth. Then he spoke like the other one. Then Dracula said to his boyars, "take him and have him impaled, for the truth, which he did not want us to know."

29. And then this Dracula would roast little children, and force their own mother to eat them. And he ordered that the breasts of many women be cut off, and he forced their men to eat them, and then he had all of them impaled.

30. And then he invited all of the beggars in his country to a great feast. After the meal, he ordered the doors in the hall where they ate and drank to be locked. And then he set fire to the house and all of them were burned. And he did this because he said that they ate the bread of people without working for it.

31. And then soon after, the king of Hungary [Matthias Corvinus] caught him and put him in prison for a long time. Later, he was baptized at Buda and showed great repentance. Therefore, the King of Hungary made this Dracula a great prince again, as before. And it is said that he did a multitude of good deeds, because he became a Christian [i.e. Catholic].

Additions to the St. Gall Manuscript

In the year 1460, on St. Bartholomew's Day, in the morning, Dracula crossed the forest with his servants and looked for all the Saxons, of both sexes, around the village of Almaş, and all those that he could gather together he ordered to be thrown, one on top of the other, like a hill, and to slaughter them like cabbage, with swords and knives. And their chaplain and the other who he did not kill immediately, he took back to his country, and there he had them hanged. And he ordered that the village and everything in it, including the people, who numbered more than 30.000, to be burned.

And then, from all the lands which are called Făgăraş, he took the people and brought them to Wallachia, men, women, and children, and he ordered that all of them be impaled.

And then, he ordered that more of his boyars be decapitated, and he took their heads and he used them to grow cabbage. After this, he invited their friends to his house and he gave them the cabbage to eat. And he said to them: "Now you eat the heads of your friends." After this he ordered that all of them be impaled.

And then he ordered that some of his people be buried naked to the navel. After this he ordered that they be shot. He also had many roasted and the skin peeled off of other.

Additions to the Strasbourg Printing of 1500

And then there was a fair in his country where the merchants had to leave all of their tents in place, just as in the daytime. During the night, Dracula went in all of their tents and took some of their money and put it in the tents of others, and he made a sign as to how much he took from or gave to each of them. And when day came, Dracula went to the tents and asked each one what he had lost, and he paid them this. But those who had found something and did not confess it, these he ordered to be impaled.

And then, once, merchants came to his country for a fair, and all of them complained that they could not make any money. When Dracula heard this, he bought all of their wares and gave them a good amount of money. Then the merchants came there again and brought other goods after the fair was finished. When Dracula found out about this, he ordered that all of them be brought before him and he said, "You are all bad men and liars. You keep complaining that you don't make any money, and as soon as you have sold your merchandise, you bring more." And he ordered that all of them be impaled.

And then, with great cunning, he had his treasure buried under water. And all of the workers, one after the other, he ordered to be killed, until the last one. And he had a boy with him whom he asked if he knew where his treasure was hidden. The boy told him that he didn't know anything about this, but he secretly found the place and Dracula killed him too, so that no one could know where it was or find his treasure.

Extract from the Chronicle of Antonius Bonfinius

The king [Matthias Corvinus] said that he was going to Walla-chia to free Dracula, to whom he had given in a lawful marriage one of his blood relatives, from the hands of the Turks. On his way there, I do not know the reason why because this was never understood clearly by anyone, he captured Dracula in Transylvania, but the other Dracula [Radu cel Frumos], whom the Turks had appointed Prince of that province, he approved of, against all expectations. The other he brought to Buda and punished him with ten years in prison.

People remember about Dracula that he was a man of unheard of cruelty and justice. About this I will say that Turkish messengers came to him to play respects, but refused to take off their turbans, accord-ing to their ancient custom, whereupon he strengthened their custom by nailing their turbans to their heads with three spikes, so that they could not take them off.

He impaled numerous Turks, and amidst them he had elegant discussions with his friends.

In addition, he invited all of the beggars, who had lost every-thing because of their laziness, the sick, and the poor to a great feast,

Vlad III Dracula

(Drawing based on a sixteenth century German manuscript)

By Octavian Ion Penda

but after they had their fill of food and wine, he had them burned to death.

And then he peeled the skin off the feet of Turkish prisoners and covered their wounds with salt, then brought goats to lick their salted soles.

He ordered a Florentine merchant, who feared and prayed for the safety of his money, to leave it in the middle of the road, and because he did not lie at all about the amount of his money, after leaving it at night, he let him go freely.

He behaved with such harshness in this barbarous country that everyone could have their things in safety, even in the middle of the forest.

In truth, later, Matthias restored him to his former rank. But he was finally killed in the war with the Turks, and his head was brought to Mehmed [II] as a gift.

Bibliography

A. Primary Sources

Armbruster, Adolf. "Jakob Unrests Ungarische Chronik," in *Revue roumaine d'histoire*, 13:3 (1974), pp. 473-508.

Bianu, I. "Ştefanu celu Mare: Câteva documente din archivulu de statu dela Milanu," in *Columna lui Traianu*, 4:1-2 (Ianuariu-Februariu, 1883), pp. 30-47.

Bisticci, Vespasiano da. *Renaissance Princes, Popes, and Prelates: The Vespasiano Memoirs, Lives of the Illustrious Men of the XVth Century.* Trans. William George and Emily Waters. New York, 1963.

Bogdan, Ioan, ed. *Documente privitoare la relaţiile Ţării Româneşti cu Braşovul şi Ţara Ungurească în secolele XV şi XVI, volumul I, 1413-1508.* Bucureşti: Institutul de Arte Grafice «Carol Göbl», 1905.

Bogdan, Ioan, ed. *Documentele lui Ştefan cel Mare.* 2 volumes. Bucureşti: Atelierele Grafice Socec & Comp., Societate Anonimă, 1913.

Bonfinius, Antonius. *Rerum Ungaricum Decades.* Volume III. I. Fogel, B. Ivanyi, L. Juhasz, eds. Leipzig, 1936.

Cazacu, Matei. *L'histoire du prince Dracula en Europe centrale et orientale (XVe siècle): Présentation, édition critique, traduction et commentaire.* Genève: Libraire Droz, 1988.

Chalcocondil, Laonic. *Expuneri istorice.* Trans. Vasile Grecu. Bucureşti: Editura Academiei, 1958.

"The Code of Stephan Dušan." Trans. Malcom Burr. Part I in *The Slavonic and East European Review,* 28:70 (November, 1949), pp. 198-217; Part II in *The Slavonic and East European Review,* 29:71 (April, 1950), pp. 516-539.

Conduratu C. Gr. *Michael Beheims Gedicht über den Woiwoden Wlad II Drakul. Mit Historischen und Kritischen Erläuterungen.* Bucureşti: Buchdruckerei "Eminescu," 1903.

Cronici turceşti privind ţările române, extrase, I, sec. XV-mijlocul sec. XVII. Mihail Guboglu and Mustafa Mehmed, eds. Bucureşti: Editura Academiei, 1966.

Da Lezze, Donado [Giovanni Maria degli Angiolelli]. *Historia Turchesca (1300-1514).* Ion Ursu, ed. Bucureşti: Ediţiunea Academiei Române, 1909.

Documente privind istoria României, veacul XVI, B. Ţara Românească, vol. III (1551-1570). Ion Ionaşcu, L. Lăzărescu-Ionescu, Barbu Câmpina, Eugen Stănescu, D. Prodan, and Mihail Roller, eds. Bucureşti: Editura Academiei, 1952.

Documenta Romaniae Historica, B. Ţara Românească, volumul I (1247-1500). P.P. Panaitescu and Damaschin Mioc, eds. Bucureşti: Editura Academiei, 1966.

Documenta Romaniae Historica, D. Relaţii între ţările române, volumul I (1222-1456). Ştefan Pascu, Constantin Cihodaru, Konrad G. Gündisch, Damaschin Mioc, and Viorica Pervain, eds. Bucureşti: Editura Academiei, 1977.

Doukas. *Decline and Fall of Byzantium to the Ottoman Turks.* Trans. Harry J. Magoulios. Detroit: Wayne State University Press, 1975.

Dragomir, Silviu. *Documente nouă privitoare la relaţiile Ţării Româneşti cu Sibiul.* Bucureşti: Cartea Românească, 1935.

Filipescu, Constantin Căpitanul [Radu Popescu]. *Istoriile domnilor Ţării Româneşti cuprinzînd istoria munteană de la început pănă la 1688.* N. Iorga, ed. Bucureşti: I.V. Socecu, 1902.

Filstich, Johann. *Încercare de istorie românească/Tentamen Historiae Vallachicae.* Adolf Armbruster, ed. Trans. Radu Constantinescu. Bucureşti: Editura Ştiinţifică şi Enciclopedică, 1979.

Górka, Olgierd. *Cronica epocei lui Ştefan cel Mare (1457-1499).* Bucureşti: M.O. Imprimeria Naţională, 1937.

Grecescu, Constantin and Dan Simonescu, eds. *Istoria Ţării Romîneşti, 1290-1690. Letopiseţul cantacuzinesc.* Bucureşti: Editura Academiei, 1960.

Gündisch, Gustav. *Urkundenbuch zur Geschichte der Deutschen in Siebenbürgen.* Vol. V (1438-1457). Bukarest: Editura Academiei, 1975.

Gündisch, Gustav. *Urkundenbuch zur Geschichte der Deutschen in Siebenbürgen.* Vol. VI (1458-1473). Bukarest: Editura Academiei, 1981.

Herodotus. *Herodotus.* Vol. II. Trans. A.D. Godley. Cambridge, MA: Harvard University Press, 1966.

Holban, Maria. *Călători străini despre ţările române.* Volume I. Bucureşti: Editura Ştiinţifică, 1968.

Hurmuzaki, Eudoxiu. *Documente privitoare la istoria românilor.* Volume I_2. Bucureşti, 1891.

Hurmuzaki, Eudoxiu. *Documente privitoare la istoria românilor.* Volume II^1. Bucureşti, 1891.

Hurmuzaki, Eudoxiu and N. Densuşianu. *Documente privitoare la istoria românilor.* Volume II^2. Bucureşti, 1891.

Hurmuzaki, Eudoxiu. *Documente privitoare la istoria românilor.* Volume VIII. Bucureşti, 1894.

Hurmuzaki, Eudoxiu and Nicolae Iorga. *Documente privitoare la istoria românilor.* Volume XV^1. Bucureşti, 1911.

Ionaşcu, Ion, Petre Bărbulescu, and Gheorghe Gheorghe. *Tratatele internaţionale ale României, 1354-1920: Texte rezumate, adnotări, bibliografie.* Bucureşti: Editura Ştiinţifică şi Enciclopedică, 1975.

Iorga, Nicolae, ed. *Acte şi fragmente cu privire la istoria Romînilor adunate din depozitele de manuscrise ale apusului.* Volume III. Bucureşti: Imprimeria Statului, 1897.

Iorga, Nicolae, ed. *Studii şi documente cu privire la istoria românilor.* Volumes III-IV. Bucureşti, 1901.

Iorga, Nicolae, ed. *Notes et extraits pour servir à l'histoire des croisades au XVe siècle. Quatrième série (1453-1476)*. Bucarest: Édition de l'Académie Roumaine, 1915.

Iorga, Nicolae, ed. *Scrisori de boieri, scrisori de domni*. 2nd edition. Vălenii-de-Munte: Aşezământul tipografic "Datina Românească," 1925.

Iorga, Nicolae. "Cronica lui Wavrin şi românii," in *Buletinul comisiei istorice a României*, no. 4 (1927).

Karadja, C. "Incunabulele povestind despre cruzimile lui Vlad Ţepeş," pp. 196-206, in *Închinare lui Nicolae Iorga cu prilejul împlinirii vârstei de 60 de ani*. Cluj, 1931.

Karadja, C. *Poema lui Michel Beheim despre cruciadele împotriva turcilor din anii 1443 şi 1444*. Vălenii-de-Munte, 1936.

Kritovoulos. *History of Mehmed the Conqueror*. Trans. Charles T. Riggs. Princeton: Princeton University Press, 1954.

Leu, Corneliu. *Plîngerea lui Dracula*. Bucureşti: Cartea Românească, 1977.

Leunclavius. *Historia Musulmana Turcorum de monumentis ipsorum exscripta*. 1591.

Mihailovic, Konstantin. *Memoirs of a Janissary*. Trans. Benjamin Stolz. Svat Soucek, ed. Ann Arbor: The University of Michigan, 1975.

Minea, Ilie. *Informţiile româneşti ale cronicii lui Ian Dlugosz*. Vălenii-de-Munte, 1926.

Monumenta Vaticana. Mathiae Corvini Hungariae regis epistolae ad Romanos Pontifices datae et ab eis acceptae. Budapest, 1891.

Nicolaescu, Ştefan. *Hrisoave şi cărţi domneşti dela Alexandru vodă Aldea, fiul lui Mircea vodă cel Bătrân, iunie 1431-iulie 1435*. Bucureşti: Cartea Românească, 1922.

Panaitescu, P.P. *Cronicile slavo-romîne din secolele XV-XVI publicate de Ion Bogdan*. Bucureşti: Editura Academiei, 1959.

Pius II. "The Commentaries of Pius II," trans. Florence Alden Gragg, in *Smith College Studies in History*. Books II and III, 25:1-4 (October,

1939-July, 1940); Books VI-IX, 35 (1951); Books X-XIII, 43 (1957). Northhampton, MA.

Popescu, Radu. *Istoriile domnilor Țării Romînești de Radu Popescu vornicul.* Constantin Grecescu, ed. București: Editura Academiei, 1963.

Sphrantzes, George. *The Fall of the Byzantine Empire.* Trans. Marios Philippides. Amherst: The University of Massachusetts Press, 1980.

Strabo. *The Geography of Strabo.* Vol. III. Trans. Horace Leonard Jones. Cambridge, MA: Harvard University Press, 1960.

Sturdza, Dimitrie A. and C. Colescu-Vartic. *Acte și documente relative la istoria renascerei României, volumul I (1391-1841).* Bucuresci: Institutul de Arte Grafice «Carol Göbl», 1900.

Szamu, Barabas. *Székely oklevéltár.* Vol. VIII. Budapest, 1934.

Tappe, Eric D. *Documents concerning Rumanian History (1427-1601).* The Hague: Mouton, 1964.

Thucydides. *The Pelopponnesian War.* Trans. Rex Warner. Harmondsworth: Penguin Books, 1985.

Tocilescu, G. *534 documente istorice slavo-române din Țara Românească și Moldova privitoare la legăturile cu Ardealul, 1246-1603.* București, 1931.

Tursun Beg. *The History of Mehmed the Conqueror.* Trans. Halil Inalcik and Rhoads Murphey. Minneapolis and Chicago: Bibliotheca Islamica, 1978.

Unrest, Jakob. "Osterreichische Chronik," in *Monumenta Germaniae Historica, Scriptores Rerum Germanicarum, Nova Series.* Vol. XI. Karl Grossman, ed. Weimar, 1957.

Ureche, Grigore. *Letopisetul Țării Moldovei.* P.P. Panaitescu, ed. București, 1958.

Ureche, Grigore, Miron Costin, and Ion Neculce. *Letopisețul Țării Moldovei.* Tatiana Celac, ed. Chișinău: Editura Hyperion, 1990.

Wey, William. *The Itineraries of William Wey, Fellow of Eton College, Published from the Bodleian Manuscript for the Roxburghe Club.* London, 1462.

Wey, William. "Iunie 1462. Biruinţa lui Vlad Ţepeş," in *Magazin istoric*, 21:11 (Noiembrie, 1987), pp. 28-29.

B. Secondary Sources

Abel, Wilhelm. *Agricultural Price Fluctuations in Europe*. New York, 1980.

Anderson, Perry. *Passages from Antiquity to Feudalism*. London: Verso Editions, 1978.

Andreescu, Ştefan. "Une information négligée sur la participation de la Valachie à la bataille de Kosovo (1448)," in *Revue des études sud-est européenes*, VI:1 (1968), pp. 85-92.

Andreescu, Ştefan. "En marge des rapports de Vlad l'Empaleur avec l'Empire Ottoman," in *Revue des études sud-est européenes*, 14:3 (1976), pp. 373-379.

Andreescu, Ştefan. *Vlad Ţepeş (Dracula): Între legendă şi adevăr istoric*. Bucureşti: Editura Minerva, 1976.

Andreescu, Stefan. "L'action de Vlad Ţepeş dans le sud-est de l'Europe en 1476," in *Revue des études sud-est européenes*, XV:2 (avril-juin, 1977), pp. 259-272.

Andreescu, Ştefan. "En marge des rapports de Vlad Ţepeş avec la Hongrie," in *Revue roumaine d'histoire*, 16:3 (1977), pp. 507-515.

Andreescu, Ştefan and Raymond T. McNally. "Exactly Where Was Dracula Captured in 1462?," in *East European Quarterly*, 23:3 (Fall, 1989), pp. 269-281.

Andreescu, Ştefan. "Quelques notes concernant Vlad l'Empaleur, Prince de Valachie," in *Revue roumaine d'histoire*, 28:1-2 (1989), pp. 123-128.

Andreescu, Ştefan. "The Heroic Figure in Romanian Political Culture: The Case of Vlad the Impaler," in *Romanian Civilization*, I:2 (Fall, 1992), pp. 29-34.

Armbruster, Adolf. "Jakob Unrests Ungarische Chronik," in *Revue roumaine d'histoire*, 13:3 (1974), pp. 473-508.

Aston, T.H. and C.H.E. Philpin. *The Brenner Debate: Agrarian Class Structure and Economic Development in Pre-Industrial Europe.* Cambridge: Cambridge University Press, 1985.

Babinger, Franz. *Mehmed the Conqueror and His Time.* Trans. Ralph Manheim. William C. Hickman, ed. Princeton: Princeton University Press, 1978.

Bârlea, Octavian. *Romania and the Romanians.* Trans. G. Mureşan and E. Moţiu. Los Angeles: American-Romanian Academy of Arts and Sciences, 1977.

Barraclough, Geoffrey, ed. *The Times Atlas of World History.* Revised edition. London: Times Books, 1984.

Binder, Paval. "Itinerarul transilvănean al lui Vlad Ţepeş," in *Revista de istorie,* 27:10 (1974), pp. 1537-1542.

Black, Cyril, ed. *Rewriting Russian History.* New York, 1964.

Bogdan, Ioan. *Vlad Ţepeş şi naraţiunile germane şi ruseşti asupra lui.* Bucureşti: Editura Librăriei Socecu & Comp., 1896.

Bogdan, Ioan. *Luptele romînilor cu turcii pănă la Mihai Viteazul.* Bucureşti: Editura Librăriei Socecu & Comp., 1898.

Bois, Guy. *The Crisis of Feudalism: Economy and Society in Eastern Normandy c. 1300-1550.* Cambridge: Cambridge University Press, 1984.

Boldur, Alexandru. *Ştefan cel Mare, voievod al Moldovei (1457-1504). Studiu de istorie socială şi politică.* Madrid: Editura Carpaţii, 1970.

Brătianu, Gheorghe I. *Sfatul domnesc şi adunarea stărilor în principatele române.* Bucureşti: Editura Enciclopedică, 1994.

Braudel, Fernand. *The Mediterranean and the Mediterranean World in the Age of Philip II.* 2 volumes. Trans. Siân Reynolds. New York: Harper and Row Publishers, 1973.

Cambridge Medieval History, Volume IV: The Eastern Roman Empire (717-1453). J.R. Tanner, ed. Cambridge: At the University Press, 1936.

Cambridge Medieval History, Volume VIII: The Close of the Middle Ages. C.W. Previté-Orton and Z.N. Brooke, eds. Cambridge: At the University Press, 1936.

Cambridge Medieval History, Volume IV: The Byzantine Empire, Part 1 — Byzantium and its Neighbors. J.M. Hussey, ed. Cambridge: At the University Press, 1966.

Câmpina, Barbu T. "Complotul boierilor şi răscoala din Ţara Românească din iulie-noiembrie, 1462," pp. 599-624, in *Studii şi referate privind istoria României.* Part I-a. Bucureşti, 1954.

Câmpina, Barbu T. "Victoria oştii lui Ţepeş asupra Sultanului Mehmed al II-lea (cu prilejul împlinirii a 500 de ani)," in *Studii: Revista de istorie*, 15:3 (1962), pp. 533-555.

Castellan, Georges. *A History of the Romanians.* Trans. Nicholas Bradley. New York: East European Monographs, Columbia University Press, 1989.

Cazacu, Matei. "La Valachie et la bataille de Kossovo (1448)," in *Revue des études sud-est europeennes*, 9:1 (1971), pp. 131-139.

Chatzidakis, Manolis and André Grabar. *Byzantine and Early Medieval Painting.* New York: Viking Press, 1965.

Cazacu, Matei. "L'impact ottoman sur les Pays Roumains et ses incidences monétaires (1452-1504)," in *Revue roumaine d'histoire*, 12:1 (1973), pp. 170-177.

Chirot, Daniel. *Social Change in a Peripheral Society: The Creation of a Balkan Colony.* New York: Academic Press, 1976.

Church, Richard William. *Miscellaneous Essays.* London and New York: MacMillan & Co., 1888.

Cihodaru, Constantin. *Alexandru cel Bun (23 aprilie 1399-1 ianuarie 1432).* Iaşi: Editura Junimea, 1984.

Ciobanu, Radu Ştefan. *Pe urmele lui Vlad Ţepeş.* Bucureşti: Editura Sport-Turism, 1979.

Ciocîltan, Virgil. "Între sultan şi împărat: Vlad Dracul în 1438," in *Revista de istorie*, 29:11 (1976), pp. 1767-1790.

Costăchel, Valeria, P.P. Panaitescu, and A. Cazacu. *Viaţa feudală în Ţara Romînească şi Moldova, sec. XIV-XVII.* Bucureşti: Editura Ştiinţifică, 1957.

Costăchescu, Mihai. *Arderea Târgului Floci şi a Ialomiţei în 1470: Un fapt necunoscut din luptele lui Ştefan cel Mare cu muntenii.* Iaşi: Institutul de Arte Grafice «Brawo», 1935.

Decei, Aurel. *Istoria imperiului otoman pînă la 1656.* Bucureşti: Editura Ştiinţifică şi Enciclopedică, 1978.

Diaconu, Petre. *Les Petchénègues au Bas-Danube.* Bucarest, 1970.

Diaconu, Petre. *Les Coumans au Bas-Danube aux XIe-XIIe siècles.* Bucarest, 1978.

Dicţionarul explicativ al limbii române DEX. Bucureşti: Editura Academiei, 1975.

Dobb, Maurice. *Studies in the Development of Capitalism.* New York: International Publishers, 1984.

Dvorik, Francis. *The Slavs in European History and Civilization.* New Brunswick, NJ: Rutgers University Press, 1962.

East, Gordon. *Géographie historique de l'Europe.* Paris, 1939.

Eliade, Mircea. *Zalmoxis, The Vanishing God: Comparative Studies in the Religions and Folklore of Dacia and Eastern Europe.* Trans. Willard R. Trask. Chicago: University of Chicago Press, 1972.

Encyclopedia of Islam. H.A.R. Gibb, J.H. Kramers et al., eds. Leiden, 1960.

Encyclopedia of Islam. B. Lewis, Ch. Pellat, and J. Scacht, eds. Leiden, 1965.

Engel, Johann Christian. *Geschichte der Moldau und Walachey.* Halle, 1804.

Fine, John V.A. *The Late Medieval Balkans: A Critical Survey from the Late Twelfth Century to the Ottoman Conquest.* Ann Arbor: University of Michigan Press, 1987.

Fischer-Galaţi, Stephen. *Man, State, and Society in East European History.* New York: Praeger Publishers, 1970.

236   The Life and Times of the Historical Dracula

Fisher, Sidney. *The Foreign Relations of Turkey, 1481-1512.* Urbana, IL: University of Illinois, 1948.

Florescu, George D. *Divanele domneşti din Ţara Românească, I (1389-1495).* Bucureşti: Institutul de Istorie Naţională din Bucureşti, 1943.

Florescu, Radu and Raymond T. McNally. *In Search of Dracula.* New York, 1970. Revised Edition: Boston and New York: Houghton Mifflin Company, 1994.

Florescu, Radu R. and Raymond T. McNally. *Dracula: A Biography of Vlad the Impaler, 1431-1476.* New York: Hawthorn Books, Inc., 1973.

Florescu, Radu R. and Raymond T. McNally. *Dracula, Prince of Many Faces: His Life and Times.* Boston: Little, Brown and Company, 1989.

Fossier, Robert, ed. *The Cambridge Illustrated History of the Middle Ages, III, 1250-1520.* Trans. Sarah Hanbury Tenison. Cambridge: Cambridge University Press, 1986.

Frazee, Charles A. *Catholics and Sultans: The Church and the Ottoman Empire, 1453-1923.* New York and London: Cambridge University Press, 1983.

Georgescu, Vlad. *The Romanians, A History.* Matei Călinescu, ed. Trans. Alexandra Bley-Vorman. Columbus, OH: Ohio State University Press, 1991.

Ghibănescu, Gh. "Vlad Ţepeş (Studiu critic)," in *Arhiva, Organul Societăţii Ştiinţifice şi Literare din Iaşi,* 8:7-8 (1897), pp. 373-417; and 8:9-10 (1897), pp. 497-520.

Gibbon, Edward. *The Decline and Fall of the Roman Empire, Volume 3: 1185 A.D.-1453 A.D.* New York: Random House, The Modern Library, 1932.

Giurescu, Constantin C. "O biserică a lui Vlad Ţepeş la Târgşor," in *Buletinul comisiei monumentelor istorice,* 17 (1924), pp. 74-75.

Giurescu, Constantin. *Istoria românilor.* Volume II[1]. Bucureşti, 1940.

Giurescu, Constantin C. "Întemeierea mitropoliei Ungro-vlahiei," in *Biserica ortodoxă romînă: Buletinul oficial al patriarhiei romîne*, 77:7-10 (iulie-octombrie, 1959), pp. 673-697.

Giurescu, Constantin. *Jurnal de călătorie în America*. Bucureşti, 1968.

Giurescu, Constantin C. *History of Bucharest*. Trans. Sorana Gorjan. Bucharest: The Publishing House for Sports and Tourism, 1976.

Giurescu, Constantin C. and Dinu C. Giurescu. *Istoria românilor*. Volume II. Bucureşti, 1976.

Giurescu, Dinu C. *Ţara Românească în veacurile XIV-XV.* Bucureşti: Editura Ştiinţifică, 1973.

Grey, Ian. *Ivan III and the Unification of Russia*. New York: Collier Books, 1967.

Grigoraş, Nicolae. *Moldova lui Ştefan cel Mare*. Iaşi: Editura Junimea, 1982.

Guboglu, Mihail. "Vlad Ţepeş şi Mehmed II," in *Revista arhivelor*, 4 (1976).

Guilmartin, John Francis. *Gunpowder and Galleys: Changing Technology and Mediterranean Warfare at Sea in the Sixteenth Century*. London, 1974.

Gündisch, Gustav. "Cu privire la relaţiile lui Vlad Ţepeş cu Transilvania în anii 1456-1458," in *Studii. Revista de istorie*, 16:3 (1963), pp. 681-696.

Gündisch, Gustav. "Vlad Ţepeş und die Sächsischen Selbstverwaltungsgebiete Siebenbürgens," in *Revue roumaine d'histoire*, 8:6 (1969), pp. 981-992.

Halecki, Oskar. *The Crusade of Varna: A Discussion of Controversial Problems*. New York: Polish Institute of Arts and Sciences in America, 1943.

Halecki, Oskar. *From Florence to Brest (1439-1596)*. 2nd edition. New York: Archon Books, 1968.

Hammer, J. de. *Histoire de l'Empire Ottoman depuis son origine jusqu'à nos jours*. Volume III. Paris, 1836.

Hasluck, F.W. *Christianity and Islam under the Sultans.* 2 volumes. Margaret Hasluck, ed. New York: Octagon Books, 1973.

Hay, Denys. *Europe in the Fourteenth and Fifteenth Centuries.* 2nd edition. London and New York, 1989.

Held, Joseph. "Peasants in Arms, 1437-1438 & 1456," in *From Hunyadi to Rákóczi: War and Society in Late Medieval and Early Modern Hungary.* János M. Bak and Béla K. Király, eds. Brooklyn: Brooklyn College Press, 1982, pp. 81-102.

Held, Joseph. *Hunyadi: Legend and Reality.* New York: East European Monographs, Columbia University Press, 1985.

Hilton, Rodney and H. Fagan. *The English Rising of 1381.* London: Lawrence and Wishart, 1950.

Hilton, Rodney. *The Decline of Serfdom in Medieval England.* London: MacMillan & Co., 1969.

Hilton, Rodney. *Bond Men Made Free: Medieval Peasant Movements and the English Rising of 1381.* New York: The Viking Press, 1973.

Hilton, Rodney. "Peasant Society, Peasant Movements, and Feudalism in Medieval Europe," in *Rural Protest: Peasant Movements and Social Change.* Henry A. Landsberger, ed. London: The MacMillan Press Ltd., 1974, pp. 67-94.

Hilton, Rodney, ed. *The Transition from Feudalism to Capitalism.* London: NLB, 1976.

Hilton, Rodney. "A Crisis of Feudalism," in *Past and Present,* 80 (August, 1978), pp. 3-19.

Hilton, Rodney. *Class Conflict and the Crisis of Feudalism: Essays in Medieval Social History.* London: The Hambledon Press, 1985.

Hitchins, Keith. "Ottoman Domination of Moldavia and Wallachia in the Sixteenth Century," in *Asian Studies One: A Collection of Papers on Aspects of Asian History and Civilization.* Balkrishna G. Gokhale, ed. Bombay, India: Popular Prakashan, 1966.

Inalcik, Halil. "Mehmed the Conqueror and His Time," in *Speculum,* 35:3 (1960), pp. 408-427.

Inalcik, Halil. *The Ottoman Empire: The Classical Age, 1300-1600.* Trans. Norman Itzkowitz and Colin Imber. New York: Praeger Publishers, 1973.

Io Mircea mare voievod şi domn. Bucureşti: Editura Meridiane, 1988.

Iorga, Nicolae. *Studii istorice asupra Chiliei şi Cetăţii-Albe.* Bucuresci: Institutul de Arte Grafice «Carol Göbl», 1899.

Iorga, Nicolae. "Lucruri nouă despre Vlad Ţepeş şi Ştefan cel Mare," in *Convorbiri literare,* 35 (1901), pp. 149-162.

Iorga, Nicolae. "Încă ceva despre Vlad Ţepeş şi Ştefan cel Mare," in *Convorbiri literare,* 38 (1904), pp. 381-382.

Iorga, Nicolae. *Istoria armatei româneşti, Vol. I, până la 1599.* Vălenii-de-Munte: Editura tipografiei «Neamul Românesc», 1910.

Iorga, Nicolae. *Istoria bisericii româneşti.* 3 volumes. Bucureşti, 1932.

Iorga, Nicolae. *Istoria literaturii religioase a românilor până la 1688.* Bucureşti, 1904.

Iorga, Nicolae. *Istoria lui Ştefan cel Mare povestită neamului românesc.* Bucureşti, 1904.

Iorga, Nicolae. *Brève histoire de l'Albanie et du peuple albanais.* Bucarest, 1919.

Iorga, Nicolae. *Histoire des roumains et de leur civilisation.* Deuxième edition. Bucarest: Cultura Naţională, 1922.

Iorga, Nicolae. *Imperiul cumanilor şi domnia lui Basaraba.* Bucureşti: Academia Română [Mem.] secţia istorică, seria III, tom. VIII, 1927-1928.

Iorga, Nicolae. *Istoria românilor, vol. IV: Cavalerii.* Bucureşti, 1937.

Iosipescu, Sergiu. "Conjunctura şi condiţionarea internaţională politico-militară a celei de a doua domnii a lui Vlad Ţepeş (1456-1462)," in *Studii şi materiale de muzeografie şi istorie militară,* 11 (1978), pp. 175-186.

Iosipescu, Sergiu. "Viziunea românească asupra războiului de cruciadă (sfîrşitul sec. al XIV-lea-începutul sec. al XVI-lea)," in *Studii de istorie şi teorie militară (Retrospective istorice, analize contemporane).* Al. Gh. Savu, ed. Bucureşti: Editura Militară, 1980, pp. 19-41.

Iosipescu, Sergiu. "Schiţă a constituirii statelor medievale româneşti," in *Revista de istorie*, 36:2 (1983), pp. 254-272.

Istoria militară a poporului român. Volume II. Bucureşti: Editura Militară, 1986.

Istoria Romîniei. Volume II. Bucureşti: Editura Academiei, 1962.

Jovius, Paulus. *A Short Treatise upon the Turkes Chronicles, compyled by Paulus Jovius, Bishop of Nucerne and dedicated to Charles the V Emperour.* Trans. Peter Ashton. London: Edwarde Whitchurch, 1546.

Kelly, J.N.D. *The Oxford Dictionary of Popes.* Oxford: Oxford University Press, 1986.

Kinross, Lord. *The Ottoman Centuries: The Rise and Fall of the Turkish Empire.* New York: William Morrow & Co., Inc., 1977.

Király, Béla K. "Society and War from Mounted Knights to the Standing Armies of the Absolute Kings: Hungary and the West," pp. 23-55, in *From Hunyadi to Rákóczi: War and Society in Late Medieval and Early Modern Hungary.* János M. Bak and Béla K. Király, eds. Brooklyn: Brooklyn College Press, 1982.

Knolles, Richard. *The Generall Historie of the Turkes from the First Beginning of that Nation to the Rising of the Othoman Familie; with All the Notable Expeditions of the Christian Princes against Them. Together with the Lives and Conquests of the Othoman Kings and Emperours.* 5th edition. London: Adam Islif, 1638.

Kriedte, Peter, Hans Medick, and Jurgen Schlumbohm, eds. *Industrialization before Industrialization: Rural Industry in the Genesis of Capitalism.* Trans. Beate Schempp. Cambridge: Cambridge University Press, 1981.

Kula, Witold. *An Economic Theory of the Feudal System: Towards a Model of the Polish Economy, 1500-1800.* Trans. Lawrence Garner. London: NLB, 1976.

Ladurie, Emmanuel LeRoy. *The Peasants of Lanmguedoc.* Trans. John Day. Urbana, IL: University of Illinois Press, 1974.

Lane, Frederic C. *Venice: A Maritime Republic.* Baltimore: Johns Hopkins University Press, 1973.

Langer, William L., ed. *An Encyclopedia of World History: Ancient, Medieval, and Modern, Chronologically Arranged.* Revised edition. Boston: Houghton, Mifflin Co., 1948.

Lis, Catharina and Hugo Soly. *Poverty and Capitalism in Pre-Industrial Europe.* Atlantic Highlands, NJ: Humanities Press, Inc., 1979.

Longworth, Philip. *The Making of Eastern Europe.* London: The MacMillan Press, 1992.

Mallett, M.E. and J.R. Hale. *The Military Organization of a Renaissance State: Venice c. 1400 to 1617.* Cambridge: Cambridge University Press, 1984.

Manolescu, Radu. "Schimbul de mărfuri între Țara Românească și Brașov în prima jumătate a secolului al XVI-lea," in *Studii și materiale de istorie medie.* Vol. II. București, 1957.

Manolescu, Radu. *Comerțul Țării Românești și Moldovei cu Brașovul (secolele XIV-XVI).* București, 1965.

McNally, Raymond T. "The Fifteenth Century Manuscript by Kritoboulos of Imbros as an Historical Source for the History of Dracula," in *East European Quarterly,* 21:1 (Spring, 1987), pp. 1-13.

McNeil, William H. *Venice: The Hinge of Europe, 1081-1797.* Chicago: University of Chicago Press, 1974.

Mehmed, Mustafa Ali. *Istoria turcilor.* București: Editura științifică și enciclopedică, 1976.

Mijatovich, Chemodil. *Constantine, the Last Emperor of the Greeks, or the Conquest of Constantinople by the Turks.* London: Sampson, Low, Marston & Co., 1892.

Miller, William. *Essays on the Latin Orient.* Cambridge: Cambridge University Press, 1921.

Miller, William. "The Last Athenian Historian: Laonikos Chalkokondyles," in *Journal of Hellenic Studies,* 42 (1922), pp. 36-49.

Minea, Ilie. "Vlad Dracul și vremea sa," in *Cercetări istorice: Revistă de istorie românească,* 4:1 (1928), pp. 5-276.

Minea, Ilie. *Cetatea Neamțului.* Iași: Tipografia "Liga Culturală," 1943.

Mitrany, David. *The Land and the Peasant in Rumania: The War and Agrarian Reform (1917-21)*. New Haven: Yale University Press, 1930.

Mosely, Philip E. "The Peasant Family: The Zadruga, or Communal Joint-Family in the Balkans and its Recent Development," in *The Cultural Approach to History*. Caroline F. Ware, ed. New York: Columbia University Press, 1940, pp. 95-108.

Moutafchieva, Vera P. *Agrarian Relations in the Ottoman Empire in the 15th and 16th Centuries*. New York: East European Monographs, Columbia University Press, 1988.

Mureşan, Camil. *Iancu de Hunedoara*. 2nd edition. Bucureşti, 1968.

Muşat, Mircea and Ion Ardeleanu. *From Ancient Dacia to Modern Romania*. Trans. Andrei Bantaş, et al. Bucureşti: Editura Ştiinţifică şi Enciclopedică, 1985.

Nandriş, Grigore. "A Philological Analysis of Dracula and Rumanian Place Names and Masculine Personal Names in *a/ea*," in *Slavonic and East European Review*, 37 (June, 1959), pp. 371-377.

Năsturel, Petre Ş. "Vlad l'Empaleur, libérateur de Hîrşova et de Ruse (1462)," in *Studiu Balcanica*, I (1970), pp. 126-128.

Neamţu, Vasile. *Istorie medie a României*. Iaşi: Universitatea "Alexandru Ioan Cuza," 1982.

Nicol, Donald M. *The End of the Byzantine Empire*. London: Edward Arnold Publishers, Ltd., 1979.

Nicolaescu, Ştefan. *Domnia lui Alexandru vodă Aldea, fiul lui Mircea cel Bătrân, 1431-1435*. Bucureşti: Cartea Românească, 1922.

Olteanu, Pandele. *Limba povestirilor slave despre Vlad Ţepeş*. Bucureşti: Editura Academiei, 1960.

Ostrogorsky, George. *History of the Byzantine State*. Trans. Joan Hussey. New Brunswick: Rutgers University Press, 1957.

Pall, Francisc. "Notes du pèlerin William Wey à propos des opérations militaires des Turcs en 1462," in *Revue historique du sud-est européen*, 22 (1945), pp. 264-266.

Pall, Francisc. "Les relations entre la Hongrie et Scanderbeg," in *Revue historique du sud-est européen*, 10:4-6 (1933), pp. 119-141.

Pall, Francisc. "Intervenţia lui Iancu de Hunedoara în Ţara Românească şi Moldova în anii 1447-1448," in *Studii: Revista de istorie*, 16:5 (1963), pp. 1049-1072.

Pall, Francisc. "Skanderbeg et Janco de Hunedoara (Jean Hunyadi)," in *Studia Albanica*, 5:1 (1968), pp. 103-118.

Panaitescu, P.P. *Mircea cel Bătrân*. Bucureşti: Casa Şcoalelor, 1944.

Panaitescu, P.P. "Les chroniques slaves de Moldavie du XVe siècle," in *Romanoslavica*, I (1958), pp. 146-168.

Panaitescu, P.P. *Interpretări româneşti: Studii de istorie economică şi socială*. 2nd edition. Ştefan S. Gorovei and Magda Magdalena Székely, eds. Bucureşti: Editura Enciclopedică, 1994.

Papacostea, Şerban. "La Moldavie état tributaire de l'Empire Ottoman au XVe siècle: le cadre international des rapports établis en 1455-1456," in *Revue roumaine d'histoire*, XIII:3 (1974), pp. 445-446.

Papacostea, Şerban. *Stephen the Great, Prince of Moldavia, 1457-1504*. Bucureşti: Editura Ştiinţifică şi Enciclopedică, 1981.

Papacostea, Şerban. *Geneza statelor feudale româneşti*. Cluj-Napoca: Editura Dacia, 1989.

Papacostea, Şerban. *Românii în secolul al XIII-lea: Între cruciată şi Imperiul Mongol*. Bucureşti: Editura Enciclopedică, 1993.

Parker, Geoffrey. *The Military Revolution: Military Innovation and the Rise of the West, 1500-1800*. Cambridge: Cambridge University Press, 1988.

Pasco, Stefan. *La révolte populaire de Transylvanie des années 1437-1438*. Bucarest: Éditions de l'Academie de la République Populaire Roumaine, 1964.

Pascu, Ştefan. *Războiul ţărănesc din anul 1514 de sub conducerea lui Gheorghe Doja*. Bucureşti, 1959.

Pascu, Ştefan. *Bobîlna*. Bucureşti: Editura Ştiinţifică, 1963.

Pascu, Ştefan, et al. eds. *Istoria medie a României.* Bucureşti: Editura Didactică şi Pedagogică, 1966.

Pascu, Ştefan. *A History of Transylvania.* Trans. D. Robert Ladd. Detroit: Wayne State University Press, 1982.

Pastor, Ludwig. *The History of the Popes from the Close of the Middle Ages.* Frederick Ignatius Antrobus, ed. Volume II, London: John Hodges, 1891; Volume III, London: Routledge and Kegan Paul, Ltd., 1949; Volume IV, London: Kegan Paul, Trench, Trübner & Co., 1894.

Pătroiu, Ion, ed. *Marele Mircea Voievod.* Bucureşti: Editura Academiei, 1987.

Petrovic, Djurdjica. "Fire-arms in the Balkans on the Eve of and After the Ottoman Conquests of the Fourteenth and Fifteenth Centuries," pp. 164-194, in *War, Technology, and Society in the Middle East.* V.J. Parry and M.E. Yapp, eds. London: Oxford University Press, 1975.

Pirenne, Henri. *Social and Economic History of Medieval Europe.* New York: Harcourt, Brace & World, Inc., n.d.

Pitcher, Donald Edgar. *An Historical Geography of the Ottoman Empire from the Earliest Times to the End of the Sixteenth Century.* Leiden: E.J. Brill, 1972.

Popescu, Niculae M. *Nifon II, patriarhul Constantinopului.* Bucureşti, 1914.

Postan, M.M. *The Medieval Economy and Society: An Economic History of Britain.* Berkeley: University of California Press, 1972.

Ranke, Leopold von. *Sämmtliche Werke: Serbien und die Türkei.* Volume 44. Leipzig, 1879.

Rosetti, Dinu V. *Săpăturile arheologice de la Snagov.* Volume I. Bucureşti, 1935.

Rosetti, Radu. *Pământul, sătenii şi stăpânii în Moldova.* Bucureşti, 1907.

Rosetti, Radu. "Stephen the Great of Moldavia and the Turkish Invasion," in *The Slavonic Review,* 6:16 (June, 1927), pp. 86-103.

Rudé, George. *Ideology and Popular Protest.* New York: Pantheon Books, 1980.

Runciman, Steven. *The Fall of Constantinople, 1453.* Cambridge: Cambridge University Press, 1965.

Sachelarie, Ovid and Nicolae Stoicescu. *Instituţii feudale din ţările române. Dicţionar.* Bucureşti: Editura Academiei, 1988.

Savu, Al. Gh. *Ştefan cel Mare. Campanii.* Bucureşti: Editura Militară, 1982.

Schevill, Ferdinand. *History of the Balkan Peninsula: From the Earliest Times to the Present Day.* New York: Frederick Ungar Publishing, 1966.

Schwoebel. *The Shadow of the Crescent: The Renaissance Image of the Turk (1453-1517).* New York, 1967.

Şerbănescu, Niculae. "Mitropoliţii Ungrovlahiei," in *Biserica ortodoxă romînă: Buletinul oficial al patriarhiei romîne,* 77:7-10 (iulie-octombrie, 1959), pp. 722-826.

Şerbănescu, Niculae. "Titulatura mitropoliţilor, jurisdicţia, hotarele şi reşedinţele mitropoliei Ungrovlahiei," in *Biserica ortodoxă romînă: Buletinul oficial al patriarhiei romîne,* 77:7-10 (iulie-octombrie, 1959), pp. 698-721.

Şerbănescu, Niculae and Nicolae Stoicescu. *Mircea cel Mare (1386-1418).* Bucureşti: Editura Institutului Biblic şi de Misiune al Bisericii Ortodoxe Române, 1987.

Seton-Watson, R.W. *A History of the Roumanians from Roman Times to the Completion of Unity.* Cambridge: At the University Press, 1934.

Setton, Kenneth M., ed. *A History of the Crusades, Volume II: The Later Crusades, 1189-1311.* Madison: University of Wisconsin Press, 1969.

Setton, Kenneth M., ed. *A History of the Crusades, Volume III: The Fourteenth and Fifteenth Centuries.* Madison: University of Wisconsin Press, 1975.

Setton, Kenneth M. *The Papacy and the Levant (1204-1571), Volume II: The Fifteenth Century.* Philadelphia: The American Philosophical Society, 1978.

Shaw, Stanford J. *History of the Ottoman Empire and Modern Turkey, Volume I: The Empire of the Gazis. The Rise and Decline of the Ottoman Empire, 1280-1808.* New York: Cambridge University Press, 1976.

Shelley, Percy Bysshe. *The Selected Poetry and Prose of Shelley.* Harold Bloom, ed. New York: New American Library, 1967.

Shelley, Percy Bysshe. *Shelley, Poetical Works.* Thomas Hutchinson, ed. Oxford: Oxford University Press, 1991.

Spinka, Matthew. *A History of Christianity in the Balkans: A Study in the Spread of Byzantine Culture among the Slavs.* Chicago: American Society of Church History, 1933.

Stahl, Henri H. *Controverse de istorie socială românească.* Bucureşti, 1969.

Stahl, Henri H. *Traditional Romanian Village Communities: The Transition from the Communal to the Capitalist Mode of Production in the Danube Region.* Trans. Daniel Chirot and Holley Coulter Chirot. Cambridge: Cambridge University Press, 1980.

Stăvăruş, Ion. *Povestiri medievale despre Vlad Ţepeş-Drăculea. Studiu critic şi antologie.* 2nd edition. Bucureşti: Editura Univers, 1993.

Stavrianos, L.S. *The Balkans since 1453.* New York: Holt, Rinehart and Winston, 1958.

Ştefănescu, Ştefan. *Ţara Românească de la Basarab "întemeietorul" pînă la Mihai Viteazul.* Bucureşti, 1971.

Ştefănescu, Ştefan. "Aspects de la vie rurale dans les principautés roumaines au Moyen Âge. Le paysage rural," in *Revue roumaine d'histoire,* 28:1-2 (1989), pp. 3-14.

Stoian, Emil. *Vlad Ţepeş: Mit şi realitate istorică.* Bucureşti: Editura Albatros, 1989.

Stoianovich, Traian. *A Study in Balkan Civilization.* New York: Alfred A. Knopf, 1967.

Stoicescu, Nicolae. *Sfatul domnesc şi marii dregători din Ţara Românească şi Moldova, sec. XIV-XVII.* Bucureşti: Editura Academiei, 1968.

Stoicescu, Nicolae. *Dicţionar al marilor dregători din Ţara Românească şi Moldova (sec. XIV-XVII).* Bucureşti: Editura Enciclopedică, 1971.

Stoicescu, Nicolae. *Vlad Ţepeş: Prince of Wallachia.* Bucharest: Editura Academiei, 1978.

Studime për epokën e Skënderbeut. 3 Vols. Tiranë, 1989.

Sugar, Peter. *A History of East Central Europe, Volume V: Southeastern Europe under Ottoman Rule, 1354-1804.* Seattle and London: University of Washington Press, 1977.

Theodorescu, B. and I. Barnea. "Cultura în cuprinsul mitropoliei Ungrovlahiei," in *Biserica ortodoxă romînă: Buletinul oficial al patriarhiei romîne,* 77:7-10 (iulie-octombrie, 1959), pp. 827-888.

Thomson, John A.F. *Popes and Princes, 1417-1517: Politics and Polity in the Late Medieval Church.* London: George Allen & Unwin, 1980.

Tihany, Leslie C. *A History of Middle Europe: From the Earliest Times to the Age of the World Wars.* New Brunswick: Rutgers University Press, 1976.

Treptow, Kurt W. "Distance and Communications in Southeastern Europe, 1593-1612," in *East European Quarterly,* 24:4 (Winter, 1990), pp. 475-482.

Treptow, Kurt W., ed. *Dracula: Essays on the Life and Times of Vlad Ţepeş.* New York: East European Monographs, Columbia University Press, 1991.

Treptow, Kurt W. "Aspects of the Campaign of 1462," in *Romanian Civilization,* 1:1 (Summer, 1992), pp. 17-27.

Treptow, Kurt W. *From Zalmoxis to Jan Palach: Studies in East European History.* New York: East European Monographs, Columbia University Press, 1992.

Treptow, Kurt W. "Ştefan cel Mare — Images of a Medieval Hero," in *Romanian Civilization,* 1:2 (Fall, 1992), pp. 35-41.

Treptow, Kurt W. "Vlad Ţepeş — An Enigma of Medieval History," in *Transylvanian Review*, 1:1 (Summer, 1992), pp. 18-28.

Treptow, Kurt W., ed. *A History of Romania*. Iaşi: The Center for Romanian Studies, 1997.

Treptow, Kurt W. "Vlad III Dracula and his Relations with the Boyars and the Church," pp. 27-40 in *Romania, Culture, and Nationalism: A Tribute to Radu Florescu*, Anthony R. De Luca and Paul D. Quinlan, eds. New York: East European Monographs, Columbia University Press, 1998.

Treptow, Kurt W., ed. *Poems and Prose of Mihai Eminescu*, Iaşi: The Center for Romanian Studies, 2000.

Tuleja, Thaddeus V. "Eugenius IV and the Crusade of Varna," in *Catholic Historical Review*, 35:3 (October, 1949), pp. 257-275.

Ursu, Ion. *Ştefan cel Mare, domn al Moldovei de la 12 Aprilie 1457 până la 2 Iulie 1504*. Bucureşti: Biblioteca istorică, 1925.

Ursu, Ion. *Ştefan cel Mare şi turcii*. Bucureşti, 1914.

Vasilescu, Alexandru A. *Urmaşii lui Mircea cel Bătrân până la Vlad Ţepeş (1418-1456), I: De la moartea lui Mircea cel Bătrân până la Vlad Dracul (1418-1437)*. Bucureşti: Institutul de Arte Grafice «Carol Göbl», 1915.

Vaughan, Dorothy M. *Europe and the Turk: A Pattern of Alliances, 1350-1700*. Liverpool: University Press, 1954.

Vaughan, Richard. *Philip the Good: The Apogee of Burgundy*. New York: Barnes & Noble, 1973.

Vernadsky, G. *Kievan Russia*. New Haven: Yale University Press, 1973.

Vucinich, Wayne S. "The Nature of Balkan Society under Ottoman Rule," in *Slavic Review*, 21:4 (June, 1962), pp. 597-616.

Ware, Timothy. *The Orthodox Church*. Harmondsworth: Penguin Books, 1985.

Xenopol, A.D. *Lupta dintre Dăneşti şi Drăculeşti*. Bucureşti: Institutul de Arte Grafice «Carol Göbl», 1907; also *Analele Academiei Române mem. sect. ist.*, seria II, tom. XXX. Bucureşti, 1907.

Index

A

B